Polemic in the Book of Hebrews

Princeton Theological Monograph Series

K. C. Hanson, Series Editor

Recent volumes in the series

David A. Ackerman
*Lo, I Tell You a Mystery:
Cross, Resurrection, and Paraenesis in the Rhetoric of 1 Corinthians*

Philip L. Mayo
*"Those Who Call Themselves Jews":
The Church and Judaism in the Apocalypse of John*

John A. Vissers
The Neo-Orthodox Theology of W. W. Bryden

Byron C. Bangert
Consenting to God and Nature

Stephen Finlan and Vladimir Kharlamov, editors
Theōsis: Deification in Christian Theology

Richard Valantasis et al., editors
*The Subjective Eye: Essays Culture, Religion, and Gender
in Honor of Margaret R. Miles*

Caryn Riswold
Coram Deo: Human Life in the Vision of God

Paul O. Ingram, editor
Constructing a Relational Cosmology

Mark A. Ellis, editor and translator
The Arminian Confession of 1621

Polemic in the Book of Hebrews
Anti-Semitism, Anti-Judaism, Supersessionism?

LLOYD KIM

Pickwick *Publications*
An imprint of *Wipf and Stock Publishers*
199 West 8th Avenue • Eugene OR 97401

POLEMIC IN THE BOOK OF HEBREWS
Anti-Semitism, Anti-Judaism, Supersessionism?
Princeton Theological Monograph Series 64

Copyright© Lloyd Kim. All rights reserved. Except for brief quotations in critical publications or reviews, no part of this book may be reproduced in any manner without prior written permission from the publisher. Write: Permissions, Wipf & Stock, 199 W. 8th Ave., Eugene, OR 97401.

ISBN 10: 1-59752-839-0
ISBN 13: 978-1-59752-8399

Cataloging-in-Publication data:

Kim, Lloyd.
Polemic in the book of Hebrews : anti-semitism, anti-Judaism, supersessionism? / Lloyd Kim.

Eugene, Ore. Pickwick, Publications, 2006
Princeton Theological Monograph Series 64

xiv + 222 p. ; 23 cm.

Includes bibliography

ISBN 10: 1-59752-839-0
ISBN 13: 978-1-59752-8399

1. Bible. N.T. Hebrews—Criticism, Interpretation, etc. 2. Christianity and other religions—Judaism—History. 3. Judaism—Relations—Christianity—History. 4. Judaism (Christian theology)—History of Doctrines—Early church, ca. 30-600. I. Title. II. Series.

BS2775.6 .K55 2006

Manufactured in the U.S.A.

Contents

Abbreviations / vii
Introduction / 1

1. The History of Scholarship on Anti-Semitism, Anti-Judaism, and Supersessionism in Hebrews / 8

2. The Method of Approach / 17

3. The Social Context of the Epistle to the Hebrews / 47

4. Priesthood and Polemic in Hebrews 7:1-19 / 62

5. Covenant and Polemic in Hebrews 8:1-13 / 100

6. Sacrifice and Polemic in Hebrews 10:1-10 / 147

Conclusion / 197
Bibliography / 202

Abbreviations

General

AB	Anchor Bible
ABD	*The Anchor Bible Dictionary,* 6 vols., edited by David Noel Freedman. New York: Doubleday, 1992
AER	American Ecclesiastical Review
AfNZK	ΑΓΓΕΛΟΣ: *Archiv für neutestamentliche Zeitgeschichte und Kulturkunde*
ALGHJ	Arbeiten zur Literatur und Geschichte des hellenistischen Judentums
AnBib	Analecta Biblica
AsTJ	*Asbury Theological Journal*
BAR	*Biblical Archeological Review*
BDAG	*A Greek-English Lexicon of the New Testament and Other Early Christian Literature.* 3d ed. Based on Walter Bauer's *Griechisch-deutsches Worterbuch zu den Schriften des Neuen Testaments und der fruhchristlichen Literatur,* 6th edition, eds. Kurt Aland and Barbara Aland, with Viktor Reichmann and on previous English editions by W. F. Arndt, F. W. Gingrich, and F. W. Danker. Chicago: University of Chicago Press, 2000
BETL	Bibliotheca Ephemeridum Theologicarum Lovaniensium
Bib	*Biblica*
Bijdr	*Bijdragen*
BJS	Brown Judaic Studies
BSac	*Bibliotheca sacra*
BST	Basel Studies of Theology
CBET	Contributions to Biblical Exegesis and Theology
CBQ	*Catholic Biblical Quarterly*

ChrCent		*Christian Century*
CJT		*Canadian Journal of Theology*
CrossCu		*Cross Currents*
CTM		*Concordia Theological Monthly*
CurBS		*Currents in Research: Biblical Studies*
Did		*Didaskalia*
EKKNT		Evangelisch-Katholischer Kommentar zum Neuen Testament
EUS		European University Studies
EvQ		*Evangelical Quarterly*
EvRT		*Evangelical Review of Theology*
ExpTim		*Expository Times*
FirT		*First Things*
FM		*Faith and Mission*
FoiVie		*Foi et vie*
GBS		Guides to Biblical Scholarship
GTJ		*Grace Theological Journal*
HNTC		Harper's New Testament Commentaries
HTR		*Harvard Theological Review*
ICC		International Critical Commentary
Int		*Interpretation*
ISBE		*The International Standard Bible Encyclopedia,* 4 vols., ed. Geoffrey W. Bromiley. Grand Rapids: Eerdmans, 1982
JBL		*Journal of Biblical Literature*
JES		*Journal of Ecumenical Studies*
JETS		*Journal of the Evangelical Theological Society*
JJS		*Journal of Jewish Studies*
JOTT		*Journal of Translation and Textlinguistics*
JPT		*Jahrbücher für protestantische Theologie*
JSNT		*Journal for the Study of the New Testament*
JSNTSS		Journal for the Study of the New Testament Supplement Series
JSOTSS		Journal for the Study of Old Testament Supplement Series
JSP		*Journal for the Study of the Pseudepigrapha*

KD	*Kerygma und Dogma*
KEK	Kritisch-exegetischer Kommentar über das Neue Testament
KTR	*King's Theological Review*
LCL	Loeb Classical Library
LibA	*Liber annuus*
LTJ	*Lutheran Theological Journal*
LXX	Septuagint
MSJ	*Master's Seminary Journal*
MT	Masoretic Text
NASB	New American Standard Bible
NCBC	New Century Bible Commentary
Neot	*Neotestamentica*
NIBCNT	New International Biblical Commentary on the New Testament
NICNT	New International Commentary on the New Testament
NIGTC	New International Greek Testament Commentary
NovT	*Novum Testamentum*
NovTSup	Novum Testamentum Supplements
NPNF[1]	*Nicene and Post-Nicene Fathers*, Series 1
NPNF[2]	*Nicene and Post-Nicene Fathers*, Series 2
NRSV	New Revised Standard Version
NTC	New Testament Commentary
NTS	*New Testament Studies*
PD	Parole de Dieu
QD	Quaestiones disputatae
QR	*Quarterly Review*
ReshScRel	*Recherches de science religieuse*
ResQ	*Restoration Quarterly*
RevExp	*Review and Expositor*
RevQ	*Revue de Qumran*
RSPT	*Revue des sciences philosophiques et théologiques*
RTR	*Reformed Theological Review*

SB	Sources Bibliques
SBLDS	Society of Biblical Literature Dissertation Series
ScEs	*Science et Esprit*
ScrHier	*Scripta Hierosolymitana*
SE	*Studia Evangelica*
SEÅ	*Svensk exegetisk årsbok*
Sem	*Semitica*
SJT	*Scottish Journal of Theology*
SNTSMS	Society for New Testament Studies Monograph Series
SOTI	Studies in Old Testament Interpretation
SR	*Studies in Religion*
SUNT	Studien zur Umwelt des Neuen Testaments
SwJT	*Southwestern Journal of Theology*
TaiJT	*Taiwan Journal of Theology*
TJ	*Trinity Journal*
TTE	*Theological Educator: A Journal of Theology and Ministry*
TynBul	*Tyndale Bulletin*
TZ	*Theologische Zeitschrift*
VT	*Vetus Testamentum*
VTSup	Vetus Testamentum Supplement
WBC	Word Biblical Commentary
WCJS	World Congress of Jewish Studies
WMANT	Wissenschaftliche Monographien zum Alten und Neuen Testament
WTJ	*Westminster Theological Journal*
WUNT	Wissenschaftliche Untersuchungen zum Neuen Testament
ZNW	*Zeitschrift für die neutestamentliche Wissenschaft und die Kunde der älteren Kirche*

Apocrypha

1–2 Macc	1–2 Maccabees
Bel	Bel and the Dragon
Jub	Jubilees

Sir	Sirach/ Ecclesiasticus
Sus	Susanna
Tob	Tobit

Dead Sea Scrolls

11QT	*Temple Scroll*
1Q34	*Liturgical Prayer a*
1Q34bis	*Liturgical Prayer b*
1QH	*Hodayot* or *Thanksgiving Hymns*
1QM	*Milhamah* or *War Scroll*
1QpHab	*Pesher Habakkuk*
1QpMic	*Pesher Micah*
1QS	*Serek Hayahad* or *Rule of the Community*
1QSa	*Rule of the Congregation* (Appendix a to 1QS)
1QSb	*Rule of Blessings* (Appendix b to 1QS)
4Q400	*Songs of the Sabbath Sacrifice*
4QFlor	*Florilegium*
4QPNah	*Pesher Nahum*
4QpsMos	*Pseudo-Moses*
CD	Cairo Genizah copy of the *Damascus Document*
MMT	*Miqsat Ma'asê ha-Torah*

Josephus

Ag.Ap.	*Against Apion*
Ant.	*Jewish Antiquities*
J.W.	*Jewish War*

Old Testament Pseudepigrapha

L.A.B.	*Liber antiquitatum biblicarum* (Pseudo-Philo)
Pss.Sol.	*Psalms of Solomon*
T. Dan	*Testament of Dan*
T.Benj.	*Testament of Benjamin*
T.Gad	*Testament of Gad*
T.Iss.	*Testament of Issachar*
T.Jos.	*Testament of Joseph*
T.Jud.	*Testament of Judah*
T.Levi	*Testament of Levi*
T.Mos.	*Testament of Moses*
T.Naph.	*Testament of Naphtali*
T.Reu.	*Testament of Reuben*
T.Sim.	*Testament of Simeon*

Philo

Alleg.Interp.	*Allegorical Interpretation*
Decalogue	*On the Decalogue*
Dreams	*On Dreams*
Drunkenness	*On Drunkenness*
Giants	*On Giants*
Heir	*Who Is the Heir?*
Her.	*Quis rerum divinarum heres sit*
Ios.	*De Iosepho*
Migr.	*De migratione Abrahami*
Migration	*On the Migration of Abraham*
Mos.	*De vita Mosis*
Mut.	*De mutatione nominum*
Opif.	*De opificio mundi*
Planting	*On Planting*
Prob.	*Quod omnis probus liber sit*

Providence	*On Providence*
QE	*Quaestiones et solutiones in Exodum*
QG	*Quaestiones et solutiones in Genesin*
Sacr.	*De sacrificiis Abelis et Caini*
Sacrifices	*On the Sacrifices of Cain and Abel*
Somn.	*De somniis*
Spec.	*De specialibus legibus*
Spec. Laws	*On the Special Laws*
Worse	*That the Worse Attacks the Better*

Seneca

Ben.	*De beneficiis*

Introduction

Is the New Testament responsible for anti-Semitism? Do the New Testament writings give rise to belligerent behavior or hateful thoughts toward Jewish people? Ever since World War II and the Jewish Holocaust, New Testament scholars have been wrestling with these kinds of questions. Most studies, however, have focused on the gospel accounts, Acts, or the Pauline epistles. Very little has been written specifically on the epistle to the Hebrews.[1] The goal of this dissertation is to determine whether the epistle to the Hebrews is anti-Semitic, anti-Judaic or supersessionistic, and if so, to what extent.

The topic itself poses several challenges. First, there does not seem to be a universal definition of anti-Semitism, nor any real consensus in the validity of distinguishing it from anti-Judaism. Second, the polemic in Hebrews seems to be directed not to the Jewish people, but rather to fundamental Jewish institutions.[2] Would then, an attack on the Jewish faith and ritual constitute anti-Semitism? Third, it is clear that the author of Hebrews[3] sees both continuity and discontinuity between Christianity

---

[1] To illustrate the disparity between the amount of work done in the Gospels, Acts, and Paul versus Hebrews regarding the question of anti-Semitism, we simply need to examine a few major studies. Gregory Baum's book, *Is the New Testament Anti-Semitic?*, contains only two sections: 1) the Gospels and the Acts of the Apostles; and 2) the epistles of Saint Paul. There is nothing written on the book of Hebrews. *Anti-Semitism in the New Testament?* by Samuel Sandmel dedicates seven chapters to the Gospels, Acts, and the Pauline writings. Only three pages are given to the epistle to the Hebrews. In Lillian Freudmann's book, *Antisemitism in the New Testament,* only nine pages are given to Hebrews, while the rest of the book focuses primarily on Paul's writings, the Gospels, and Acts. In the book *Anti-Semitism and Early Christianity: Issues of Polemic and Faith*, seven articles are dedicated to Jesus, Paul, the Gospels, and the deutero-Pauline writings, while only one deals with the book of Hebrews (and not exclusively).

[2] William Lane identifies the following as polemical passages in Hebrews: 7:18-19; 8:7; 8:13; 9:8-10; 10:1-4; 10:9; "Polemic in Hebrews and the Catholic Epistles," in *Anti-Semitism and Early Christianity: Issues of Polemic and Faith*, ed. C. Evans and D. Hagner (Minneapolis: Fortress, 1993) 166–98. These passages describe polemic against the Levitical priesthood, sacrificial ritual, Jewish law, Mosaic covenant, and temple.

[3] Though it is unknown for certain whether the author was male or female, I will use male

and Judaism. Though there are indeed strong words against the Levitical priesthood, Mosaic Covenant, and Levitical sacrifices,[4] there are also words of praise for Jewish men and women in the history of Israel.[5] Though the author speaks against the law,[6] he frequently quotes Scripture to support his arguments.[7] Though he seems to encourage his readers to separate from Judaism,[8] he also promotes a faith that is deeply rooted in Jewish thought and history. How then are we to understand his polemic in light of Christianity's birth from her Jewish roots? Is the author advocating supersessionism?

Defining Anti-Semitism and Anti-Judaism

Anti-Semitism versus Anti-Judaism

John Gager makes a clear distinction between anti-Semitism and anti-Judaism. He defines anti-Semitism as "hostile statements about Jews and Judaism on the part of Gentiles." He defines "anti-Judaism" as a primarily religious and theological disagreement with Judaism. The real difference according to Gager is that anti-Semitism is uninformed hostility from those on the outside, while anti-Judaism is a more informed critique from those on the inside or at least familiar with the Jewish faith.[9] This distinction implies that anti-Semitism is irrational, belligerent behavior, while anti-Judaism is thoughtful, non-aggressive dialogue.

Several scholars follow Gager in distinguishing anti-Judaism from anti-Semitism.[10] Craig Evans defines anti-Judaism as opposition to Judaism

---

pronouns for convenience when referring to the author. Donald Hagner notes that Priscilla is a possible candidate for the authorship of Hebrews. See Donald Hagner, "Interpreting the Epistle to the Hebrews," in *The Literature and Meaning of Scripture*, ed. Morris A. Inch and C. Hassell Bullock (Grand Rapids: Baker, 1981) 221.

[4] Heb 7:11-19, 8:6-13, 10:1-10.

[5] Heb 3:5; 7:1-10; 11:4-38.

[6] Heb 7:18-19, 28; 10:1.

[7] Heb 1:5-13; 2:6-8, 12-13; 3:7-11, 15; 4:3-7; 5:5-6; 7:17, 21; 8:8-12; 10:5-7, 16-17; 12:5-6; 13:6.

[8] See chapter 3. Cf. Heb 13:10, 13.

[9] John G. Gager, *The Origins of Anti-Semitism: Attitudes Toward Judaism in Pagan and Christian Antiquity* (New York: Oxford University Press, 1983) 8.

[10] See also Robert A. Guelich, "Anti-Semitism and/ or Anti-Judaism in Mark?" and Donald Hagner, "Paul's Quarrel with Judaism," in *Anti-Semitism and Early Christianity*, 80–81, 128–29.

as a religion, while anti-Semitism is opposition to the Jewish people.[11] Scot McKnight also makes this distinction, but further describes anti-Semitism as "irrational, personal, racial prejudice against Jews because they are Jews," and anti-Judaism as "the religious polemic exercised especially by early Christians who thought rejecting Jesus as Messiah was abandoning God's covenant with Israel."[12] Though he uses the term "anti-Judaism," he admits that it too may not be the most appropriate term in light of the fact that the earliest Christians saw themselves as true Jews or the true Israel. Therefore they were not against Judaism per se, but rather against non-Messianic Judaism.[13] McKnight stresses that the real issue is not that Christians have disagreed with Jews over matters of religion, but how they have expressed their disagreements.[14] James Dunn in an article entitled, "The Question of anti-Semitism in the New Testament,"[15] also makes several clarifications regarding the term "anti-Semitism." First he questions the appropriateness of the term in light of the fact that it emerged in the nineteenth century referring to hostility toward Jews based on racial or ethnic differences. Hostility toward Jews prior to the nineteenth century was based primarily on religious differences.[16] It is this fact that has prompted the use of the term "anti-Judaism". Dunn finds this term helpful in that it focuses the discussion on the Jewish religion, but argues that it too needs further clarification. First, it assumes that there is a uniform view of Judaism, universally agreed upon by all its constituents. Second, it assumes a prejudice against the religion from those on the outside. [17]

Qualifying the Term "Anti-Judaism"

Dunn acknowledges Douglas Hare's distinctions between three different kinds of "anti-Judaism": 1) prophetic anti-Judaism, which describes internal critiques of Judaism by Jews; 2) Jewish-Christian anti-Judaism, which are criticisms of Judaism by Jews who believe Jesus is Messiah; and

---

[11] Craig Evans, "Faith and Polemic: The New Testament and First-Century Judaism," in *Anti-Semitism and Early Christianity*, 1.

[12] Scot McKnight, "A Loyal Critic: Matthew's Polemic with Judaism in Theological Perspective," in *Anti-Semitism and Early Christianity*, 56–57.

[13] Ibid., 56; see also 57 n. 5.

[14] Ibid., 57 n. 4.

[15] James D.G. Dunn, "The Question of Anti-Semitism in the New Testament Writings of the Period," in *Jews and Christians: the Parting of the Ways A.D. 70 to 135*, rev. ed., ed. James D. G. Dunn (Grand Rapids: Eerdmans, 1999) 177–211.

[16] Ibid., 179–80.

[17] Ibid., 180.

3) Gentilizing anti-Judaism, which rejects Israel, emphasizing the Gentile character of Christianity.[18] Yet Dunn does not believe these distinctions go far enough. The real problem comes from the fact that Judaism cannot be defined as a monolithic, uniform religious movement. He cites Jacob Neusner's work, which argues for several varieties of Judaism.[19] The lack of consensus on one, single, normative Judaism makes the term "anti-Judaism" somewhat question begging. Which "Judaism" is being attacked? Therefore in any discussion on this subject, these particular nuances of Judaism in the first century need to be considered.

Anti-Judaism as Anti-Semitism

Though there are several scholars who clearly distinguish anti-Judaism from 19th century anti-Semitism, there are others who continue to describe the New Testament as containing anti-Semitism. Samuel Sandmel admits that the term "anti-Semitism" is inappropriate in connection with the New Testament, in light of the fact that the term has 19th century roots. Yet he continues to use the term throughout his book.[20] Though Rosemary Radford Reuther also admits a distinction between anti-Judaism and anti-Semitism, she believes that the anti-Judaism implicit in Christian interpretations of Scripture find "social expression in anti-Semitism."[21] Gavin I. Langmuir also questions whether the efforts of scholars, who have tried to prove that Christian anti-Judaism was distinct and separate from pagan anti-Semitism were successful. He states that Christian scholars were not able to prove an empirical difference between Christian hostilities toward Jews and pagan hostilities. Thus he concludes, "Their historical investigations only demonstrated ever more clearly an undeniable connection be-

---

[18] Douglas R. A. Hare, "The Rejection of the Jews in the Synoptics and Acts," in *Anti-Semitism and the Foundations of Christianity*, ed. A.T. Davies (New York: Paulist, 1979), 28-32. John Gager clarifies the term "prophetic anti-Judaism" to mean an internal debate within Judaism where the *meaning* and *control* of the essential symbols of the faith (temple, Torah, ritual commandments) were in debate rather than the symbols themselves (Gager 1983, 9).

[19] Jacob Neusner, "Varieties of Judaism in the Formative Age," in *Formative Judaism: Second Series* (BJS 41; Chico: Scholars, 1983) 59–89.

[20] Samuel Sandmel, *Anti-Semitism in the New Testament?* (Philadelphia: Fortress, 1978), xix-xxi.

[21] Rosemary Radford Ruether, *Faith and Fratricide* (1974; reprinted, Eugene, Ore.: Wipf & Stock, 1996) 116.

tween Christian hostility in the first century and the horrors of twentieth-century antisemitism."[22]

Hatred and Hostility

Thus we must ask, is the distinction between anti-Judaism and anti-Semitism merely a word game, not really getting to the heart of the issue? Is not the real concern hatred and hostility toward the Jewish people, regardless of the basis of the hatred (theological or racial)? What difference does it really make to a person who receives hate whether it is based on the fact that they look different or whether they believe different things?[23] Therefore, if we adopt the term "anti-Judaism" to distinguish it from nineteenth-century anti-Semitism, we must acknowledge that its extreme forms can be just as morally base as current strands of anti-Semitism.

Douglas Hare's distinctions of anti-Judaism seem to imply that internal critiques are somehow less damaging than external critiques. Yet in each of his categories, there are perhaps extreme forms of rhetoric that promote hatred toward the Jews or some segment of them. Even internal criticisms by fellow Jews vary in degree of harshness and influence. Though these critics may not be properly labeled as anti-Semites, they could be called traitors, who may be even more offensive to their fellow Jewish brothers and sisters.

As we turn our attention to the book of Hebrews, it clear that its polemic is not directly directed against the Jewish people (the term Ἰουδαῖος is not found in the epistle)[24] but to fundamental Jewish institutions. The language against the Levitical priesthood (and law), the Mosaic covenant, and the sacrificial ritual is quite severe.[25] Therefore as we work through the individual passages, we need to evaluate the extent to which the identity of the Jews was tied to these fundamental Jewish institutions and to what degree if any these passages promote hatred or antagonism toward Jews. This will help us evaluate whether the polemic against these religious symbols constitutes a belligerent form of anti-Judaism.

---

[22] Gavin I. Langmuir, *History, Religion, and Antisemitism* (Berkeley: University of California Press, 1990) 276.

[23] We must also note that attacking someone's religion is often more offensive than attacking one's appearance.

[24] When the author refers to Jews, he designates them "the (your) fathers" (1:1, 3:9, 8:9). See Clark M. Williamson, "Anti-Judaism in Hebrews?" *Int* 57 (2003) 270.

[25] Heb 7:18-19; 8:7; 8:13; 10:1-4; 10:9.

Defining Supersessionism

Traditionally, supersessionism implies a complete abandonment of Israel by God, with the church as Israel's replacement. Franklin Littell identifies supersessionism as having two foci: "(1) God is finished with the Jews; (2) the 'new Israel' (the Christian church) takes the place of the Jewish people as the carrier of history."[26] After the Holocaust, there has been a strong denouncement of supersessionism in favor of a more open, accepting view of Judaism.[27] Donald Bloesch writes that in the contemporary approach, "Israel has its own unique contribution to be a light to the nations; and the church is another light, but not one that surpasses or supersedes Israel."[28]

When the discussion is framed in such a manner it seems that only two options are available. If one believes in the exclusive claims of Christianity, he or she is a supersessionist (= God has abandoned Israel; the Christian religion replaces Judaism). The only other option seems to be to embrace contemporary Judaism as an equally acceptable religion, doing away with the uniqueness and necessity of Jesus as Messiah. It seems

---

[26] Franklin H. Littell, *The Crucifixion of the Jews* (New York: Harper & Row, 1975) 30.

[27] In the declaration, *Nostra aetate,* signed by Pope Paul VI in 1965, the Catholic Church officially rejected older views of supersessionism. The document states, "the Jews should not be spoken of as rejected or accursed as if this followed from holy Scripture" (*Documents of Vatican II,* ed. Austin P. Flannery [Grand Rapids: Eerdmans, 1975] 741). For more statements by the Roman Catholic Church against supersessionism, see Eugene J. Fisher, "The Church's Teaching on Supersessionism," *BAR* 17 (1991) 58. In addition, in 1987, the General Assembly of the Presbyterian Church (U.S.A.) approved a document entitled, *A Theological Understanding of the Relationship between Christians and Jews* (New York: Office of the General Assembly, 1987). In this document, which was not an official position paper but commended to the church for study and reflection, these two statements were made:

> 2. We affirm that the church, elected in Jesus Christ, has been engrafted into the people of God established by the covenant with Abraham, Isaac, and Jacob. Therefore, Christians have not replaced Jews (*A Theological Understanding*, 8).
> 3. We affirm that both the church and the Jewish people are elected by God for witness to the world and that the relationship of the church to contemporary Jews is based on that gracious and irrevocable election of both (*A Theological Understanding*, 10).

For an evaluation of the paper see Robert R. Hann, "Supersessionism, Engraftment, and Jewish-Christian Dialogue: Reflections on the Presbyterian Statement on Jewish-Christian Relations," *JES* 27 (1990) 327–42. For more ecumenical statements see Thomas Breidenthal, "Neighbor-Christology: Reconstructing Christianity Before Supersessionism," *Cross Currents* 49 (1999) 319 n. 1.

[28] Donald G. Bloesch, "'All Israel Will Be Saved': Supersessionism and the Biblical Witness," *Int* 43 (1989) 131.

that this dichotomy is too simplistic and rigid to do justice to the complex dynamics of Christianity's emergence from Judaism.[29]

Therefore, as we examine various polemical passages in Hebrews we need to ask what specifically is being superseded? Is the text arguing for the replacement of the Jewish people, or simply Jewish practices and institutions? And if the passage does indicate the replacement of specific elements of Judaism, what takes their place? Are they completely new institutions, or things that are informed and foreshadowed by the old? There can be a supersession of Jewish practices and institutions that need not imply a complete abandonment by God of the Jewish people.

---

[29] See Donald Hagner, "A Positive Theology of Judaism from the New Testament," *SEÅ* 69 (2004) 7–28.

1

The History of Scholarship on Anti-Semitism, Anti-Judaism, and Supersessionism in Hebrews

General Trends

BEFORE World War II, only a few scholars took up the issue of anti-Semitism and the New Testament. Notable are G. F. Moore, James Parkes, and A. Lukyn Williams.[1] They argued that there were many anti-Judaic statements in early Christian literature. After World War II, several more studies addressed this issue. Jules Isaac's work, *Jésus et Israel,* published in 1948,[2] argued that the New Testament presented a contemptuous picture of the Jews and the Jewish religion. He questioned whether the Christian religion could ever separate itself from its implicit anti-Semitic roots.

Following Isaac was Marcel Simon's *Verus Israel* originally published in 1948, with a second edition in 1964.[3] Simon made a crucial distinction between "anti-Jewish polemic" and "Christian anti-Semitism." The first describes the effort by Christians to distinguish themselves ideologically

---

[1] See G. F. Moore, "Christian Writers on Judaism," *HTR* 14 (1921) 197–254; James Parkes, *The Conflict of the Church and the Synagogue: A Study in the Origins of Antisemitism* (Philadelphia: Jewish Publication Society of America, 1961); A. L. Williams, *Adversus Judaeos: A Bird's Eye View of Christian Apologiae until the Renaissance* (Cambridge: Cambridge University, 1935).

[2] A revised edition was published in 1959, and an English translation was produced in 1971: Jules Isaac, *Jesus and Israel* (New York: Holt, Rinehart and Winston, 1971).

[3] Marcel Simon, *Verus Israel: étude sur les relations entre chrétiens et juifs dans l'empire romain (135–425)* (Paris: Boccard, 1948). For the English translation see Marcel Simon, *Verus Israel: A Study of the Relations between Christians and Jews in the Roman Empire (135–425),* trans. H. McKeating (Oxford: Oxford University Press, 1986).

from Jews. The second represents hostility towards Jews in general, but mainly as a result of their refusal to accept Christian claims. This began the attempt to distinguish between justifiable rational polemic and violent acts or belligerent words.

Two scholars who have attempted to respond to Isaac are F. Lovsky[4] and Gregory Baum. Lovsky tries to protect the New Testament from Isaac's anti-Semitic claim by arguing that anti-Semitism before Christianity actually had a much larger influence on early Christianity than Isaac admits. Secondly, Isaac does not distinguish between anti-Judaism and anti-Semitism. Lovsky argues that there is no anti-Semitism in the New Testament—except possibly in John. However, there is indeed anti-Judaism. Gregory Baum began trying to defend the New Testament from charges of being anti-Semitic by attributing anti-Semitism of Christians to later historical developments. Yet as he continued to dialogue with others,[5] he changed his mind. He now believes that the New Testament is anti-Jewish and that a few marginal corrections will not clear its name.[6]

Much of the discussion following the holocaust revolved around making theological room for the Jewish religion. Catholic and Protestant scholars have attempted to show that the Jewish and Christian faiths are actually one, though mediated through different covenants or types of covenants.[7] These studies have primarily focused on ecclesiology, redefining the believing community.

J. Coert Rylaarsdam begins by identifying two covenants in the Old Testament, one made with Israel and the other made with David. He argues that the covenant with Israel was the older *berith*, which was a covenant of religious confederacy.[8] This covenant is more of a historically oriented covenant, while the Davidic is more eschatologically oriented.[9] Rylaarsdam sees Christianity's uniqueness as a Jewish sect as simply a re-prioritizing of the Davidic covenant over against the one made with Israel.

---

[4] Lovsky, *Antisémitisme et mystère d'Israel* (Paris: A Michel, 1955).

[5] Especially Rosemary Radford Ruether; see the introduction to *Faith and Fratricide* (1974; reprinted, Eugene, Ore.: Wipf & Stock, 1996).

[6] Gregory Baum, introduction to *Faith and Fratricide,* by Rosemary Radford Ruether 7.

[7] Alan Davies identifies Paul Tillich and Reinhold Niebuhr as two theologians who support the theory of two covenants: *Antisemitism and the Christian Mind* (New York: Herder and Herder, 1969) 145–46. In addition, J. Coert Rylaarsdam has also promoted this view.

[8] Rylaarsdam, "Jewish-Christian Relationships: The Two Covenants and the Dilemmas of Christology," in *Grace upon Grace,* ed. J. I. Cook (Grand Rapids: Eerdmans, 1975) 72.

[9] Ibid., 79.

He argues that both of these covenants are found in the New Testament, creating an opportunity for dialogue between Judaism and Christianity.[10]

Rosemary Radford Ruether, in her book *Faith and Fratricide*, published in 1974, contributed to the discussion by asking whether the Christian gospel itself contains elements of anti-Jewish trends. She identifies the claim, "Jesus is Messiah," as the source and origin of anti-Semitism in Christian thought. For by claiming Jesus as the Christ, one necessarily refutes the synagogue reading of Scripture. Therefore all the early Christian writings were bent on proving that the church alone had the hermeneutical key to understand Scripture. This implied that the Jews were reading Scripture incorrectly. It is this crucial distinction that Radford describes as the "left hand of Christology." She argues that it is difficult to say, "Jesus is the Messiah," without saying at the same time, "the Jews be damned."[11] Thus the gospel itself has created the divide between the synagogue and the church.

More recently, some scholars have tried to combine several different reasons for anti-Judaism and anti-Semitism within the Christian faith.[12] For example, Gavin I. Langmuir points to the fact that the Christian sect of Judaism was inherently anti-Judaic in order to distinguish itself and propagate itself. "For motives common to most sects, the adherents of the new Christian religions were necessarily anti-Judaic in the sense that they had to demonstrate the superiority of their Christian religions to any Judaic religions."[13] Langmuir sees the emergence of anti-Semitism coming from the disbelief of the Jews in Jesus, the accusation of deicide, and the idea that God was punishing the Jews for their disbelief.[14]

---

[10] Ibid., 83.

[11] Ruether, *Faith and Fratricide*, 246.

[12] Miriam S. Taylor focuses her research on the early patristic writings and concludes that Christian anti-Judaism was not a result of competition with Judaism for converts, Jewish persecution, or inherited pagan or Christian prejudices. Rather it was motivated theologically to help shape early Christian identity. See Miriam S. Taylor, *Anti-Judaism and the Early Christian Identity: A Critique of the Scholarly Consensus*, Studia post-biblica 46 (Leiden: Brill, 1995).

[13] Gavin I. Langmuir, *History, Religion, and Anti-Semitism* (Berkeley: University of California, 1990), 282.

[14] Langmuir, *History, Religion, and Anti-Semitism*, 285.

Focus on Hebrews

Negative Views of the Epistle

Although Hebrews has not been the focus of the debate in regard to the question of anti-Semitism in the New Testament,[15] there have been some pretty serious charges laid against it. With the majority of scholars, Lillian Freudmann argues that Hebrews was written to persuade Christians who were tempted to revert back to Judaism.[16] However, she asserts that the author of Hebrews twisted Old Testament passages to demonstrate the superiority of Christianity over Judaism.[17] Freudmann concludes that this type of exegesis "transmitted an anti-Torah, anti-Jewish, and antisemitic ideology."[18] She accuses the author of intentionally manipulating Old Testament passages to present a negative view of Judaism and those who hold on to Jewish practices.

John Gager, in his book *The Origins of Anti-Semitism,* admits that Hebrews does not make any explicit attack against the Jewish people, but rather the Jewish faith. Yet this attack is of such a radical nature, he cannot categorize it as simply a critique from within Judaism.[19] He concludes that Hebrews is "the most sustained and systematic case against Judaizing to be found anywhere in Christian literature of the first century."[20]

Samuel Sandmel does not see the book of Hebrews as vilifying Judaism. He argues that the book is really addressing the ancient Judaism of Scripture, rather than the Jews of the generation in which it was written. However, he does see the epistle as supersessionist. Hebrews describes

---

[15] A recent article by Clark M. Williamson has brought more attention to the question of anti-Judaism in Hebrews. See Clark M. Williamson, "Anti-Judaism in Hebrews?" *Int* 57 (2003) 266–79. He frames the discussion on the question of anti-Judaism in Hebrews by distinguishing "yes" and "no" types. While this article is a helpful beginning, it does not distinguish adequately the various approaches used by the "no" types. Furthermore, Williamson does not leave room for an anti-Judaism that is simply a "theological disagreement;" rather he defines the term only in a negative sense, inevitably leading to anti-Semitism (Williamson, 277).

[16] Lillian C. Freudmann, *Antisemitism in the New Testament* (Lanham, Md.: University Press of America, 1994) 150.

[17] Ibid., 158.

[18] Ibid.

[19] John G. Gager, *The Origins of Anti-Semitism: Attitudes Toward Judaism in Pagan and Christian Antiquity* (New York: Oxford University, 1983) 183.

[20] Ibid., 184.

Christianity as the pinnacle and perfection of ancient Judaism.²¹ Sandmel writes, "In summary, it is the ancient Judaism with which Hebrews deals, regarding it as the worthy but imperfect preparation for the perfection which is Christianity. The Christ has superseded the Law; Christianity has superseded Judaism."²²

Hunt proposes that Hebrews is actually an early anti-Judaic treatise that Paul took over adding chapter 13. Much of his argument is based on stylistic differences and the fact that Hebrews 13:22 mentions that the author only wrote briefly. Noting that the epistle itself is not brief, he imagines Paul writing a short addendum to a pre-existing anti-Judaic tract. He also points out that many of the anti-Judaic tracts of the time were entitled πρὸς Ἰουδαίους. Thus the title, Πρὸς Ἑβραίους was not "To the Hebrews," but "Against the Hebrews."²³

Positive Views of the Epistle

Emphasis on Continuity

Other scholars do not find Hebrews to be hostile to Jewish people. These works can be divided into essentially three different types. The first is the approach that seeks to mitigate the discontinuity and polemical nature of the book. For example, William Lane first discusses the structure of Hebrews as oscillating between exposition and exhortation. He points out that the exhortation is really the focus of the book, and the exposition only serves to support the exhortation.²⁴ This is important because Lane sees no discontinuity or pejorative terms against Judaism in the exhortation sections.²⁵ He understands the radical statements in Hebrews 7-10,

---

[21] Samuel Sandmel, *Anti-Semitism in the New Testament?* (Philadelphia: Fortress, 1978) 121.

[22] Ibid., 122. See also N. A. Beck, *Mature Christianity in the 21ˢᵗ Century: The Recognition and Repudiation of the Anti-Jewish Polemic of the New Testament*, 2d ed. (New York: Crossroad, 1994).

[23] B. P. W. S Hunt, "The Epistle to the Hebrews or against the Hebrews? Anti-Judaic Treatise?" *SE* 2 (1964) 408.

[24] John Walters argues similarly in his analysis of the structure of Hebrews. He cites Barnabus Lindars as the one who has rightly identified the climax of the epistle to fall not in the doctrinal sections, but in the final hortatory section; Barnabas Lindars, "The Rhetorical Structure of Hebrews," *NTS* 35 (1989) 392 n. 2; J. R. Walters, "The Rhetorical Arrangement of Hebrews," *AsTJ* 51 (1996) 59–70.

[25] Robert W. Wall and William Lane, "Polemic in Hebrews and the Catholic Epistles," in *Anti-Semitism and Early Christianity*, eds. Craig Evans and Donald Hagner (Minneapolis: Fortress, 1993), 173. See also William Lane, *Hebrews 1–8*, WBC 47a (Dallas: Word, 1991) cxxv–xxxv.

not as polemic, but as reflections on Old Testament prophecies. He argues that the author of Hebrews wants to emphasize the fulfillment of God's promises, the very thing that is questioned by his readers (Klassen argues similarly).[26] Lane concludes that the book of Hebrews is not trying to convince Christians who are tempted to abandon their Christian faith for Judaism, but those who are tempted to abandon their belief in God altogether.[27] He writes, "The premise that Hebrews engages in any form of anti-Judaic polemic, however, is untenable."[28]

In reference to the new covenant language found in Hebrews 8, Dieter Sänger states that the "new" covenant from a Jewish perspective never had in mind the "casting off" of the Jews, rather it was a renewal of the old covenant.[29] He also argues that early Christians saw themselves as part of Judaism.[30] Thus in a context where one's view of Torah and *halakah* were often debated, Christians were just one voice among many. Sänger believes that Christians simply turned to Jesus in their critique of the cultural and legal aspects of the law.[31]

BALANCE OF CONTINUITY AND DISCONTINUITY

Another approach seeks to balance both the continuity and discontinuity in the epistle. Yet the discontinuity is never identified as anti-Semitism, but rather anti-Judaism. Donald Hagner asserts that though there may be anti-Judaism—a theological disagreement with Judaism—in the epistle, there certainly is no warrant for anti-Semitism—hostility toward Jews. He also points out that the strong discontinuity within Hebrews is more

---

[26] William Klassen, "To the Hebrews or against the Hebrews? Anti-Judaism and the Epistle to the Hebrews," in *Anti-Judaism in Early Christianity*, Vol. 2 of *Separation and Polemic*, ed. Stephen G. Wilson (Waterloo, Ont.: Wilfred Laurier University Press, 1986) 1–16.

[27] Wall and Lane, "Polemic in Hebrews and the Catholic Epistles," 184.

[28] Lane, *Hebrews 1–8*, cxxxv. A fuller analysis of Lane's approach is found below in the conclusion of chapter 3, pages 60-61; chapter 4, pages 95-97; and chapter 5, pages 145-46.

[29] See also Marie E. Isaacs, "Hebrews," in *Early Christian Thought in Its Jewish Context*, ed. J. Barclay and J. Sweet (Cambridge: Cambridge University Press, 1996) 158.

[30] Other scholars make this same point. See Tim Perry, "The Historical Jesus, Anti-Judaism, and the Christology of Hebrews: A Theological Reflection," *Did* 10 (1999) 74; C. P. Anderson, "Who Are the Heirs of the New Age in the Epistle to the Hebrews?," in *Apocalyptic and the New Testament: Essays in Honor of J. Louis Martyn*, ed. Joel Marcus and Marion L. Soards, JSNTSS 24 (Sheffield: JSOT Press, 1989) 273; and Isaacs, "Hebrews," 157.

[31] Dieter Sänger, "Neues Testament und Antijudaismus: Versuch einer exegetischen und hermeneutischen Vergewisserung im innerchristlichen Gespräch," *KD 34* (1988) 210–31.

of an intra-Jewish debate. Finally, Hagner mentions the sociological phenomenon that those who depart from one religious faith to another often become the harshest critics of the faith they left.[32]

Donald Bloesch notes that Hebrews seems to promote supersessionism, but at the same time it venerates the Old Testament saints. There is both continuity and discontinuity in the epistle. He writes,

> The Epistle to the Hebrews could possibly be designated as a supersessionist book, since the author insists that the Old Testament sacrificial system and priesthood have been superseded by the all-sufficient sacrifice of Jesus Christ and his efficacious intercession as our one High Priest. Yet even here Old Testament heroes and heroines are celebrated as models of true faith in God. One passage intimates that the faith of Israel finally apprehends its object through the sanctifying of the church (Heb 11:40).[33]

Therefore Bloesch seems to qualify the term "supersession" to speak of the replacement of Jewish institutions and not necessarily the replacement of the Jewish people.

Rhetorical Approach

The third approach to the question of anti-Semitism in Hebrews has been the use of rhetorical analysis. Luke Timothy Johnson deals with the question of anti-Jewish language in the New Testament by placing it in its cultural context. His main point is that slander among competing religious and philosophical schools was actually quite common. Johnson argues that early Christianity was likely thought of as a sect of Judaism, which had to survive in the midst of a majority of non-Messianic sects. Therefore, the language of slander should be expected because Christians were a marginalized group among a majority.[34]

Since Judaism was quite Hellenized at the time, one can see a parallel between the Jewish sects and the Greek philosophical schools.[35] Johnson demonstrates how the philosophers through several various writings used very strong language in their attacks on other groups. He also examines some Jewish writings and finds similar polemic. "The main thing such

---

[32] Donald Hagner, *Encountering the Book of Hebrews* (Grand Rapids: Baker Academic, 2002) 35–36.

[33] Bloesch, "All Israel Will Be Saved," 139.

[34] Luke Timothy Johnson, "The New Testament's Anti-Jewish Slander and the Conventions of Ancient Polemic," *JBL* 108 (1989) 423–24.

[35] Ibid., 429.

slander signified, therefore, was that someone was an opponent. . . . The slander was not affected by facts. A particular Platonist may be a good person, but that does not affect the way Platonists as such are to be described."[36] Johnson concludes: 1) in the context, Christians (Messianists) had reason to be critical of other groups; 2) their slander was quite mild compared with others; 3) their use of rhetoric was more to conjure up certain feelings about a group than to scientifically describe exactly what they were; and 4) both Messianic and non-Messianic Jews used the rhetoric of Hellenistic Philosophical schools.[37]

David A. deSilva approaches the question of anti-Judaism in Hebrews by using socio-rhetorical analysis. He argues that the author of Hebrews was not arguing against the Levitical priesthood, but was simply using rhetoric to highlight the greatness of Jesus' priesthood. He suggests that the author was using *encomia*, "speeches in praise of some person and his or her achievements."[38] Thus the author simply picked a type or pattern to which he could compare Jesus. It was not a poor reflection upon the Levitical priests per se, but they were chosen simply because they were a pattern that Jesus' ministry followed. In this way, the author was better able to bring out the salvation historical element of Jesus' priestly ministry. It follows that the author's goal was to cause his audience to feel a sense of privilege and honor in experiencing something unavailable to previous generations. DeSilva does not see the rhetorical goal as simply a polemic against those who are tempted to fall back into Judaism.[39]

DeSilva's insights are helpful in bringing out the rhetorical function of the author's use of *synkrisis* within his examination of honor-shame language in the epistle. It seems reasonable that the author's comparison of Jesus with Moses in 3:1-6 does not intend to denigrate Moses, but rather to praise Jesus. Yet it is more difficult to argue the same as we examine the author's comparison between Christ's priesthood, covenant, and sacrifice and that of the Levitical priesthood (and law), Mosaic covenant, and Levitical sacrifices. Can we reasonably believe that there was no sense of polemic in this language?[40] Clearly the author did not want his readers to

---

[36] Ibid., 433.

[37] Ibid., 441.

[38] David A. deSilva, *Perseverance in Gratitude: A Socio-Rhetorical Commentary on the Epistle 'to the Hebrews'* (Grand Rapids: Eerdmans, 2000) 263.

[39] Ibid., 264.

[40] The author describes 1) the law as "weak" and "useless" (7:18); 2) the Mosaic covenant as having "fault" (8:7) and becoming obsolete (8:13); and 3) the ineffectiveness of bull and goat sacrifices in taking away sins (10:4), cf. 13:10.

participate in the Levitical priesthood, the Mosaic covenant, and Levitical sacrifices. Therefore, it stands to reason that he did intend to paint these older institutions in a negative light, because of a real threat of reversion. Luke Timothy Johnson points out that strong polemical language signifies that someone was indeed an opponent.[41]

In deSilva's approach, many insights are gleaned from examining the epistle through the lens of the patron-client relationship and honor-shame language. Yet de Silva does not explore the sociological function of conflict language in the epistle. He assumes too quickly that polemics are not at work in Hebrews.

---

[41] Johnson, "The New Testament's Anti-Jewish Slander," 433.

2

The Method of Approach

We shall approach the question of anti-Semitism, anti-Judaism, and supersessionism in Hebrews by applying the socio-rhetorical method to three specific polemical passages: Heb 7:1-19, 8:1-13, and 10:1-10.[1] The socio-rhetorical approach will be particularly helpful in this study because it blends together rhetorical criticism, social-scientific criticism, as well as other modern methods.[2] In this chapter, we will first review rhetorical and socio-scientific studies on Hebrews. Then, we will describe and evaluate the socio-rhetorical approach.

Review of Rhetorical Approaches to Hebrews

General Trends

The socio-rhetorical approach has its roots in rhetorical criticism, which can be divided into three major trajectories: literary-aesthetic studies, rhetorical criticism, and the "new rhetoric" of Chaim Perelman and Lucie Olbrechts-Tyteca.[3]

LITERARY-AESTHETIC STUDIES

The modern history of rhetorical criticism began with James Muilenburg's 1968 Presidential address to the Society of Biblical Literature. At that fo-

---

[1] These passages represent the most radical statements against Judaism in the epistle to the Hebrews. Though there are other passages that might also indicate anti-Semitic, anti-Judaic, or supersessionist statements (cf. 3:3; 9:8-10; 13:10), they are not as radical or clearly identified as speaking against Judaism.

[2] Vernon K. Robbins, *Exploring the Texture of Texts: A Guide to Socio-Rhetorical Interpretation* (Valley Forge, Pa.: Trinity, 1996) 1.

[3] Chaim Perelman and Lucie Olbrechts-Tyteca, *The New Rhetoric: A Treatise on Argumentation* (Notre Dame: University of Notre Dame Press, 1969).

rum, he asked what would come after form criticism.[4] Muilenburg wanted to move beyond form criticism, which did not do enough to examine authorial creativity and composition. He also wanted to head off the new literary critical movement, which seemed to discount any historical considerations when examining a text.[5] Amos Niven Wilder also promoted a rhetorical approach that was historically grounded. He did not want to separate form from content.[6] However, what has emerged from Muilenburg's and Wilder's work is a view that rhetorical criticism is primarily an examination of the aesthetics or literary properties of the text.

RHETORICAL CRITICISM

A second movement promoted by George A. Kennedy is referred to as "rhetorical criticism." Kennedy shifted the focus from rhetoric as literary artistry to rhetoric as the art of persuasion, using classical Greek rhetoric as his guide.[7] Though he was not the first to adopt this more technical definition of rhetoric for New Testament interpretation, he was perhaps the most influential.[8] He distinguishes rhetorical criticism from (new) literary criticism in that literary criticism is concerned with how modern readers read these ancient documents, while rhetorical criticism seeks to discern how the ancient readers read the works in their own context.[9]

---

[4] Burton L. Mack, *Rhetoric and the New Testament*, GBS (Minneapolis: Fortress, 1990) 12.

[5] Mack, *Rhetoric and the New Testament*, 12.

[6] Amos N. Wilder, *Early Christian Rhetoric: The Language of the Gospel* (Cambridge: Harvard University Press, 1964) 25–26.

[7] George Kennedy, *New Testament Interpretation through Rhetorical Criticism* (Chapel Hill: University of North Carolina Press, 1984) 3. Kennedy draws many of his rhetorical categories from Aristotle's *Rhetoric*. He also notes Cicero's works *On Invention* and *Partitions of Oratory*, and Quintilian's work, *On the Education of the Orator*. See Kennedy, *New Testament Interpretation*, 12–13.

[8] Some identify Hans Dieter Betz's work, "The Literary Composition and Function of Paul's Letter to the Galatians," NTS 21 (1975) 353–79 as the beginning of a new era in New Testament scholarship. Cf. Betz, *Galatians: A Commentary on Paul's Letter to the Churches in Galatia*, Hermeneia (Philadelphia: Fortress, 1979). See Carl Joachim Classen, *Rhetorical Criticism of the New Testament*, WUNT 128 (Tübingen: Mohr/Siebeck, 2000) 1–2.

[9] Kennedy, *New Testament Interpretation*, 5. Kennedy has come under recent criticism for his assertion that the New Testament writings primarily follow Greco-Roman rhetorical forms. Roland Meynet argues that the New Testament writings more appropriately follow Jewish rhetorical forms; Meynet, *Rhetorical Analysis: An Introduction to Biblical Rhetoric*, JSOTSS 256 (Sheffield: Sheffield Academic Press, 1998) 21–22. Meynet distinguishes Hebrew rhetoric from Greco-Roman rhetoric in three ways: 1) Jewish rhetoric is more con-

Kennedy outlines an approach that begins with identifying the rhetorical unit. He defines a unit as that which has a beginning, middle, and an end.[10] He notes that one must look for signs that indicate a proem and epilogue (i.e., *inclusios*, etc.). Once the unit is determined, one must turn to form criticism and seek to define the rhetorical situation or *Sitz im Leben* of the text, specifically the situation in which the reader was to make some response.[11] This can be facilitated by identifying the text as deliberative, judicial, or epideictic and then determining the rhetorical problem (objections that the audience may have had against the speaker).[12] Next would be an examination of the arrangement of the material, paying attention to the argument and its use of deductive or inductive reasoning.[13] Once this is complete then one should look over the entire unit and ask whether it was successful in meeting its rhetorical goal.[14]

The "New Rhetoric"

A third trajectory is described as the "new rhetoric." Burton Mack argues that the publication of Chaim Perelman and L. Olbrechts-Tyteca's English translation of *The New Rhetoric: A Treatise on Argumentation*[15] moved the discipline from seeing rhetoric as simply an analysis of style and aesthetics, to seeing it as argumentation.[16] Though this movement is similar to

---

crete than abstract; 2) it uses parataxis more than hypotaxis; and 3) it is more involutive than linear (173–75). Kennedy defends the idea that we can look at the New Testament using Greek rhetorical categories, even though it was written in-between two cultures. He bases his premise on the widespread Hellenization of the Near East and points to the works of Josephus and Philo as examples. Kennedy also makes a lengthy argument that Jesus and Paul were at least acquainted with Greek rhetoric if not formally trained. Thus he argues that it is historically and philosophically legitimate to use classical Greek rhetoric in analyzing the New Testament. He does note, however, that one must be aware of other influences, such as the Jewish chiasmus, in the unique rhetoric of the New Testament (Kennedy, 8–12). Whether one defines the New Testament as uniquely Hebraic with some parallel to Greco-Roman forms or primarily Greco-Roman with some Jewish influence seems to depend on the specific New Testament writing. Instead of thinking in binary terms of either Hellenistic or Jewish, it may be better to view each writing on a continuous spectrum between these two extremes.

[10] Kennedy, *New Testament Interpretation*, 34.
[11] Ibid., 35.
[12] Ibid., 36.
[13] Ibid., 37.
[14] Ibid., 38.
[15] Perelman and Olbrechts-Tyteca, *The New Rhetoric*.
[16] Mack, *Rhetoric and the New Testament*, 14.

Kennedy's rhetorical criticism, it emphasizes the social situation behind the text much more than Kennedy's approach and focuses less on how the text follows Greco-Roman rhetorical forms. Perelman and Olbrechts-Tyteca bring out the fact that the social situation in which the argument was made is an important factor in understanding the persuasive force of an argument.

> All language is the language of a community, be this a community bound by biological ties, or by the practice of a common discipline or technique. The terms used, their meanings, their definition, can only be understood in the context of the habits, ways of thought, methods, external circumstances, and traditions known to the users of those terms.[17]

Perelman and Olbrechts-Tyteca wanted to focus on the audience and the social context as well as the speaker and the speech. This led naturally to examining the rhetoric of a text in hopes of reconstructing the social history behind the text. This approach takes rhetorical criticism out of the context of analysis of style and ornamentation, and into the realm of a social theory of language.[18] The reader can trace back each writing to a particular Christian persuasion and its view of authority. Then one can rank the various authorities and evaluate whether or not the use of these authorities has persuasive force.[19] This third trajectory comes closest to socio-rhetorical criticism.

Focus on Hebrews

The history of scholarship of rhetorical criticism applied to Hebrews follows the three trajectories mentioned above.

---

[17] Perelman and Olbrechts-Tyteca, *The New Rhetoric*, 513.

[18] Mack, *Rhetoric and the New Testament*, 15–16. See also C. Clifton Black, "Rhetorical Criticism," in *Hearing the New Testament: Strategies for Interpretation*, ed. Joel Green (Grand Rapids: Eerdmans, 1995) 263–64.

[19] Mack, *Rhetoric and the New Testament*, 23–24. Mack notes the highly polemical nature of Christian rhetoric, which makes ample use of comparison and contrast with the surrounding culture in defining itself. He argues that this type of rhetoric often presents a straw man in the polemic and creates "inauthentic discourse." Thus much of the New Testament shows the Christian perspective as superior, or paints the opponents unfairly or inadequately (96).

LITERARY-AESTHETIC STUDIES

Structural Analyses

Perhaps the best examples of the kind of rhetorical approach promoted by Muilenburg applied to the epistle to the Hebrews are the structural analyses of Leon Vaganay, Albert Vanhoye, and Wolfgang Nauck. Though they ended up with different results, they all focused on the literary character of the epistle.

Leon Vaganay's work is thought to be the beginning of the modern discussion on the structure of Hebrews.[20] He was perhaps the first to apply his knowledge of the rhetorical aspects of the book to his structural analysis.[21] Perhaps most notable was his identification of "hook" words used to connect sections together.[22] His approach led him to a five-part structure, which was thematically chiastic or concentric.

Albert Vanhoye followed Vaganay, but was able to synthesize the work of others as well. He identified the principal techniques used by the author in constructing the epistle: 1) announcement of the topics to be discussed; 2) *inclusios*, which determine the boundaries of the topics; 3) variation of literary genre (exposition or *paraenesis*); 4) words, which characterize a development; 5) use of "hook" words; and 6) symmetric arrangement.[23] Using these devices he proposed a symmetrically arranged structure, with only minor differences from Vaganay.[24]

Wolfgang Nauck departed from the Vaganay/Vanhoye outline and revised Otto Michel's three-part structure as an alternate view.[25] He marked the end of the first section of Hebrews as 4:13 in light of the parallel he saw between 1:2b-3 and 4:12-13. He also saw a parallel between 4:14-16 and 10:19-23. Thus he identifies the beginning of the second section as

---

[20] George H. Guthrie, *The Structure of Hebrews: A Text-Linguistic Analysis*, NovTSup 73 (Leiden: Brill, 1994; Grand Rapids: Baker, 1998) 11–12.

[21] Though Vaganay's work preceded Muilenburg's 1968 address, Muilenburg is still heralded as the one who initiated the major shift in New Testament scholarship toward rhetorical criticism.

[22] Leon Vaganay, "Le Plan de L'Épître aux Hébreux," in *Mémorial Lagrange*, ed. L.-H. Vincent (Paris: Gabalda, 1940) 271–72.

[23] Albert Vanhoye, *Structure and Message of the Epistle to the Hebrews*, trans. James Swetnam, Subsidia Biblica 12 (Rome: Pontifical Biblical Institute Press, 1989) 20.

[24] Ibid., 40a-b.

[25] Wolfgang Nauck, "Zum Aufbau des Hebräerbriefes," in *Judentum, Urchristentum, Kirche: Festschrift für Joachim Jeremias*, ed. Walther Eltester, BZNW 26 (Berlin: Töpelmann, 1960) 199–206.

4:14 and the end as 10:31.[26] The final section (10:32-13:17) begins and ends with similar exhortations.[27]

Semiotic Discourse Approach

Since Muilenburg, many scholars have concentrated simply on the aesthetics of the text, moving away from historical considerations. Andries Snyman in an article entitled, "Hebrews 6:4-6: From a Semiotic Discourse Perspective,"[28] focuses on the text rather than the sender, recipient, or its history. The semiotic approach is derived from a structural approach to linguistics, which was one of the many approaches that moved away from a focus on the history of the text to the text itself.[29]

The basic premise of the approach is that meaningful relations occur not simply between words in a sentence, but also among larger groups—like sentences, pericopes, paragraphs, etc. One must understand these relationships in order to understand the flow of the argument. Three layers of meaning are identified: 1) the declarative, which simply describes the text as it is predicated lexically and semantically;[30] 2) the structural, which describes the clustering of individual cola into larger units (pericope) based on semantic considerations;[31] and 3) the intentional, which describes the purpose or message of the discourse.[32]

After a brief evaluation of the method, Snyman applies it to Heb 6:4-6, which seems to indicate that it is impossible for apostates to repent and be brought back into the fold of God. On the declarative level the author states very simply, "those who have tasted the heavenly gift, etc., and then abandoned their faith cannot be brought back to repentance again."[33] On the structural level, the statement that his readers are babes in the faith prepares them for the warning in the following section. The author is arguing that his readers should not be reluctant to grow in their faith. Rather,

---

[26] Otto Michel ended the second section at 10:18. See Otto Michel, *Der Brief an die Hebräer*, 13th ed., KEK (Göttingen: Vandenhoeck & Ruprecht, 1975) 29–35.

[27] Nauck, "Zum Aufbau des Hebräerbriefes," 200–203.

[28] Andries H. Snyman, "Hebrews 6:4-6: From a Semiotic Discourse Perspective," in *Discourse Analysis and the New Testament: Approaches and Results*, ed. Stanley E. Porter and Jeffery T. Reed, JSNTSS 170 (Sheffield: Sheffield Academic Press, 1999) 354–68.

[29] Ibid., 354.

[30] Ibid., 356.

[31] Ibid., 357.

[32] Ibid.

[33] Ibid., 365.

they should seek to know the full significance of Jesus as their high priest. But before the author proceeds to teach them this significance, he warns them of the real danger of apostasy.[34] On the intentional level, this passage challenges its audience to right action by eliciting an emotional response. Snyman sees it serving the purpose of the larger message in 5:11-6:20, namely, to call his readers to remain faithful to their faith.[35]

RHETORICAL CRITICISM

General Studies

There have been several general studies on the book of Hebrews following the pattern of George A. Kennedy. Walter G. Übelacker, for instance, argues that Hebrews is an example of deliberative discourse written to persuade the audience to make a choice. Übelacker divides up the sections of the epistle as follows: 1:1-4 is identified as *Prooemium* (*exordium*); 1:5—2:18 is *Narratio* with *Propositio* in 2:17-18; 3:1—12:29 is *Argumentatio* with *probatio* and *refutatio*; 13:1-21 is *Peroratio*; and 13:22-25 is *Postscriptum*. The literary character of 1:1—13:21 is identified as a "word of encouragement." [36]

Übelacker begins with the idea that the text is a unity, and must be seen as a unity. He argues that from an analysis of the literary character we come to understand the basic thoughts of organization.[37] The warning sections in Hebrews are identified as *paraklesis* just as the author himself calls his work a word of *paraklesis* (encouragement). Übelacker also distinguishes between direct warnings and indirect warnings. The direct warnings are admonitions and can be categorized as *paraenesis*. The indirect, however, he describes as "Evaluation" or "Appeal".[38]

In another study, Thomas H. Olbricht discusses the rhetorical technique of amplification as it is applied to the epistle to the Hebrews. The term is Aristotle's and describes a way of fleshing out an argument by demonstrating a person's value or worth by comparing him with men of notable reputation. Olbricht comments on the structure of Hebrews and

---

[34] Ibid.
[35] Ibid., 367.
[36] Walter Übelacker, *Der Hebräerbrief als Appell* (Stockhom: Almqvist & Wiksell, 1989) 224.
[37] Ibid., 17.
[38] Ibid., 32.

then compares its use of amplification with funereal oratory in classical Greece and in the early Christian fathers.[39]

In his study of funeral sermons, he notes a common pattern and then applies this knowledge to the structure of Hebrews. He finds significant parallels between Hebrews and the eulogies of Isocrates on Evagoras and Gregory Nazianzen on Basil the Great.[40] Taking the general categories of funeral discourses, Olbricht identifies three main sections in Hebrews: 1) *exordium* (1:1-4); 2) *encomium* (1:5—13:16); and 3) the final exhortation and prayer (13:17-25). Under *encomium* there are further divisions that speak of: 1) Jesus' family and birth (1:5—3:13); 2) his endowments, upbringing, and education (3:14—6:12); 3) his life, occupation, achievements, fortune (6:13—10:39); and 4) an ongoing comparison with great men (11:1—13:16).[41]

Olbricht argues that the author of Hebrews seeks to present Jesus as superior in order to challenge his readers to action and to perseverance. In his analysis of the author's comparison between Christ and angels, Olbricht notes that the power of the argument resides in the fact that several Old Testament texts are quoted to support the argument.[42] Ironically, this is precisely where the use of amplification in Hebrews differs with Greek speeches. In Greek orations the evidence of the superiority is empirically verified. The primary evidence in Hebrews comes from sacred texts. The only empirical evidence offered according to Olbricht is the fact of Christ's death.[43]

In Hebrews 7–10, Christ is compared with Levitical priests and their sacrifices. The superiority of Christ extends beyond that of persons as he is

---

[39] Thomas H. Olbricht, "Hebrews as Amplification," in *Rhetoric and the New Testament: Essays from the 1992 Heidelberg Conference,* ed. Stanley E. Porter and Thomas H. Olbricht, JSNTSS 90 (Sheffield: Sheffield Academic Press, 1993) 375.

[40] Ibid., 378.

[41] Ibid. Olbricht notes the use of amplification in comparing Christ to a whole series of heroes. This practice, which typically occurred at the end of an exhortation, was found in both classical Greek eulogies and the eulogies of the early church fathers. Olbricht argues that the comparison in Hebrews 11 was not so much to show the superiority of Christ over these men, but rather the superior position of the contemporary believers over the heroes of the past. Because the contemporary believers were able to focus on Jesus, they were superior to those in the past who did not receive the promises but looked only to shadows and types. See ibid., 386–87.

[42] Ibid., 382.

[43] Ibid., 383. Though Greek sermons did not use Scripture as evidence, the eulogies of the early church fathers often did. See for example, Gregory Nazianzen's *Panegyric on S. Basil* (NPNF[2] 7:395–422).

also shown to be superior to the sacrifice itself. Furthermore, the location of the sacrifice is amplified.[44] Again the evidence does not come from empirical data or even his own experience, but from Scripture. Since much of the saving work of Christ took place in heaven, there is a lack of empirical earthly evidence. However, the comparison between the earthly and heavenly temple was based both on observation and Scripture.[45]

One scholar who attempts to utilize the insights of form criticism and rhetorical analysis is Steve Stanley. He has contributed to the on going study of the structure of the epistle to the Hebrews by balancing three important perspectives or considerations in determining structure: literary genre, rhetorical character, and content.[46]

Stanley argues that the literary genre of the epistle is fundamentally a homily. He bases this insight mainly from the epistle's self-identification as a "word of exhortation" (13:22). Stanley cites Lawrence Wills' study, which attempts to establish the "word of exhortation" as a sermonic form in early Christianity and Hellenistic Judaism.[47] Wills first notes the use of the phrase in Acts 13:15, where Paul speaks during a synagogue service. He identifies three sections to the exhortation that Paul gives in the subsequent verses: 1) authoritative examples (*exempla*); 2) a conclusion based on the authoritative *exempla*; and 3) an exhortation. This forms the general pattern for all "words of exhortation."[48] Wills then examines several other early Christian and Hellenistic Jewish sermons also finding this same pattern.[49] He argues that the "word of exhortation" does not follow classical Greco-Roman forms, but comes from innovations of Greek oratory

---

[44] Olbricht, "Hebrews as Amplification," 384.

[45] Ibid., 385.

[46] Steve Stanley, "The Structure of Hebrews from Three Perspectives," *TynBul* 45 (1994) 245–71.

[47] Ibid., 248. See Lawrence Wills, "The Form of the Sermon in Hellenistic Judaism and Early Christianity," *HTR* 77 (1984) 277–99.

[48] Ibid., 279.

[49] Wills examines Hebrews, *1 Clement*, Peter's sermon in Solomon's Portico (Acts 3:12-26), Peter's Pentecost sermon (2:14-40), Paul's speech on the Areopagus (17:24-27), Paul's speech at Miletus to the elders of the church at Ephesus (20:17-35), 2 Corinthians 6:14-7:1, 1 Corinthians 10:1-14, the letters of Ignatius of Antioch, and others. He also looks at Jewish sources and finds this pattern in Jeremiah 7:1-8:3, Ezekiel 20, *Testaments of the Twelve Patriarchs, Jewish War*, and others (ibid., 278–96).

in the fifth century BC.⁵⁰ The identification of Hebrews as a homily has obvious benefits in determining its structure.⁵¹

The second perspective that he considers is the rhetorical character of Hebrews. Stanley cites Vanhoye's work in identifying several important literary markers in determining structure, but argues that there is still a great deal of subjectivity in demarcating the precise divisions.

It is for this reason that the third perspective or content of the epistle is also important to keep in mind. If a particular structure is at odds with the content of the epistle itself, then it must be reevaluated.⁵² The structure should be seen as a servant of the content. Stanley distinguishes between the doctrinal sections, which mainly deal with the superiority of Christ and all that he brings, and the *paraenetic* sections, which demand fidelity to Christ and the Christian community.⁵³ In coordinating these two sections, he argues that the message of Hebrews is "Christ's priestly ministry demands fidelity to the new relationship with God that he mediates."⁵⁴ With all three of these perspectives in mind, Stanley then outlines his structure of Hebrews.⁵⁵

C. F. Evans argues that though most people recognize that the letter to the Hebrews uses Greco-Roman forms of rhetoric, they tend to discount the importance of the form in influencing the actual content of the speech.⁵⁶ His short study is devoted to examining how the form of the speech (rhetoric) is related to its content. He first notes the extensive use by the author of *synkrisis*, which he identifies as a branch of the encomiastic tradition that focused on praising those who were excellent. The way praise or blame is given is by way of comparison. Sometimes it is a comparison of opposites, but more often it is a comparison of similar

---

⁵⁰ Ibid., 296–97. C. Clifton Black II responds to Wills' work by arguing that the word of exhortation form does indeed follow the classical conventions of Greco-Roman rhetoric. He argues that Wills' understanding of classical forms and structures is overly restrictive; Black, "The Rhetorical Form of the Hellenistic Jewish and Early Christian Sermon: A Response to Lawrence Wills," *HTR* 81 (1988) 1–17, esp. 4–11.

⁵¹ Stanley understands this particular homily to be an exposition of Psalm 110, which he finds in all the major sections of the book. This clue also aids him in his structural analysis (Stanley "The Structure of Hebrews," 253–54).

⁵² Ibid., 256. See also James Swetnam, "Form and Content of Hebrew 1–6," *Bib* 53 (1972) 268–85.

⁵³ Stanley, "The Structure of Hebrews," 262–63.

⁵⁴ Ibid., 263.

⁵⁵ For the actual structure, see ibid., 270–71.

⁵⁶ C. F. Evans, *The Theology of Rhetoric: The Epistle to the Hebrews* (London: Dr. Williams Trust, 1988) 3.

things.⁵⁷ Evans discusses the specific uses of this technique in highlighting the superiority of Christ's revelation, priesthood, sacrifice, etc.

Evans also discusses Christology. He notes that the author uses *synkrisis* to demonstrate that Jesus is the eschatological Messiah. Thus the types that prefigured Jesus are replaced and demoted when compared to Jesus (i.e., he is like Moses in faithfulness, but is superior to him as Son).⁵⁸ It is this use of *synkrisis* that leads Evans to believe that the Christology of Hebrews is properly identified as a divine-hero Christology.⁵⁹

Studies on Specific Passages

Several other studies on specific texts have emerged using rhetorical criticism. One study on Heb 2:10 examines the use of πρέπειν and rhetorical propriety.⁶⁰ Alan Mitchell argues that the author of Hebrews was influenced by the idea of propriety in rhetoric when he wrote that it was appropriate for God to perfect Jesus through suffering. The rhetorical concept of τὸ πρέπον is concerned with both what is appropriate for the speaker and the audience. Therefore by using this concept one is able to analyze the appropriateness of God perfecting his Son as well as the appropriateness of the act for the needs of the audience.⁶¹ He notes that propriety in Greek rhetoric involves the proper use of *ethos, pathos,* and *logos* to persuade one's audience.⁶²

The use of πρέπειν in Heb 2:10 follows a pattern in classical Greek.⁶³ Mitchell identifies God as the persuasive speaker in Christ. He is described throughout the epistle as one who seeks to bring men into salvation, despite the hardened response of previous generations. His steadfast communication to his people is a reflection of his character. "And so what makes God's part in Jesus' suffering both fitting and persuasive is how it discloses the character of God (ἦθος) and appeals to human emotions (πάθος)

---

⁵⁷ Ibid., 5–6.

⁵⁸ Ibid., 17.

⁵⁹ Ibid., 18.

⁶⁰ Alan C. Mitchell, "The Use of πρέπειν and Rhetorical Propriety in Hebrews 2:10," *CBQ* 54 (1992) 681–701.

⁶¹ Ibid., 682–83.

⁶² Craig Koester also analyzes Hebrews' rhetorical effectiveness using these categories. He examines the logic of the argument, the emotional appeal to persuade, and the character of God as the author. See Craig R. Koester, *The Epistle to the Hebrews,* AB 36 (New York: Doubleday, 2001) 87–92.

⁶³ Mitchell, "The Use of πρέπειν," 688.

when highlighting the continual divine initiative."[64] Mitchell also surveys other passages describing how the author highlights God's *ethos* in order to appeal to the *pathos* of the audience. He concludes by stating that this rhetorical concept of propriety illumines God's constant effort to communicate to human beings, culminating in the suffering and death of Jesus. This is important in helping the author win back those who were questioning the value of Jesus' death.[65]

In another study, David Worley assumes the author of Hebrews was influenced by rhetorical training in human litigant oaths. Most commentators have understood the two immutable things in Heb 6:12-20 as God's oath and God's promises. He argues that the author was in fact thinking of God's oath-taking and oath-witness. Worley compares the rhetoric of Greek orators, who "colored and maximized"[66] oaths sworn by litigants in the courtroom with the rhetoric of Heb 6:12-20. In the Greek court system one litigant could challenge his opponent to take an oath or swear to his god that his words were true. If the other agreed and made an oath, then the matter was settled. Yet more often the case, someone offered to voluntarily take an oath to validate his own claims. This was commonly described as "fleeing to the oath."[67]

In the process of giving oaths, lawyers were trained to color the oath either as fraudulent (minimize) or credible (maximize). They would minimize the oath by arguing that the person issuing the oath was a liar or a man of ill-reputation. In order to maximize an oath the lawyer would describe the man's integrity and character.[68] Worley then notes the similarities between the oath language in Hebrews and the rhetoric of the Greek courtroom. "God swore by no one greater. . . . For men swear by a greater and the oath brings a final settlement to every human dispute. . . . He became a witness to the oath . . . it is impossible for God to lie we who have fled [to God's oath] . . . ."[69] The author's familiarity with the litigant oath seems to be in the background of this language. Worley points out that the author maximizes the oath given by God in a way a Greek lawyer might

---

[64] Ibid., 694.

[65] Ibid., 701.

[66] David R. Worley, "Fleeing to Two Immutable Things: God's Oath Taking and Oath Witnessing," *ResQ* 36 (1994) 223.

[67] Ibid., 224.

[68] Ibid., 224–5.

[69] Ibid., 225.

for his client. Yet there is certainly an adaptation of the rhetoric considering God is the one making the oath.[70]

One would expect the author to continue to discuss the character of God as trustworthy, but rather he highlights the willingness of God to act as oath-witness. This is how Worley translates the phrase ἐμεσίτευσεν ὅρκῳ, "God acts as a μεσίτης, i.e., as a witness who thereby guarantees [the oath]."[71] The language of "God not being able to lie" also maximizes the oath (6:18). Thus Worley argues that the two immutable things the author has in mind are God's dependability in keeping his promissory oath and his unwavering testimony to his own oath taking.[72] The author's choice of words describing those "who have fled" refers to those who flee to God's oath for assurance and encouragement. Unlike in litigant cases, where the person flees to his own oath, the readers of this epistle have a better hope in fleeing to God's oath.[73]

Michael Cosby examines the rhetorical techniques used in Hebrews 11 to persuade the readers to a certain action. He puts a great deal of emphasis on how the text was heard by the audience.[74] Cosby begins by noting that Greek writing was typically written to be heard. So that even for individual use, texts were read aloud.[75] He then discusses the form of Hebrews 11 surveying several different opinions by various scholars. After his own examination of several ancient example lists, he concludes that it is still debatable whether the author used a particular literary form or a Jewish source in composing chapter 11.[76]

Cosby continues his examination of Hebrews 11 by pointing out the *anaphoric*[77] use of πίστει in 11:3-31. He argues that the reason why the author chose this technique was to communicate that many more examples could be used if space and time permitted. This is accomplished by

---

[70] Ibid., 226.

[71] Ibid., 227.

[72] Ibid.

[73] Ibid., 228.

[74] Michael R. Cosby, *The Rhetorical Composition and Function of Hebrews 11: In Light of Example Lists in Antiquity* (Macon, Ga.: Mercer University Press, 1988) 5. See also idem, "The Rhetorical Composition of Hebrews 11," *JBL* 107 (1988) 257–73.

[75] Cosby, *Rhetorical Composition*, 6.

[76] Ibid., 12.

[77] This refers to the repetition of the same element at the beginning of several successive sections.

creating a sort of rhythm of expression.[78] He adds that faith is presented as the motivation for the great deeds of the saints in the past.[79]

The author of Hebrews uses *asyndeton*[80] to highlight the idea that time is limited (11:32-34). The lists that are employed refrain from using conjunctions, which speed up the movement of the text and demonstrate vigor or passion.[81] Cosby points out that there is a staccato pattern that is very effective in penetrating one's mind with so many (it seems) examples of people who have exercised this kind of faith.[82] The list as it is read affects the emotions of the hearer and attempts to bring about bravery and courage in the times of suffering.[83]

Another technique in these lists is that of *antithesis*, in which two contradictory statements or options are placed side by side. The intent is to compare the hero's action with the potential action of the contemporary reader. Thus Moses despised the pleasures of Egypt to suffer with his people Israel.[84] This is a very powerful technique to encourage certain actions. Cosby also notes the minor uses of hyperbole, paronomasia, and circumlocution, which enhance and strengthen the other more important techniques.[85]

Following Cosby's general argument that there is probably not one "example list" literary form, Gareth Lee Cockerill focuses more on how the author arranged his example list in Hebrews 11 to serve his own rhetorical purpose.[86] He argues that v. 35 is key to the examples of faith contained in vv. 32-38, which he identifies as the climactic passage of the chapter.[87] Cockerill identifies the list of examples in vv. 33-35a as describing those who have triumphed in faith. This is balanced by the list in 35b-38, which describes those who have suffered. Verse 35 is the turning point "where

---

[78] Cosby, *Rhetorical Composition*, 42.

[79] Ibid., 48.

[80] This refers to the omission of conjunctions.

[81] Cosby, *Rhetorical Composition*, 59–60.

[82] Ibid., 63.

[83] Ibid., 65.

[84] Ibid., 75–76.

[85] Ibid., 84.

[86] G. L. Cockerill, "The Better Resurrection: Heb 11:35," *TynBul* 51 (2000) 215–34. See also Alan D. Bulley, "Death and Rhetoric in the Hebrews 'Hymn of Faith," *SR* 25 (1996) 409–23. Bulley argues that Heb 11:1-40 is an example of epideictic rhetoric, praising the elders of the church with the deliberative goal of exhorting faithfulness in the midst of suffering and death (410).

[87] Cockerill, "The Better Resurrection," 220.

those who were raised from the dead are compared to those who braved death by the power of faith in the 'better resurrection.'"[88]

Cockerill identifies Abel and Enoch as the prototypical examples of faith. Abel faced suffering and death because he had faith in a better resurrection and Enoch escaped death by being translated into heaven.[89] Verse 28 is a transitional verse separating the lives of those who suffered in faith with those who triumphed in faith. Verses 8-27 describe those who have faced persecution and suffering, while verses 28-35a describes those who have triumphed (usually militarily) by faith.[90] Verse 39 concludes the section by mentioning that though these heroes died in faith, they did not receive what had been promised. Thus Cockerill states that they all anticipated the "better resurrection." His analysis serves to answer the larger question whether the author of Hebrews was concerned with the resurrection. He concludes that though the resurrection was not primary in the Christology of Hebrews, it was used as a strong motivation to encourage perseverance for those who were suffering in this life.[91]

The "New Rhetoric"

There have also been studies on Hebrews that focus on the rhetoric in Hebrews as argument. The analysis does not focus so much on the author's use of Greco-Roman rhetorical forms but on identifying the social situation behind the text by examining the argument in Hebrews. Most of these studies have focused on particular passages in Hebrews.

Peter Enns examines how the author of Hebrews recontextualized Psalm 95 to address the specific needs of his audience. In his article, "Interpretation of Psalm 95 in Hebrews 3.1-4.13,"[92] he notes that the author does not use Psalm 95 as a proof text to support previous statements, but simply exposits and applies it to his situation. He believes that the author wants his audience to see themselves as those who are figuratively in the wilderness.[93]

---

[88] Ibid., 222.
[89] Ibid., 224.
[90] Ibid., 231–32.
[91] Ibid., 234.
[92] Peter Enns, "Interpretation of Psalm 95 in Hebrews 3.1—4.13," in *Early Christian Interpretation of the Scriptures of Israel: Investigations and Proposals*, ed. Craig Evans and James Sanders, JSNTSS 148 (Sheffield: Sheffield Academic Press, 1997) 352–63.
[93] Ibid., 352–53.

Enns begins by noting the important emendations the author makes when quoting the LXX. The author inserts the conjunction διός in v. 10, essentially changing the meaning of the phrase from, "Where your fathers tested, they tried, and saw my works. I was angry with that generation for forty years" to "Your fathers tested with scrutiny and saw my works for forty years. Therefore, [διός] I was angry with this generation."[94] The point of the change is to highlight the fact that the wilderness episode was not to be seen in a negative light. God was not angry with them for the forty years they were in the wilderness, but he was angry *after* their disobedience. The author wants to paint the wilderness time period positively, because he sees the church currently in the wilderness, so to speak. Therefore by identifying the wilderness time period positively, he also affirms that the current time of his audience is a time of blessing.[95]

One obvious problem with Enns's analysis is the fact that 3:17 clearly describes God being angry with the wilderness community for forty years. Enns believes this highlights the contrast between the New Testament community and the Old. The Old Testament community suffered under God's anger, but the New Testament community experienced God's wonders or works.[96] Yet it seems reasonable that quoting the LXX as it was originally written could have made this same contrast. Why would the author of Hebrews intentionally misquote the "word of God," to make one theological point, and then contradict it in his own analysis?

Also focusing on use of Old Testament Scripture in Hebrews, Karen Jobes uses new rhetorical analysis to help explain the variant quotation of Psalm 40 in Heb 10:5-7.[97] Instead of hypothesizing that the author quoted a corrupted text, Jobes argues that the author purposefully misquoted the Psalm for his own rhetorical purposes.[98] She notes in a detailed analysis

---

[94] Ibid., 353.

[95] Ibid., 354.

[96] Ibid., 355. Enns also examines the author's emendation of ἐδοκίμασεν in the LXX to ἐν δοκιμασία in v. 9. The LXX reading would be, "Your fathers tested, they tried my works." But in Hebrews we have, "Your fathers tested with scrutiny my works." This distinction paints the wilderness generation in a more negative light. See ibid., 356.

[97] Karen H. Jobes, "The Function of Paronomasia in Hebrews 10:5-7," *TJ* 13 (1992) 181–91; and idem, "Rhetorical Achievement in the Hebrews 10 'Misquote' of Psalm 40," *Bib* 72 (1991) 387–96.

[98] Jobes, "Rhetorical Achievement," 389. There are four variations of the text of Hebrews compared to the LXX: 1) σῶμα is found in verse 5 instead of ὠτία; 2) ὁλοκαυτώματα is substituted in verse 6 for the singular form ὁλοκαύτωμα; 3) εὐδόκησας is substituted for ᾔτησας in verse 6; and 4) ὁ θεός and τὸ θέλημά σου are transposed in verse 7 and the remainder of the verse is omitted (Jobes, "Function of Paronomasia," 182–3).

that the variant changes produce phonetic assonance with other words in the quotation, which is the rhetorical technique of *paronomasia*.[99] This particular technique functioned to bring attention to specific elements of the argument.[100] Perhaps the most important variation is the change from "ears" to "body" in verse 5. In contrast to the many burnt offerings, God has prepared a body for Jesus as the once-for-all sacrifice. The assonance produced by this change eloquently embellishes the argument creating a catchy tune easy to remember.[101] Thus the author of Hebrews alters the text of Psalm 40 in order to show the discontinuity with the past and to persuade his hearers that in these last days God spoke to them in his Son.[102]

In a short article entitled, "The Use of Antithesis in Hebrews 8–10,"[103] Harold Attridge demonstrates the rhetorical mastery of the author of Hebrews. Attridge first describes the social context of the epistle as one in which Christians were often ambivalent toward their Jewish past.[104] He then identifies several antitheses used in chapters 8-10: opposition of flesh and spirit, earth and heaven, many and one, old and new, and external and internal.[105] Attridge argues that the sacrifice of Christ, which combines many of these antitheses, is uniquely qualified to inaugurate the new covenant of Jeremiah 31:31.[106] In the climactic section (10:1-10), the Christ utters Psalm 40:7-9 (6-8 MT) as he comes into the world (10:5). A fleshly body is prepared for the divine Son. Thus in Jesus the heavenly/earthly antithesis is brought together (10:5). How then can the believer receive internal cleansing and spiritual renewal from external rituals? It is by faith in Jesus, who conformed to the will of God, that one is sanctified and overcomes the internal/ external antithesis. Attridge concludes that the author of Hebrews uses exegetical rhetoric to resolve antithetical oppositions and suggests that perhaps this type of rhetoric helped Christians who were ambivalent to their Jewish past.[107]

---

[99] Jobes, "The Function of Paronomasia," 184.
[100] Ibid., 185.
[101] Ibid., 189.
[102] Ibid., 191.
[103] Harold W. Attridge, "The Uses of Antithesis in Hebrews 8–10," *HTR* 79 (1986) 1–9.
[104] Ibid., 1.
[105] Ibid., 5.
[106] Ibid.
[107] Ibid., 8–9.

One scholar who attempts to weave aspects of the three major approaches mentioned above (literary aesthetic, rhetorical criticism, "new rhetoric") in his analysis of the structure of Hebrews is George Guthrie. After a lengthy survey of the history of scholarship on the subject, he suggests that a text-linguistic analysis incorporates the concerns of the new rhetorical criticism, rhetorical criticism, and literary analysis. He also notes that one must take into account the unique literary conventions of the first century.[108]

In his analysis Guthrie focuses on cohesion shifts, where the unity of a text changes. These shifts are marked off by changes in genre, topic, conjunction, logical relationships, consistency of grammar, verb tense, person and number, lexical repetition, and consistency of temporal and spatial indicators. By examining these shifts, one is able to identify new units and sub-units.[109] Guthrie also uses the rhetorical convention of *inclusio* in determining structure.[110] Finally, he argues that the two genres of exposition and hortatory material each share the same goal in calling the hearers to endure. "The expositional material builds toward the goal by focusing on the appointed high priest as a superior basis for endurance. The hortatory passages move toward the goal by reiteration of warnings, promises, and examples used to challenge the hearers to endure."[111]

Review of Social Scientific Approaches to Hebrews

General Trends

Bruce J. Malina identifies John H. Elliot as the one who coined the term social-scientific criticism in 1993.[112] Originally it was called sociological criticism, but was changed because of the different meanings of "sociological" in the United States and Europe. Malina also notes that sociological

---

[108] George H. Guthrie, *The Structure of Hebrews: A Text-Linguistic Analysis*, NovTSup 73 (Leiden: Brill, 1994; Biblical Studies Library; Grand Rapids: Baker, 1998) 45.

[109] Ibid., 54.

[110] Ibid., 76–89.

[111] Ibid., 146.

[112] Bruce J. Malina, "Rhetorical Criticism and Social-Scientific Criticism: Why Won't Romanticism Leave Us Alone?" in *Rhetoric Scripture and Theology: Essays from the 1994 Pretoria Conference,* ed. Stanley E. Porter and Thomas H. Olbricht, JSNTSS 131 (Sheffield: Sheffield Academic Press, 1996) 73. Cf. John H. Elliott, *What Is Social-Scientific Criticism?* GBS (Minneapolis: Fortress, 1993).

studies of the New Testament are mainly social descriptions and social history.[113] The term, "social-scientific criticism," however, is more general and includes all types of social sciences applied to New Testament interpretation.

The goal of social scientific criticism is to find out what an initial audience understood when a speech was given or a document was read aloud.[114] The approach used to achieve the goal is to examine the social systems, which reveal meaning in a given social interaction. These social interactions are presumed in the writing and reading of the New Testament documents. Malina presupposes that meaning is rooted in one's "enculturation, socialization, interrelationships and interactions."[115] Elliott comments, "Sociological exegesis asks not only what a text said 'then and there' but also how and why that text was designed to function, and what its impact upon the life and activity of its recipients and formulators was intended to be."[116]

Dale Martin identifies two major trends in the social scientific criticism movement.[117] One movement is characterized by those who seek to use traditional historical-critical methods to investigate the "social world" of early Christianity.[118] This is what Malina referred to as sociological criticism above, which focused primarily on creating "social histories." The other movement is characterized by those who seek to use sociological or anthropological models to explain the historical texts.[119] Martin admits, however, that these are not two absolutely distinct movements, using completely different methods.

One example of a study seeking to identify the social history behind New Testament writings is the article by Wayne Meeks, "The Man from Heaven in Johannine Sectarianism."[120] Meeks examines the gospel of John

---

[113] Malina, "Rhetorical Criticism and Social-Scientific Criticism," 73–4.

[114] Ibid., 74.

[115] Ibid., 75.

[116] John H. Elliott, *A Home for the Homeless: A Sociological Exegesis of 1 Peter, Its Situation and Strategy* (Philadelphia: Fortress, 1981) 7–8.

[117] Dale Martin, "Social-Scientific Criticism," in *To Each its Own Meaning*, ed. Steven L. McKenzie and Stephen R. Haynes (Louisville: Westminster John Knox, 1993) 103–20.

[118] Ibid., 107. Martin identifies John G. Gager, Wayne A. Meeks, L. William Countryman, and Howard Clark Kee as "social historians."

[119] Martin, "Social-Scientific Criticism," 107. Martin identifies John H. Elliott, Jerome H. Neyrey, Bruce J. Malina, Antoinette Clark Wire as "social scientists".

[120] Wayne Meeks, "The Man from Heaven in Johannine Sectarianism," *JBL* 91 (1972) 44–72.

using concepts of sectarianism taken from the "sociology of knowledge" theories of Peter Berger and Thomas Luckmann.[121] In his article, Meeks argues that Jesus is portrayed as one rejected by his own people to reflect the social conflict between the Johannine community and the synagogue. Meeks claims that one of the primary functions of the gospel is to legitimize and solidify the community's identity, which was likely isolated from the larger society and attacked by it.[122]

An example of a social-scientific approach that seeks to use a particular model in analyzing texts comes from the work of Bruce Malina. His particular approach in reading texts is what he calls the scenario model. In this model he assumes that language is used to communicate meaning to another, or "a realization of meanings in a social system."[123] In essence he seeks to "develop a set of scenarios that fit the social system realized in the language of the Bible."[124] He identifies rhetorical criticism as one tool used to detect these scenarios. Malina speaks of persuasion as a major goal of the New Testament authors. Most of their persuasive work attempts to keep the readers from being persuaded by others or to establish behavior patterns which were previously unknown.[125]

To illustrate how this model is applied, we shall look at Malina's discussion on the clean and unclean or sacred and profane distinction in the ancient world.[126] He argues that social lines are needed to determine what is set-apart and what is common. For Malina, "purity" is "about the general cultural map of social time and space, about arrangements within the space thus defined, and especially about the boundaries separating the inside from the outside."[127] He sees the sacred and profane as subsets of purity rules determining what is included and what is excluded. The process of restoring things to their proper order can be described as purifying or cleansing.[128]

Malina also mentions the fact that purity rules are to bring about prosperity in a society. Those who violate these rules, however, only bring

---

[121] See Peter L. Berger and Thomas Luckmann, *The Social Construction of Reality: A Treatise in the Sociology of Knowledge* (Garden City, N.Y.: Doubleday, 1966).

[122] Meeks, "The Man from Heaven," 70.

[123] Malina, "Rhetorical Criticism and Social-Scientific Criticism," 81.

[124] Ibid.

[125] Ibid., 82.

[126] Bruce J. Malina, *The New Testament World: Insights from Cultural Anthropology*, 3d ed. (Louisville: Westminster John Knox, 2001) 161–97.

[127] Ibid., 164.

[128] Ibid., 165.

about danger to themselves and to others.¹²⁹ Malina argues that in the first-century world the main goal was to maintain one's inherited position in society. One's position was directly connected to his prosperity and his harmonious relationship with others. Thus it was very important how others viewed a person.¹³⁰ The purity laws were there to help foster these harmonious relationships. For example, sacrifices functioned not so much for God, but for the people to maintain their right standing before God. They needed his affirmation and evaluation of their worth and value.¹³¹

Malina notes that Jesus seems to reject many of the Jewish purity rituals: touching, cleansing, interacting with things and people impure and acting on sacred days. He argues, however, that Jesus accepts the general system of purity regulations, but questions the social abuse of these rules. The regulations are not to keep people from coming to God, but rather they are to facilitate access to God.¹³² Paul, on the other hand goes further and declares all things clean in Christ, rejecting both the Jewish and the Greek understanding of holiness, purity, and sacredness. For Christians in the Pauline tradition, the temple was the church gathered. Those who belonged to the community were those in Christ; outsiders were those not in Christ. Purity rituals no longer distinguished who was "in" or "out," but rather one's relationship to Christ determined who belonged. In addition, all times were sacred for those on the inside of the community. Thus there was no need to observe days, months, seasons, and years.¹³³

Focus on Hebrews

Social Histories

The social scientific studies on Hebrews can be divided into the two general movements mentioned above. One example of a study that takes more of a "social history" approach is the work of William Lane. Lane offers

---

¹²⁹ Ibid., 170.

¹³⁰ Malina distinguishes between the dyadic personality and the individual personality. The dyadic personality describes someone who perceives himself or herself in terms of how others see him or her. He or she needs others to know and define who he or she is. The individual personality describes someone who sees others as distinct and unique and forms his or her own definition of self. Malina argues that the individual personality was quite foreign to the ancient world, which was dominated by the dyadic personality; ibid., 62–63.

¹³¹ Ibid., 185–86.

¹³² Ibid., 188.

¹³³ Ibid., 191–96.

some insight into the setting of Hebrews from a social perspective.[134] He first argues that the epistle has Rome as its setting.[135] He then identifies the recipients as a house church of the city, which had its roots in the Jewish Hellenistic synagogue.[136]

After examining the social dynamics of a Roman household, Lane points out that the church in Hebrews is identified primarily as the household of God, with Jesus as the presider over the house.[137] "The extension of protection, the exercise of administrative responsibility, and the provision of supervision and nurture are his [Jesus] responsibility, analogous to the role of the head of the household in Greco-Roman society."[138] Lane argues that the strained relationship between the community addressed and its leaders intimated in 13:17-18 is perhaps one occasion for the use of the household metaphor. By describing the church as a household, the author of Hebrews hopes "to bring the two groups together in a social context of shared cordiality."[139]

Lane also suggests that the real tension that emerged came because the current leaders mentioned in 13:17 were not the owners of the houses of the house churches. These owners, as hosts and patrons had a certain social standing and authority over the members. Yet the leadership structures in these house churches were not based on patronage, but "charismatic endowment and service to the congregation."[140] Those who had the gift of preaching within the community emerged as the leaders. Thus he imagines that the implicit tensions were caused by power struggles within the house church movement.[141]

---

[134] William Lane, "Social Perspective on Roman Christianity During the Formative Years from Nero to Nerva: Romans, Hebrews, 1 Clement," in *Judaism and Christianity in First-Century Rome,* ed. Karl P. Donfried and Peter Richardson (Grand Rapids: Eerdmans, 1998) 196–244.

[135] Lane's argument for Rome as the location of Hebrews is as follows: 1) The generosity of those addressed in Hebrews is consistent with an affluent Roman church (Heb 6:10-11; 10:33-34, cf. Ignatius, Romans, Dionysius of Corinth, Eusebius, *Church History* 4.23.10); 2) the description of sufferings is consistent with the edict of Claudius in Rome in 49 AD; and 3) the leadership identified as ἡγούμενοι in the epistle is consistent with the community of Rome (Heb 13:7, 17, 24); ibid., 215.

[136] Ibid., 216.

[137] Ibid., 218.

[138] Ibid.

[139] Ibid., 222.

[140] Ibid., 224.

[141] Ibid., 223.

Craig Koester describes the social history of the community addressed in Hebrews in three phases: 1) proclamation and conversion; 2) persecution and solidarity; and 3) friction and malaise.[142] Drawing from clues within the epistle itself, Koester states that the first phase involved Christian evangelists forming the community through preaching and baptism. During this phase, the confession of faith played an important role in uniting its members from different social classes and distinguishing them from those on the outside. Baptism was not a rite of passage as much as a boundary marker identifying who was in and who was out.[143] The second phase was characterized by physical hostilities and persecution against the community by non-Christians. Koester sees the reference in 10:32-34 of the members visiting those in prison, losing property, and receiving physical persecution as descriptive of this phase.[144] The final phase gave way to a more subtle type of conflict, where Christians were verbally harassed and marginalized in society. There was a general malaise and a tendency to neglect the faith and community meetings. Koester argues that the epistle was written in this third phase of the community's formation.[145]

He also argues that the Christian community fit neither the Jewish subculture nor the Greco-Roman culture and needed to reaffirm its own identity. Koester sees the author of the epistle appropriating and transforming Jewish and Greco-Roman images to reinforce the community's identity and confession. For example, the author transforms the Jewish idea of priesthood and temple and appropriates these Jewish religious symbols for his own purposes.[146] In addition, the unique character of Christ's sacrifice draws not only from Jewish sacrificial imagery, but also Greco-Roman cultic imagery. Sacrifices were offered at many sanctuaries throughout the Greco-Roman world.[147]

Social Scientific Studies

In a more specialized study, Harold Attridge interacts with Leo Perdue in determining the social function of the paraenetic sections of Hebrews.[148]

---

[142] Koester, *Hebrews*, 64–72.

[143] Ibid., 66–67.

[144] Ibid., 67.

[145] Ibid., 71–72.

[146] Ibid., 77.

[147] Ibid., 79.

[148] Harold W. Attridge, "Paraenesis in a Homily (λόγος παρακλήσεως): The Possible Location of, and Socialization in, the 'Epistle to the Hebrews,'" *Semeia* 50 (1990) 211–

He does not see the epistle fitting in any of the four functions of hortatory literature as defined by Perdue: protreptic (that which seeks to persuade someone to convert), socialization, legitimation, or conflict.[149] It does not seek to convert, because it addresses those who already share common values and religious beliefs. Nor does it socialize its audience into a particular segment of society, giving instructions about social roles or states. However, there is some indication that the epistle may function in legitimizing the Christian community. The references to imitate the community's leaders (13:7) and to obey them (13:17) seem to legitimate the authority structure of the community. Yet it would be difficult to argue that the whole epistle was written for this particular function.[150] Attridge also admits that the epistle does reflect a situation of conflict (10:32-24; 12:4; and others). But he also argues that this particular function does not account for the epistle as a whole.[151]

Attridge suggests that the function of the hortatory sections of the epistle is not primarily to engage in polemic, but to confirm the validity of the social world of the community. It is to "reinforce the identity of a social sub-group in such a way as not to isolate it from its environment."[152] The community experiencing suffering is not to separate from the society but to engage it with its values and commitments. This particular function falls somewhere in between Perdue's categories of legitimation and socialization.[153]

Following up on Attridge's suggestion that the epistle may function to legitimize the community, Iutisone Salevao produced a more thorough work on the subject. He argues that the sociological concept of "legitimation" successfully explains the "correlation between theology, situation, and the strategy of the letter [to the Hebrews]."[154] He approaches the epistle using sociological exegesis, drawing from the work of Peter Berger and Thomas Luckmann.[155] Salevao describes legitimation as the different ways

---

26.

[149] Leo G. Perdue, "The Social Character of Paraenesis and Paraenetic Literature," *Semeia* 50 (1990) 5–39, esp. 23–26.

[150] Attridge, "Paraenesis," 218.

[151] Ibid., 219–20.

[152] Ibid., 223.

[153] Perdue, "Social Character," 25–26.

[154] Iutisone Salevao, *Legitimation in the Letter to the Hebrews*, JSNTSS 219 (Sheffield: Sheffield Academic, 2002) 5.

[155] Peter L. Berger and Thomas Luckmann, *The Social Construction of Reality: A Treatise in the Sociology of Knowledge* (Garden City, N.Y.: Doubleday, 1966).

in which a society is explained and justified to its members. "Employed as a sociological model, legitimation relates to the genesis and maintenance of a society and its social institutions; it explains and justifies the existence and continuation of the social world."[156]

Salevao describes the situation behind the epistle to the Hebrews in sociological terms. There were separatist members of the community promoting theological views, which were in direct conflict with the views and practices of the community. Some of these separatists still held on to their former religion of Judaism. Saleveo argues that the community in Hebrews was a sect, which he understands as a clearly defined entity, separate and distinct from Judaism. He then shows how the author uses the doctrine of the impossibility of a second repentance in 6:4-6 to curb the threat of deviation from the norms of the community. In addition the author employed a superiority/inferiority structure, which helped maintain the symbolic universe of the Christian community. Finally Saleveo examines the use of the language of Hebrews as a legitimating tool.[157]

John Dunnill's monograph, *Covenant and Sacrifice in the Letter to the Hebrews* attempts to use both sociological and structuralist approaches in its examination of the epistle to the Hebrews.[158] Dunnill defines the author as the authorial presence within the text and derives his social reconstruction from textual clues.[159] He identifies the addressees of the epistle as a small group of churches who are experiencing persecution from the outside and disillusionment from the inside. To encourage them, the author of the epistle uses the rich imagery of household, which Dunnill notes is even more basic than nation, or clan. The author wants to bring his community, which likely felt cut off from its social and religious past and uncertain about its future,[160] back to Melchizedek, the ancient priest and king.

Dunnill uses anthropological insights primarily for the sake of comparison. For instance, after citing some anthropological works comparing gift-giving and -receiving and formal trade, he draws the parallel between

---

[156] Salevao, *Legitimation*, 6, 53–54.

[157] Ibid., 70–71.

[158] John Dunnill, *Covenant and Sacrifice in the Letter to the Hebrews*, SNTSMS 75 (Cambridge: Cambridge University, 1992).

[159] Ibid., 14.

[160] Ibid., 37–39.

the old covenant system, which seemed to work more on the basis of trade, and the new system, which is based on the idea of gift giving.[161]

Similar to the approach of Snyman, Dunnill moves away from traditional historical criticism in his use of structuralism. Yet he goes further than Snyman in seeking to bring out the modern reader's contribution to meaning.[162] He wants to understand the text, "better than the author himself, and better than the first readers too."[163] He substantiates his right to do so by noting that the author of Hebrews himself is claiming to know the Levitical symbols better than the original author or the first readers.

In conclusion, Dunnill writes, "Hebrews claims for itself the image of a liturgy, a symbolic action in the sacred sphere: more particularly, a covenant-renewal rite, of which the book's words comprise a long prophetic exhortation."[164] Dunnill sees the author of Hebrews drawing from Old Testament cultic symbolism and re-interpreting it in the light of Christ. He argues that the structuralist method helps put the particulars of the letter into a larger system or context, unraveling deeper, more opaque meanings. Dunnill contrasts this with historical methods, which tend to reduce the unusual and ambiguous to conformity.

Socio-Rhetorical Approach

Description of Method

From our survey we have seen attempts from rhetorical critics to use sociological insights and attempts from social scientific critics to use rhetorical criticism. The "new rhetoric" of Chaim Perelman and Lucie Olbrechts-Tyteca is keenly sensitive to the social situation that stands behind the text and the work of Bruce Malina demonstrates his dependence on rhetorical criticism. Another scholar who also sees a very close relationship between these two approaches is Vernon Robbins.[165] He defines socio-rhetorical criticism as a discipline that combines the use of social-scientific approach-

---

[161] Ibid., 243–44.

[162] Ibid., 9.

[163] Ibid., 116.

[164] Ibid., 261.

[165] See Vernon K. Robbins, *Exploring the Texture of Texts: A Guide to Socio-Rhetorical Interpretation* (Valley Forge, Pa.: Trinity, 1996) and *The Tapestry of Early Christian Discourse: Rhetoric, Society, and Ideology* (London: Routledge, 1996). Hens-Piazza proposes a slightly different socio-rhetorical approach applied mainly to Old Testament texts. See Gina Hens-Piazza, *Of Methods, Monarchs, and Meanings: A Sociorhetorical Approach to Exegesis*, SOTI 3 (Macon, Ga.: Mercer University Press, 1996).

es with analysis of how a text uses subjects and topics to communicate thoughts, arguments, speeches, etc. Robbins states, "Thus, socio-rhetorical criticism integrates the ways people use language with the ways they live in the world."[166] He identifies several textures of a text, but notes that not all of the textures have to be explored when using the method. The first texture he mentions is the inner texture, which deals with things like the repetition of words, *inclusios*, alternation of speech and storytelling, different ways arguments are presented, and the aesthetic feel of the text.[167]

The second texture is the intertexture, which has to do with life outside the text. Robbins distinguishes several types. Oral-scribal intertexture deals with how language was used in the social context of the time. Social intertexture explores family structures, political arrangements, distribution of goods and services, etc. Cultural intertexture describes how people determine their importance, their responsibility to the world, etc. Historical intertexture is concerned with events that happen outside of the text and are recorded as narrative within the text.[168]

The "social and cultural" texture deals with sociological and anthropological theory. It asks how the text communicates what the world outside the text is like or at least what it is like from the perspective of the text. It seeks to discern how the text perceives how one should live in the world or how one can change the world.[169] Ideological texture deals with how the language of the text aligns itself with or against other groups or persons (i.e. feminist readings). It asks questions about the social location of the author and its recipients.[170] This texture is narrower than the social and cultural texture in that it does not simply ask how the text aligns itself with or against other views, but it describes the particular view itself.

---

[166] Robbins, *Exploring*, 1.

[167] Ibid., 3.

[168] Ibid., 3, 40–70.

[169] Ibid., 71.

[170] Robbins identifies cultural categories that help identify one's cultural location (the manner which one presents one's propositions, arguments, and reasons to oneself and others): 1) dominant culture rhetoric (these are norms, values, and attitudes presupposed in the social structure); 2) subculture rhetoric (imitates the norms and values of the dominant culture but claims to support them better than the dominant culture); 3) counterculture rhetoric (rejects the dominant subculture and responds to it); and 4) contraculture rhetoric (a short lived response to the dominant culture that does not formulate its response from a set of values, but just reacts negatively to certain dominant values or norms) (ibid., 86–87).

Finally there is sacred texture, which deals with the unique relationship of humans with the divine.[171]

David deSilva has done much work using this method.[172] In his book entitled, *Despising Shame: Honor Discourse and Community Maintenance in the Epistle to the Hebrews*,[173] he examines the honor/shame language in Hebrews within the larger honor/shame culture in the Mediterranean world. He first looks at Classical and Hellenistic texts to determine the dominant cultural view of what constituted honor and shame in the ancient world. He then examines the honor and shame language in groups that are counter-cultural or have set themselves apart from the dominant group. The last part of his study involves a detailed analysis of the book of Hebrews, identifying the recipients as a counter-cultural group. They are those who have been rejected from the dominant culture and explore counter-definitions of honorable and shameful behavior. The author of Hebrews appeals to his reader's sense of honor and shame especially in relation to God and hopes to establish that God's view of them is more important than society's view of them.[174]

In an article entitled, "Hebrews 6:4-8: A Socio-Rhetorical Investigation (Part 1)," deSilva walks through the method outlined by Vernon Robbins and applies it to a specific passage.[175] He argues that the rhetorical goal of the epistle is to dissuade those who are drifting away or shrinking back in their Christian commitment.[176] The exhortation beginning in 6:1 presents two options before the readers, either press on to maturity or fall away. He notes the repetitive use of participles in the argument describing an unspecified group of people.[177] These people are those who have received God's gifts. The mention of the heavenly gift (6:4) draws deSilva into a

---

[171] Ibid., 4.

[172] See David A. deSilva, *Perseverance in Gratitude: A Socio-Rhetorical Commentary on the Epistle 'to the Hebrews'* (Grand Rapids: Eerdmans, 2000).

[173] David A. deSilva, *Despising Shame: Honor Discourse and Community Maintenance in the Epistle to the Hebrews*, SBLDS 152 (Atlanta: Scholars, 1995).

[174] Ibid., 23–27.

[175] David Arthur deSilva, "Heb 6:4-8: A Socio-Rhetorical Investigation (Part 1)," *TynBul* 50 (1999) 33–57. Part II is *TynBul* 50 (1999) 225–36 and describes the ideology promoted in the passage and how it serves the author's rhetorical goals. See also deSilva, *Perseverance in Gratitude*, 219–44.

[176] DeSilva, "Heb 6:4-8 (Part 1)," 39–40. De Silva does not see any direct polemic at work in the epistle against the dominant Jewish society. He does not believe there is a threat of reversion back to Judaism. See above chapter 1, pages 15-16.

[177] Ibid., 42.

lengthy discussion of the social intertexture of patron-client relationships.[178] The people are obviously the clients and God is the patron. DeSilva cites Seneca, *De beneficiis* in describing the reciprocal obligations understood in this relationship. Those who would receive benefits were obligated to repay their benefactors by giving them honor and thereby increase their fame and reputation.[179] Those who show contempt to their benefactors were to be punished and barred from future benefits.

DeSilva argues that the readers of the epistle were tempted to value friendship with the world more than God's patronage. Thus their shrinking back from their Christian commitments would make it impossible for God to renew them to repentance, according to the social order of patron-client relations.[180] He draws from both Greek and Jewish sources in identifying the oral-scribal intertexture, which informs the agricultural illustration in 6:7-8. He argues that similar agricultural examples in both Isaiah 5:1-7 and Philo's *De agricultura* 9-18 reinforce the idea of fulfilling one's obligation of reciprocity.[181]

Evaluation of the Socio-Rhetorical Approach

The socio-rhetorical approach outlined by Vernon Robbins proves to be a valuable tool in approaching the New Testament texts from a variety of perspectives. Its interweaving of disciplines produces a richer, thicker understanding of the text. Nevertheless, one must discuss its limitations and weaknesses.

R. Alan Culpepper affirms much of what Robbins says regarding the inner texture but rightly adds that it should also include analysis of the narrator, plot, characters, settings, and other aspects of the narrative or discourse.[182] This refinement of the inner texture should produce studies that better balance insights from rhetorical criticism with insights from new literary criticism. Culpepper also notes that under intertexture, Robbins fails

---

[178] Ibid., 45. See also idem, "Exchanging Favor for Wrath: Apostasy," *JBL* 115 (1996) 91–116.

[179] DeSilva, "Heb 6:4-8 (Part 1)," 45–46. Cf. Seneca, *Ben.* 2.22.1; 2.24.2.

[180] Ibid., 48. Cf. Seneca, *Ben.* 3.1.1.

[181] Ibid., 52–54. De Silva is not arguing that the author of Hebrews used either of these as a direct source.

[182] R. Alan Culpepper, "Mapping the Textures of the New Testament Criticism: A Response to Socio-Rhetorical Criticism," *JSNT* 70 (1998) 73.

to include any analysis of the text's genre.[183] Certainly genre analysis will greatly assist in the understanding of a text and should be considered.

Under the category of "social and cultural" texture, one is to make use of social scientific methods. Stephen Barton enumerates some potential weaknesses of social scientific approaches: 1) they may anachronistically apply modern Western models and theories to an ancient settings without taking into account the differences in cultures; 2) they run the risk of explaining away true religious experience by describing actions and behaviors exclusively in sociological terms; 3) they have their roots in the atheistic philosophy of the Enlightenment.[184] Certainly the use of these sociological models should be sensitive to the culture and context of the time.

In Robbins' section on ideological texture we are to examine our own social and cultural location as well as the writer's. Certainly this particular texture is important for the purposes of this dissertation, yet it also poses the greatest challenge. There is the very obvious issue of subjectivity in exploring this texture. Are all ideological readings of equal merit, or are some readings unacceptable? Some controls or boundaries in determining acceptable ideological readings are needed. The approach in this dissertation will be to use the insights from the other textures as a general guide in exploring the ideological texture. Ideological readings should be grounded upon solid inner texture and intertextural research. Finally, Robbins' section on sacred texture is vague and without sufficient example and illustration. Nevertheless, this approach will be extremely helpful in adding new insights to the questions posed by this dissertation.

---

[183] Ibid., 74. Robbins responds by arguing that we need to move beyond literary genres to rhetorical genres (different forms of speech); Robbins, "Response," *JSNT* 70 (1998) 103. Yet, there seems to be a close connection between literary genre and rhetorical genre. Why should we neglect to consider the literary form of the text for the purpose of exegesis?

[184] Stephen C. Barton, "Historical Criticism and Social-Scientific Perspectives in New Testament Study," in *Hearing the New Testament: Strategies for Interpretation*, ed. Joel B. Green (Grand Rapids: Eerdmans, 1995) 74–76.

3

The Social Context of the Epistle to the Hebrews

In order to determine whether the epistle to the Hebrews is anti-Semitic, anti-Judaic, or supersessionist, we need to identify the precise relationship between the community in Hebrews and the larger Jewish society. Did the author and the community of Hebrews see themselves as Jews, a faction of the larger Jewish society, a sect of Judaism, or a completely different religion? In other words, at what stage in the separation of Christianity from Judaism was the community in Hebrews? This social dynamic of separation will be important in understanding the rhetorical and social function of the polemic in Hebrews.

In the survey above of different approaches to the question of anti-Semitism/ anti-Judaism in Hebrews, we note a general trend. Those who argue that the epistle is not anti-Semitic/anti-Judaic tend to emphasize the continuity or close relationship between the community in Hebrews and the larger Jewish society.[1] Those who argue that the epistle is anti-Semitic or anti-Judaic tend to emphasize the discontinuity between Judaism and the community in Hebrews.[2] The difficulty of course is the fact that the epistle has both elements of continuity and discontinuity.

Faction or Sect

Even from a cursory reading of Hebrews, one can easily exclude extreme statements of continuity or discontinuity. The community in Hebrews cannot be considered part of mainstream Judaism. Its polemic against the Levitical priesthood (7:11-19, 28), Mosaic covenant (8:1-13), and the Levitical sacrifices (10:1-10) make this clear. At the same time, the com-

---

[1] See Chapter 1, pages 12-13.
[2] See Chapter 1, pages 11-12.

munity was not completely separate from its Jewish roots. The author's use of Scripture,[3] veneration of Old Testament saints,[4] and ample allusions to Old Testament institutions[5] demonstrate the author's awareness of the community's Jewish history. With these extremes excluded, we shall proceed to ask whether the community was a faction of Judaism or a sect of Judaism.

Definition of Terms

Torrey Seland working with Bruce Malina defines a faction or coalition as an alliance of different people only for a limited time and purpose.[6] Malina and Seland see the people of Israel rooted in the Temple and Torah as the "corporate group" from which the different factions and coalitions emerged. These groups formed in protest against the Temple aristocracy and its control over the social, economic, and cultural life of Jewish Palestine.[7] What is key in this description is the fact that these factions were seen as those fully included under the larger umbrella of Judaism.

John Elliott argues that early Christianity should be seen as a faction along side that of the Pharisees, disciples of John the Baptist, etc.[8] He notes that

> ... all conflicting Palestinian coalitions, including the Jesus faction, remain inseparable parts of and ideologically bound to the ἔθνος of Israel. Though their specific group interests, goals, strategies, and ideologies vary in their rivalries with one another, they nevertheless all remained social entities within, and not separated from, the corporate body of Israel.[9]

---

[3] Cf. Heb 1:5-13; 2:6-8, 12-13; 3:7-11, 15; 4:3-7; 5:5-6; 7:17, 21; 8:8-12; 10:5-7, 16-17, 37-38, et al.

[4] Cf. 3:1-6; 7:1-10; 11:4-40.

[5] Cf. 5:1-4; 9:1-28, et al.

[6] Torrey Seland, "Jesus as a Faction Leader: On the Exit of the Category 'Sect,'" in *Context*, ed. P. W. Böckman and R. E. Kristiansen (Trondheim: TAPIR, 1987), 197-211. The idea of a coalition or faction comes from Jeremy Boissevain's anthropological research. See Jeremy Boissevain, *Friends of Friends: Networks, Manipulators and Coalitions* (Oxford: Blackwell, 1974) 171.

[7] Bruce J. Malina, "A Conflict Approach to Mark 7," *Forum* 4 (1988) 25.

[8] John H. Elliott, "Phases in the Social Formation of Early Christianity from Faction to Sect—A Social Scientific Perspective," in *Recruitment, Conquest, and Conflict: Strategies in Judaism, Early Christianity, and the Greco-Roman World*, ed. Peder Borgen et al. (Atlanta: Scholars, 1998) 285.

[9] Elliott, "Phases," 287.

The problem is that the term faction does not adequately describe the movement as it disengages itself from its previous group and structure. Therefore, Elliot suggests that the idea of sect better describes the later Jesus movement. He follows Bryan Wilson's understanding of sect as:

> A clearly defined community; it is of a size which permits only a minimal range of diversity of conduct; it seeks itself to rigidify a pattern of conduct and to make coherent its structure of values; it contends actively against every other organization of values and ideals, and against every other social context possible for its adherents, offering itself as an all-embracing, divinely prescribed society. The sect is not only an ideological unit, it is, to greater or lesser degree, a social unit, seeking to enforce behavior on those who accept belief, and seeking every occasion to draw the faithful apart from the rest of society and into the company of each other…the sect, as a protest group, has always developed its own distinctive ethic, belief and practices, against the background of the wider society; its own protest is conditioned by the economic, social, ideological and religious circumstances prevailing at the time of its emergence and development.[10]

Evidence of Separation in Hebrews

Elliott enumerates the changing conditions that describe the rift between Christianity and Judaism:

1) There is an increased tension over Jesus as Messiah, Torah observance, Temple allegiance, purity rules and boundaries, and harassment and punishment from Jewish authorities.
2) There is recruitment of Gentiles and Samaritans, and others previously excluded by the Torah.
3) There is a claim that Christianity alone is the true Israel and the final realization of its expectations.[11]
4) There is a replacement of major institutions.[12]
5) There is a view that the parent group was different from the faction.

---

[10] Bryan R. Wilson, *Sects and Society: A Sociological Study of the Elim Tabernacle, Christian Science, and Christadelphians* (Berkeley: University of California Press, 1961) 1.

[11] Elliott, "Phases," 288.

[12] Ibid., 288–89.

6) There are statements from the parent group that the faction no longer holds to the values and commitments of the parent group.
7) There is acknowledgement from the society at large that the faction is distinct from the parent group, usually with the application of a new name or label (Christians).[13]

As we examine these conditions, it is clear that many of them are found in Hebrews. The first, third, and fourth certainly apply to the epistle. Clearly the author presupposes that Jesus is the promised Messiah.[14] In addition the author speaks of: 1) the sacrificial law as weak and useless;[15] 2) a heavenly sanctuary over against the earthly tabernacle;[16] 3) the limitations of purity laws and the removal of boundaries;[17] and 4) persecution, which may have come from other Jews.[18] The author does indeed paint the community as the recipients of God's word in the last days (1:2) and those who have access to the heavenly Jerusalem (12:22). Finally, the author argues that Jesus' priesthood fulfills the Levitical, his new covenant makes obsolete the old covenant, and his final sacrifice ends all other sacrifices.[19]

The fifth and sixth criteria above seem to be present in various degrees. There is certainly a sense that the community in the epistle is different from the parent group,[20] but the extent of that difference is difficult to determine. Many commentators have argued that the problem addressed in the epistle is that some of the members of the Christian community were reverting back to Judaism.[21] It seems that this is indeed an underly-

---

[13] Ibid., 289.

[14] See Heb 1:2, 5, 9; 2:6-8; 3:6.

[15] Heb 7:18. Cf. 7:28.

[16] Cf. Heb 9:1-11, 24.

[17] Cf. Heb 9:10; 10:19; 12:22ff., 13:10. See also Iutisone Salevao, *Legitimation in the Letter to the Hebrews*, JSNTSS 219 (Sheffield: Sheffield Academic, 2002) 194.

[18] Cf. Heb 10:32-34; 13:3. Those responsible for the early persecution mentioned in 10:32-34 are not disclosed. It does seem possible, however, to imagine Jewish families or relatives unleashing social persecution or perhaps even repossessing the inheritance of those who aligned themselves with the followers of Jesus. See Craig R. Koester, *The Epistle to the Hebrews: A New Translation with Introduction and Commentary*, AB 36 (New York: Doubleday, 2001) 69.

[19] Cf. Heb 7:11-19, 28; 8:13, 10:5-10.

[20] Cf. Heb 13:10-13.

[21] This is the majority view among scholars. See Paul Ellingworth, *The Epistle to the Hebrews: A Commentary on the Greek Text*, NIGTC (Grand Rapids: Eerdmans, 1993) 80; Harold W. Attridge, *The Epistle to the Hebrews: A Commentary on the Epistle to the Hebrews*,

ing problem. This fact alone demonstrates a clear difference between the community in Hebrews and its parent group.

It is reasonable to assume that if those in the Hebrews' community were tempted to revert back to Judaism, then members of the dominant Jewish society probably played some role in persuading them to come back. Perhaps family members were urging their wayward relatives to come back to the Jewish cult and sacrifices.[22] This would indirectly indicate that the dominant Jewish society did not see the community of Hebrews as holding to its values and beliefs. Furthermore, if one assumes that the persecution mentioned in 10:32-34 came in part from other Jews, then we have reason to believe that the larger Jewish society acknowledged that the recipients of this letter no longer held to their core commitments and values.

There is little evidence of the second and seventh criteria above. The epistle makes no explicit mention of recruiting non-Jews or Gentiles. However, some of the language in the epistle indicate a need to show hospitality toward strangers (13:2). There is no evidence in the epistle that the larger non-Jewish society sees the community addressed in the epistle as separate from their Jewish heritage. The label "Christian" is not found in the epistle.

On the whole, however, the community more aptly is described as a sect of Judaism.[23] The new revelation of Jesus Christ in the last days (1:1-2) has forced the community to reevaluate and reinterpret their Jewish faith. It is clear from our analysis above that they saw themselves as a separate entity from the larger Jewish society. The epistle marks the stage of a

---

Hermeneia (Philadelphia: Fortress, 1989) 10–13. Koester, *Hebrews*, 71; F. F. Bruce, *The Epistle to the Hebrews*, rev. ed., NICNT (Grand Rapids: Eerdmans, 1990) 9, 155; Barnabas Lindars, *Theology of the Letter to the Hebrews* (Cambridge: Cambridge University Press, 1991) 10–11; William Loader, *Sohn und Hoherpriester*, WMANT 53 (Neukirchen-Vluyn: Neukirchener, 1981), 258; James D. G. Dunn, *The Partings of the Ways: Between Christianity and Judaism and Their Significance for the Character of Christianity* (Philadelphia: Trinity 1990); Philip E. Hughes, *A Commentary on the Epistle to the Hebrews* (Grand Rapids: Eerdmans, 1977) 260; Robert H. Culpepper, "The High Priesthood and Sacrifice of Christ in the Epistle to the Hebrews," *TTE* 32 (1985) 46; Horbury, "The Aaronic Priesthood in the Epistle to the Hebrews," 43–71.

[22] The language that describes the community in Hebrews as members of the "household of God" (3:6) would provide some encouragement to those who have left their household to join the community.

[23] Elliott believes that within a generation of Jesus' death the Christian movement shifted from a faction to a sect. See Elliott, "Phases in the Social Formation," 301. However, it is safe to assume that different Christian communities progressed at different rates in distinguishing themselves from Judaism. Cf. Salevao, *Legitimation*, 246–47.

maturing Christianity that is more independent from Judaism.[24] Though the community promoted by the author of Hebrews seeks to retain its Jewish roots and history, it is a separate social entity, distinguished from and marginalized by the dominant Jewish society.[25] What inevitably results in these kinds of transitions is conflict. Elliott notes as well, "the sectarian struggle with the parent body was intense precisely because it was a family conflict."[26]

Socio-Rhetorical Function of the Polemic in Hebrews

Counter-Cultural Rhetoric

Assuming then that the community in Hebrews saw itself as a separate entity from the larger Jewish society, we can better determine the kind of rhetoric used in the epistle. Vernon Robbins identifies five different types of rhetoric: dominant culture rhetoric, subculture rhetoric, counterculture rhetoric, contraculture rhetoric, and liminal culture rhetoric.[27] Dominant culture rhetoric is the language of the group in power. Subculture rhetoric "imitates the attitudes, values, dispositions, and norms of the dominant culture rhetoric, and it claims to enact them better than the members of the dominant status."[28] Counterculture rhetoric rejects characteristics of the dominant culture, setting forth a new future for the group and establishing institutions that facilitate independence from the dominant society. The hope is that the dominant society will eventually adopt and accept the new vision voluntarily. Contracultural rhetoric is more of a short-lived negative reaction or response to the dominant culture. Liminal

---

[24] Samuel Sandmel, *The First Christian Century in Judaism and Christianity: Certainties and Uncertainties* (New York: Oxford University Press, 1969) 172–73.

[25] Several scholars have argued that the community in Hebrews had separated itself from the synagogue. See Luke Timothy Johnson, "The New Testament's Anti-Jewish Slander and the Conventions of Ancient Polemic," *JBL* 108 (1989) 423–24; Lindars, *The Theology of the Letter to the Hebrews*, 11; John Dunnill, *Covenant and Sacrifice in the Letter to the Hebrews* (Cambridge: Cambridge University Press, 1992) 24–25; Pamela M. Eisenbaum, *The Jewish Heroes of Christian History: Hebrews 11 in Literary Context*, SBLDS 156 (Atlanta: Scholars, 1997) 10; and Salevao, *Legitimation*, 192–93. For a contrary view see William Lane, *Hebrews 1–8*, WBC 47A (Dallas: Word, 1991) cxxvii.

[26] Elliott, "Phases," 301.

[27] Vernon K. Robbins, *Exploring the Texture of Texts: A Guide to Socio-Rhetorical Interpretation* (Valley Forge, Pa.: Trinity, 1996) 86–88.

[28] Ibid., 86.

culture rhetoric is for those on the edge of the society, not able to establish for themselves a clear identity and is often inconsistent and incoherent.[29]

For the purposes of this work we will assume the dominant culture is the Jewish culture from which the community in Hebrews emerged.[30] The majority position that the readers were tempted to revert back to Jewish sacrificial rituals, presupposes that the readers were by and large Jewish Christians living in a larger Jewish context.[31]

From our analysis above, it is clear that the rhetoric used in the epistle is not the dominant culture or even sub-culture rhetoric. Unlike the Second Temple Jewish writings,[32] the author of Hebrews does not assume that the Levitical priesthood, the Mosaic covenant, and the Levitical sacrifices will remain as the definitive priesthood, covenant, and sacrificial system for the Jewish people. The author speaks very clearly of a better priesthood, covenant, and sacrifice implying a better future for the community as a whole.[33] At the same time, the author is not using contracultural or liminal rhetoric. He is not simply reacting negatively to the dominant culture or speaking incoherently as someone on the edge of society. What seems to be driving his rhetoric is a very thoughtful and well reasoned theology grounded upon the person, work, and teaching of Jesus Christ. Therefore, the rhetoric can best be characterized as counter-cultural rhetoric.

---

[29] Ibid., 86–88.

[30] Certainly the recipients of the epistle lived in the secular Greco-Roman culture as well. But this work is focused on the question of the relationship between the community in Hebrews and the dominant Jewish community.

[31] See Lane, *Hebrews 1–8* , xlvii–lv; Attridge, *Hebrews*, 1–13; Donald Hagner, *Hebrews*, NIBC 14 (Peabody, Mass: Hendrickson, 1990) 1–11; and Koester, *Hebrews*, 42–48. For a contrary view see Geerhardus Vos, *The Teaching of the Epistle to the Hebrews*, ed. and rev. J. Vos (1956; reprinted Eugene, Ore.: Wipf and Stock, 1998) 11–23. Vos argues that the original readers were Gentile Christians. This view was originally proposed by E. M. Röth, *Epistolam vulgo "ad Hebraeos" inscriptam non ad Hebreos, id est christianos genere judaeos* (Frankfurt: Schmerberi, 1836) and followed by H. von Soden, "Der Hebräerbrief," *Jahrbücher für protestantische Theologie* 10 (1884) 435–93, 627–56; and J. A. Moffatt, *Critical and Exegetical Commentary on the Epistle to the Hebrews*, ICC (Edinburgh: T. & T. Clark, 1924).

[32] Certainly it is difficult to identify even one of the many Jewish movements as the dominant Jewish culture. It may be misleading to state that the Jews in power accurately represented the larger Jewish society. Therefore, for the purposes of this dissertation, we will assume that all the Jewish writings surveyed—taken as a whole—give a composite picture of the dominant Jewish culture.

[33] Cf. Heb 7:11-19, 28; 8:1-13; 10:1-10.

Social Function of the Polemic

But what is the social function of the polemical passages in Hebrews? Richard Johnson and Iutisone Salevao offer two different answers to this question. Our approach will follow Salevao's with some modification.

Conversion/Outreach in Hebrews?

Richard W. Johnson argues that the social function of the Levitical critique in Hebrews is to "minimize the role of ritual in the spiritual life of the society."[34] The author of Hebrews' intention would be to make Christianity more appealing to those on the outside. Thus the function of the polemic in Hebrews is ultimately for missions or conversion. Johnson uses Mary Douglas' Group/Grid paradigm to identify first-century Judaism and Christianity's basic attitude toward ritual.[35] Douglas classifies societies according to two parameters: 1) group, or the experience of a defined social unit; and 2) grid, or the rules that govern one's relationship to others.[36] A society can be either strong or weak in either of these categories. What results are four different types: 1) weak group/strong grid, which describes a complex society where roles are assigned and accepted; 2) weak group/weak grid, where individualism is predominant; 3) strong group/strong grid, where the institution and hierarchy are respected and loyalty is rewarded; and 4) strong group/weak grid, where there is factionalism with only the external boundary set and all else is open to question.[37]

Johnson's general argument is that first-century Judaism fits the strong group/strong grid paradigm, where very strict boundary markers were set and there were very clear rules and regulations regarding social roles. He then identifies the implied ideal society promoted by Hebrews as weak group/weak grid in comparison to first-century Judaism. This is based on: 1) the epistles' lack of nationalistic rhetoric and "insider versus outsider" language; and 2) the absence of an elevated leadership status.[38] With these identifications made, Johnson notes that only the weak group/weak grid

---

[34] Richard Warren Johnson, *Going Outside the Camp: The Sociological Function of the Levitical Critique in the Epistle to the Hebrews*, JSNTSS 209 (Sheffield: Sheffield Academic, 2001) 153. Though Johnson focuses specifically on the Levitical priesthood and sacrifices, the Mosaic covenant is also implicitly in view.

[35] Mary Douglas, *Natural Symbols: Explorations in Cosmology*, 3d ed. (New York: Pantheon, 1982).

[36] Ibid., viii.

[37] See Johnson, *Going Outside the Camp*, 21.

[38] Ibid., 97.

society is open to outsiders.[39] Therefore, the critique of the Levitical cult, served to minimize ritual in the implied ideal society and better equip the readers to carry out the world mission of the church.[40] Johnson writes,

> The move from non-missionary Judaism to a society committed to world mission does constitute a significant social change that should be accompanied by a thorough revision of cosmology. This 'conversion' to Christianity, as understood by the author, necessitated his thorough reevaluation of the levitical cultus.[41]

One of the weaknesses of this argument is already noted by Johnson himself. His assessment of the implied ideal society in Hebrews as a weak group/ weak grid society is based on arguments from silence.[42] Furthermore, he establishes the missionary character of Christianity on data outside of Hebrews. Hebrews itself says very little about missions or Gentiles, indicating that it is perhaps concerned with other matters.[43] Finally the actual critique of the Levitical cult in Hebrews was never based on the fact that it excluded those outside the community.[44] Though the Levitical critique in Hebrews could have functioned secondarily to encourage missions, this does not seem to be the overriding emphasis.

---

[39] Ibid., 142.

[40] Ibid., 153. Charles Anderson, who does not necessarily disagree with the idea that the epistle has in mind conversion, would argue that it has ethnic Jews primarily in mind as the object of its evangelism. He carefully examines the references made to Abraham in Hebrews (Genesis 22) and contrasts them with the references to Abraham that Paul utilizes (Genesis 15, 17). Anderson concludes that the author of Hebrews was not as interested in the Gentile mission as Paul; Charles P. Anderson, "Who are the Heirs of the New Age in the Epistle to the Hebrews?" in *Apocalyptic and the New Testament: Essays in Honor of J. Louis Martyn,* ed. Joel Marcus and Marion L. Soards, JSNTSS 24 (Sheffield: Sheffield Academic, 1989) 258–68).

[41] Johnson, *Going Outside the Camp,* 150.

[42] Ibid., 98.

[43] Anderson notes that Gentiles are never mentioned in the epistle. See Anderson, "Heirs," 258.

[44] Hebrews does seem to contrast the relative accessibility to God through the Levitical priesthood and the priesthood of Christ (4:16; 10:19-22). But we must remember that the accessibility is for those on the inside of the community. According to Hebrews, Christianity is better not because it is more accepting of those on the outside, but because it provides greater access to all on the inside.

Legitimation in Hebrews

Iutisone Salevao argues that Hebrews reflects a conflict between an outgroup with its parent group. The issue he identifies in the community is that some of the members were still practicing elements of the Jewish cult and were tempted to revert back to Judaism.[45] With this in mind, he suggests that the function of the Levitical critique was to legitimate the symbolic universe of the author.[46] Salevao focuses more on the subversive tactics used in deprecating the alternative view, namely Judaism.

Salevao agrees with Berger and Luckmann who state that the confrontation between two different groups or societies is a major occasion for the development and employment of "universe-maintaining" conceptualizations.[47] "Two societies confronting each other with conflicting universes will both develop conceptual machineries designed to maintain their respective universes."[48] Salevao believes that by the time Hebrews was written Christianity and Judaism were for the most part two separate religions, defining Christianity as a sect.[49] This is important because a threat posed by a competing society is much more serious than intra-societal conflicts (deviation or heresy). The reason is that the competing society challenges the validity of one's definitions of reality. It offers an alternative symbolic universe, which it claims to be equal or superior to one's own. If the claim is believed, one's own universe is rendered redundant or inferior.[50]

Adopting a conflict model, Salevao identifies in Hebrews the use of a superiority/ inferiority dialectic to legitimize its proposed symbolic universe. The author of Hebrews uses typology within this superior/inferior framework. Typology implicitly assumes that the type is inferior to the anti-type. The fact that these concepts were implicit in the language allows the author to construct his view of the world around these categories.[51] Though noting that typology has its roots in Judaism, Salevao affirms that New Testament typology was unique in that it was a fulfilled typology. "By this is meant that Christian typology interpreted each of the Old Testament types as ultimately no more than prophecies or pointers to

---

[45] Salevao, *Legitimation*, 340.

[46] A threat to the existing community provides the need for legitimation.

[47] Salevao, *Legitimation*, 339.

[48] Peter L. Berger and Thomas Luckmann, *The Social Construct of Reality: A Treatise in the Sociology of Knowledge* (Garden City, N.Y.: Doubleday, 1967) 126–27.

[49] Salevao, *Legitimation*, 246–47.

[50] Ibid., 340–41. See also Berger and Luckmann, *The Social Construct of Reality*, 125.

[51] Salevao, *Legitimation*, 346.

the reality which had taken place in the Christian dispensation, and particularly in Christ."[52] Thus, typology plays an important role in apologetics against Judaism. It highlights the uniqueness of Christ and legitimizes Christianity in its environment.[53]

For example, we can see the relationship between Melchizedek and Christ as one of type and anti-type. Jesus is the anti-type of the Melchizedekian priesthood. Though there are similarities between Jesus and Melchizedek, Jesus is superior as the anti-type.[54] The argument that follows from Hebrews 7:1-10 is that since Melchizedek is superior to Abraham (and Levi), and Jesus is superior to Melchizedek, then Jesus' priesthood is superior to the Levitical priesthood.

In addition to typology, Salevao notes that the use of the term τελείωσις "perfection" or "completion"[55] also serves a legitimizing function. The use of the term is to help construct reality for the readers. It is used to define and epitomize the new covenantal order[56] and help identify the reader's status in relation to Judaism. Those in the author's community have been made perfect, while those who remain connected to the dominant Jewish society have not been made perfect.[57] This language of perfection is also used to deconstruct the old order. By highlighting the superiority of the new, the inferiority of the old is also highlighted.[58]

Thus Salevao argues that the author of Hebrews describes the superiority of Christianity and the inferiority of Judaism in the midst of this conflict between these separate societies. Salevao does not, however, believe it was the author's intention to engage in a direct confrontation with

---

[52] Ibid., 348.

[53] Ibid., 348.

[54] Ibid., 372. See also Harold S. Songer, "A Superior Priesthood: Hebrews 4:14-7:27," *RevExp* 82 (1985) 355.

[55] Cf. Heb 2:10; 5:9; 7:11, 19, 28; 9:9; 10:1, 14; 11:40; 12:23.

[56] Salevao, *Legitimation*, 401.

[57] Heb 10:1, 14. Perfection in Hebrews refers to more than moral or ethical perfection. It includes internal cleansing from sin and guilt, but it also has an eschatological sense, in which a person's relationship with God is consummated and all the barriers blocking that relationship are removed. See David G. Peterson, *Hebrews and Perfection: An Examination of the Concept of Perfection in the 'Epistle to the Hebrews,'* SNTSMS 47 (Cambridge: Cambridge University Press, 1982) 127–28; Koester, *Hebrews*, 122–23; Franz Delitzsch, *Commentary on the Epistle to the Hebrews* (2 vols; trans. Thomas L. Kingsbury; (1871; reprinted, Minneapolis: Klock & Klock, 1978) 350; A. B. Bruce, *The Epistle to the Hebrews* (Edinburgh: T. & T. Clark, 1899) 263; Hugh Montefiore, *A Commentary on the Epistle to the Hebrews* (New York: Harper & Row, 1964) 124.

[58] Salevao, *Legitimation*, 402.

the whole of Judaism. Rather he was against some of his own members continuing to adhere to certain Jewish practices and beliefs, and their tendency to revert back to Judaism. "His purpose was therefore more moderate than a full-scale unprovoked attack on the Jewish religion as such."[59]

We certainly agree with Salevao that the language used by the author seeks to legitimize Jesus' priesthood in the ongoing conflict between the Christian community and the dominant Jewish community. However, what is missing is the role of these polemical texts in socializing and confirming those already in the community. The author of Hebrews is not simply addressing those who are tempted to revert back to Judaism, but the entire community, whose faith may have been shaken by those seeking to return to Judaism.

Structure / Anti-Structure Model

We suggest the adoption of a structure/ anti-structure model that deals not only with legitimizing the community to those who are thinking of reverting back to Judaism, but also reinforcing the values and norms of the entire community. Leo Perdue explores how paraenesis, or moral instruction functions within in a community.[60] He begins by positing two social models—the "order" model, and the "conflict" model. In the "order" model, paraenesis serves to retain the status quo, giving structure and stability to the society by reinforcing duty, obligations, and morals.[61] In the "conflict" model, paraenesis seeks to subvert the existing social order for a new order.[62] The problem of course is the fact that many forms of paraenesis seem to reflect both order and conflict. And so Perdue suggests the "structure/ anti-structure" model of Victor Turner, which views society moving back and forth between structure and anti-structure. Turner identifies three stages in this process: separation, margin or *limen*, and aggregation or reincorporation. Separation describes an individual divorcing himself or herself from the existing social structure.[63] Margin has two phases: 1) the death of their previous social identity with its norms; and 2) the new birth into a new social role and structure. In the first phase,

---

[59] Ibid., 340.

[60] Leo G. Perdue, "The Social Character of Paraenesis and Paraenetic Literature," *Semeia* 50 (1990) 5–39.

[61] Ibid., 6–8.

[62] Ibid., 8–9.

[63] "Separation" can also describe a group divorcing themselves from the existing social structure.

paraenesis is subversive and seeks to invalidate the existing social order. In the second phase, paraenesis functions to instruct the new members into the new roles and responsibilities they will assume as they are reincorporated into society.[64]

In this model, it is assumed that one is simply changing their social status within the same society or community. Yet, Turner acknowledges that those who separate may indeed completely reject the former society and in fact create an alternative social structure and hierarchy.[65] In this model, paraenesis functions to subvert the former social structure and to validate and reinforce the norms and values of the new structure.

This model seems to fit well the situation presented in the epistle to the Hebrews. The counter-cultural rhetoric used in the epistle functions first to invalidate the previous institutions that regulated the community's relationship with God and second to promote and maintain the new institutions inaugurated by Jesus Christ. The author presents to his readers two alternative societies: the former society characterized by the dominant Jewish culture and the counter-cultural society promoted by the author. The ramifications of the annulment of the previous priestly institution and law, covenant, and sacrifice require an entirely different social and hierarchical structure. Because of the far-reaching social consequences of being associated with the alternative society, the author must use rhetoric that leaves his readers with little choice but to adopt and/or remain in the new structure. This rhetoric addresses the entire community by reinforcing beliefs and socializing those who are immature.

It is within this sociological model of structure/anti-structure that we see the author of Hebrews confirming, legitimizing, and socializing his community, while at the same time, seeking to subvert allegiance to the dominant Jewish ritual practices and covenant.[66]

---

[64] Perdue, "The Social Character of Paraenesis," 10. Cf. Victor Turner, *The Forest of Symbols* (Ithaca, N.Y.: Cornell University Press, 1967) 94.

[65] Perdue, "The Social Character of Paraenesis," 10–11.

[66] Perdue offers five general social functions of paraenesis: conversion, confirmation, socialization, legitimation, and conflict. When paraenesis is used for conversion it seeks to persuade the audience to turn from one course to another. When it is used for confirmation it simply confirms the validity of the morals and values propagated and encourages the hearers to continue on the path already set. Legitimation is most needed when the group or society is questioned or under attack. Finally, subversive, anti-traditional (conflict) paraenesis seeks to undermine the legitimacy of the prevailing social order, leading to its destruction or fragmentation. It is this kind of paraenesis that establishes social boundaries by constructing a new social order (ibid., 23–26).

Conclusion

From our discussion of the social context of the letter to the Hebrews, it is clear that the community addressed was separate from the dominant Jewish society. And yet there was still some contact with the dominant culture by members of the community. It is likely that some in the Hebrews community were tempted to revert back to the dominant form of Judaism and therefore, needed to be encouraged to remain steadfast in their commitment to the community in Hebrews.

Our conclusion then rules out the approach to the question of anti-Judaism in Hebrews that seeks to minimize the sectarian nature of the community. William Lane, for instance, questions the majority opinion that Hebrews addresses Jewish Christians who were thinking of retreating back to Judaism.[67] He does not see a counter-cultural sectarian dynamic in the epistle. Rather he argues that the author is simply reflecting upon Scripture in the Judaic tradition of homiletical midrash.[68] The strong statements against Judaism are simply deductions from the Scripture texts the author quotes.

According to Lane, the author is not in any direct polemic with Judaism. This he believes is shown by the fact that the exhortations that are derived from his Scriptural reflections demonstrate no separation or discontinuity with Judaism.[69] Rather the author is encouraging his readers, who have grown lax in their commitment to the Christian message, to give heed to God's revelation in Jesus Christ.[70] The pejorative words the author uses in describing Judaism are not for the purpose of combating a Jewish threat, but a pastoral strategy in encouraging his community members to greater faith and commitment to God.[71] Lane writes, "His [author of Hebrews] concern was not that members of the community would simply return to the synagogue but that they would turn away from the living God altogether (3:12-13)."[72]

---

[67] Lane, *Hebrews 1–8*, cxxvii. See also David A. deSilva, *Perseverance in Gratitude: A Socio-Rhetorical Commentary on the Epistle 'to the Hebrews'* (Grand Rapids: Eerdmans, 2000) 264.

[68] Lane, *Hebrews 1–8*, cxxvi.

[69] Ibid., cxxvii.

[70] Ibid., lvi. See also David A. deSilva, "Heb 6:4-8: A Socio-Rhetorical Investigation (Part 1)," *TynBul* 50 (1999) 33–57, esp. 39–40.

[71] Lane, *Hebrews 1–8*, cxxxiii

[72] Ibid., cxxxiv.

Though there certainly was continuity with Judaism, the community in Hebrews was clearly seeking to distinguish itself from its parent group. Lane only seems to want to tell half of the story. It is true that the author wanted his readers to be strengthened in their commitment to God, but he also wanted them to distance themselves from the larger Jewish community. If the author's real interest was simply to persuade apathetic Jewish-Christians to get serious about their faith, he did not have to: 1) choose to reflect on texts that imply discontinuity with Judaism; or 2) make pejorative statements about the Levitical priesthood and law, Mosaic covenant, and Levitical sacrifices. Encouraging apathetic Jewish-Christians does not have to come at the cost of deprecating specific Jewish institutions. The severe polemical language in Hebrews demonstrates that a real threat to the legitimacy of the community in Hebrews existed.[73]

---

[73] As mentioned above, Perdue argues that legitimation is most needed when the group or society is questioned or under attack; Perdue, "The Social Character of Paraenesis," 23–26.

4

Priesthood and Polemic in Hebrews 7:1-19

IN this chapter, we will examine the polemical rhetoric used in Hebrews 7:1-19. We will seek to determine how this passage functions in the social context in which it was given. This examination will help evaluate to what extent if any this text can be considered anti-Semitic, anti-Judaic or supersessionist.

There will be three major sections to this chapter. In the first section, we will explore the role, function, and significance of the Levitical Priesthood in Second Temple Jewish writings.[1] In the second section we will examine Hebrews 7:1-19, in order to determine the socio-rhetorical goal of the author. In the final section we will discuss to what degree, if any, the author of Hebrews' rhetoric constitutes anti-Semitism, anti-Judaism, or supersessionism.

---

[1] Though these writing are quite diverse and reflect the opinion of quite different segments of the Jewish community, together they can help us discern the specific role the covenant played in the life, identity, and culture of the larger, dominant Jewish community. We will exclude rabbinic literature in our discussion because of the difficulty in determining the precise date of certain ideas or traditions. See Jacob Neusner, "The Use of the Later Rabbinic Evidence for the Study of Paul," in *Approaches to Ancient Judaism,* vol. 2, ed. W. S. Green, BJS 9 (Missoula, Mont.: Scholars, 1980) 43–64; E. P. Sanders, "Puzzling out Rabbinic Judaism," in *Approaches to Ancient Judaism,* vol. 2, ed. W. S. Green, BJS 9 (Missoula, Mont.: Scholars, 1980) 65–80; and Alan F. Segal, "Covenant in Rabbinic Writings." *SR* 14 (1985) 55–56. Though it is true that rabbinic literature may reflect practices and ideas characteristic of Second Temple Judaism, distinguishing what was part of the early tradition and what reflects a later time period is difficult. More often than not, only those ideas and concepts in Rabbinic Judaism that parallel those in sectarian writings in the Second Temple period are thought to be reflections of the earlier period. This approach renders the study of rabbinic literature pointless for our purposes, if it only confirms what is already known about Second Temple Judaism.

Levitical Priesthood and Law in the Second Temple Period

In order to understand how the message of Hebrews 7:1-19 was received in its Jewish context, we must determine the role, significance, and importance of the Levitical priesthood in the larger Jewish community. If the Levitical priesthood and law were so fundamentally tied to the identity of Jews, then it could be argued that attacking the Levitical priesthood and law was tantamount to attacking Judaism or the Jewish people. In addition, we will also examine how Second Temple Jewish writers used polemic against the priesthood to further their own socio-rhetorical goals. This will shed light on how the author of Hebrews uses his polemic.

What becomes clear as we survey several different Second Temple writings is the fact that the Jews held in high regard the Levitical priesthood as an institution. As the God appointed office to regulate Israel's cultic relationship with God, the priesthood itself is venerated. And yet because of its importance and significance in the community, several writers criticize individual priests for corrupting and denigrating the office by their unlawful behavior and attitudes.

We shall see that many of these authors use polemical language to sharply define the identity of their community as sub-culture and contra-culture factions and in the case of the Dead Sea writings as a counter-cultural sect. By criticizing the Levitical priests in power, these sub-groups seek to legitimize their own group.

For most of the Second Temple writings, what lies behind both the veneration of the Levitical priesthood as well as the critique of individual priests are the Hebrew Scriptures themselves. What is consistent about the Scriptures' description of the Israelite priesthood is the fact that it was an honorable office ordained by God[2] and that it was a hereditary office assigned specifically to the tribe of Levi.[3] The role of the priest in the community certainly developed throughout the history of Israel. And though the history itself is quite debated, what remains fairly consistent is the importance of the Levitical ancestry for priests. John M. Scholer argues, "however muddled the historical picture, the hereditary lineage

---

[2] Exodus 28:1; Lev 21:10; Num 3:12, 41.

[3] Exodus 28:1; Lev 1:5-7; 8:1-3; 21:1; 22:1-4; Num 1:47-51; 3:5-9. Certainly not all Levites became priests but only those from the tribe of Levi were given the opportunity. We should note, however, that the right to the office of priest is different from instances in which individuals perform priestly functions. There are instances in which non-Levites perform priestly acts without censure (Gen 22:31, 54; 46:1; Judg 6:20-28; 1 Sam 6:14-15; 2 Sam 6:13-18; 1 Kgs 18:30-38).

of the priests remains fairly consistent: only descendants of the tribe of Levi possess legitimate access to the priesthood throughout the history of Israel."[4]

Even though the priesthood may have been quite prominent at the time of the return of the Jews from the Babylonian exile, it was not free from criticism. Malachi 1:6-2:9 criticizes the priests for offering blemished sacrifices and showing partiality in carrying out the law. Nehemiah sharply rebukes Eliashib, the priest in charge of the temple, for preparing a room in the temple for a secular Ammonite named Tobiah (Neh 13:4-9). Furthermore, Eliashib was also rebuked for allowing one of his daughters to marry a foreigner, Sanballat the Horonite (Neh 13:27-29).[5]

Apocrypha and Pseudepigrapha

First and Second Maccabees

First Maccabees[6] demonstrates both a high regard for the priesthood as well as critiques of individual priests. During the time of this writing, Judah's political status under the Seleucid Empire was one of semi-autonomy. It was at this time that the high priest played a prominent role. The importance of the priesthood is demonstrated by the fact that the Seleucids intervened in the appointment of Alcimus, not the governor, but the high priest.[7]

The author of 1 Maccabees was calling his readers to greater covenant faithfulness in the face of Gentile threats. He sought to undermine those Jews who were more sympathetic to Gentile powers and authorities.[8] First Maccabees describes Alcimus as "ungodly", a traitor, a murderer, a liar, and

---

[4] John M. Scholer, *Proleptic Priests: Priesthood in the Epistle to the Hebrews*, JSNTSS 49 (Sheffield: JSOT Press, 1991) 14. See also Menahem Haran, *Temples and Temple Service in Ancient Israel* (Oxford: Clarendon, 1978) 64–71. Haran notes that though the sources differ as to how the priests functioned in the community, they all agree that the priesthood was given to the tribe of Levi alone.

[5] Ezra 10:18 also describes priests marrying foreign wives.

[6] The date of this work is between the death of John Hyrcanus (104 BC), whose ascension is mentioned at the end of the narrative, and Pompey's incursion into Jerusalem (63 BC). See David A. deSilva, *Introducing the Apocrypha: Message, Context, and Significance* (Grand Rapids: Baker, 2002) 248.

[7] 1 Macc 7:4-11. Cf. Aelred Cody, *A History of Old Testament Priesthood*, AnBib 35 (Rome: Pontifical Biblical Institute Press, 1969) 175–77.

[8] See deSilva, *Introducing the Apocrypha*, 244.

a slanderer.[9] The polemic against Alcimus was motivated by the fact that he was a member of the Hellenistic faction promoting the agenda of the Seleucid king.[10]

Furthermore, the revolt against the Seleucids was in fact led by the Hasmonean priestly family of Mattathias. It was this priestly family – well recognized even by the foreigners as leaders in the community[11] – that refused to participate in the idolatry instituted by Antiochus IV and in fact killed those on their way to sacrifice to pagan gods, including one Jew who was going to comply with the foreigners (1 Macc 2:23-27).

Second Maccabees also seeks to persuade its readers to resist the Hellenization of their Jewish culture and faith. Second Maccabees 4 describes the great struggle for the office of high priest in Jerusalem.[12] The language in this chapter exposes the political nature of the priesthood and its corruption. Referring to Menelaus, who replaced Jason as high priest, the author writes,

> But he, when presented to the king, extolled him with an air of authority, and secured the high priesthood for himself, outbidding Jason by three hundred talents of silver. After receiving the king's orders he returned, possessing no qualification for the high priesthood, but having the hot temper of a cruel tyrant and the rage of a savage wild beast (2 Macc 4:24-25 NRSV).[13]

The critique of the priesthood in 1 Maccabees functions to legitimize the Hasmonean dynasty and further subvert any allegiance to Gentile powers or their appointed priests. Boundaries are set up by this rhetoric, defining who is on the inside and who is excluded. By painting the high priests as evil, wicked, compromisers the author leaves his readers little choice but to reject them. The implication of course is that the priests are not performing faithfully their God given task in leading the people and

---

[9] 1 Macc 7:9, 15–16, 25.

[10] See deSilva, *Introducing the Apocrypha*, 245, 263; Larry R Helyer, *Exploring Jewish Literature of the Second Temple Period: A Guide for New Testament Students* (Downers Grove, Ill.: Inter Varsity, 2002) 157.

[11] 1 Macc 2:17.

[12] The dating of 2 Maccabees is difficult because it is thought to be the result of an editor or redactor of a much longer work. Supposing that it was completed after 1 Maccabees would make the earliest date around 85 BC. Since there is evidence of its influence in Hebrews and 4 Maccabees, its latest date is about AD 50. However, it was likely written before 63 BC, given that it portrays a positive relationship with Rome (4:11; 8:10, 36; 11:34-36). See deSilva, *Introducing the Apocrypha*, 269.

[13] All Apocrypha quotations are taken from the New Revised Standard Version.

regulating Israel's relationship with God. Second Maccabees has the goal of maintaining commitment to Jewish values and culture. DeSilva writes, "It seeks not to legitimate a dynasty but rather to demonstrate the ongoing legitimacy of Deuteronomy's philosophy of history as can be traced out in recent events, as well as the legitimacy of the Jerusalem temple as the focal point of God's protective care and concern."[14] Thus the polemic against the priesthood in 2 Maccabees also seeks to subvert allegiance to the dominant Gentile culture and strengthen fidelity to the Jewish faith.

Sirach/Ecclesiasticus

The Wisdom of Ben Sira or Sirach is representative of a conservative voice in the first decades of the second century BC.[15] In this writing the author seeks to encourage his readers to give proper respect and reverence to the priests (7:29,31; 50:1ff.). The glory and honor of the priesthood come from the fact that God himself ordained it. Sirach 45:6-7 states, "He (God) exalted Aaron, a holy man like Moses who was his brother, of the tribe of Levi. He made an everlasting covenant with him, and gave him the priesthood of the people. He blessed him with stateliness, and put a glorious robe on him."[16]

According to Sirach, the priests continued in their cultic role offering sacrifices, incense, and perfume, making expiation for the people, and blessing them in the name of the Lord (Sir 45:6-26). They were appointed to regulate the relationship between God and his people. In addition the priests functioned as teachers in the community (Sir 45:17). And the practice of receiving support from the offerings of the people was also maintained (Sir 45:20ff).

In painting a positive picture of the priesthood, Ben Sira seeks to encourage his readers to remain faithful to the Torah prescribed means of approaching God in worship. His rhetoric functions to confirm the value of the Levitical priesthood, as well as socialize his readers as to how they should relate to the cult.

---

[14] See deSilva, *Introducing the Apocrypha*, 266.

[15] The date of this work is between 196 and 175 BC. Mention of the high priesthood of Simon II and no mention of Jason, the younger son of Simon II, guides our dating. See deSilva, *Introducing the Apocrypha*, 153, 157–58.

[16] Cf. Sir 45:16, 20-21.

Testament of Moses

The author of the *Testament of Moses*[17] writes against the priests of his day,

> For they will not follow the truth of God, but certain of them will pollute the high altar by [four to six letters are lost] the offerings which they place before the Lord. They are not (truly) priests (at all), but slaves, yea sons of slaves. For those who are the leaders, their teachers, in those times will become admirers of avaricious persons, accepting (polluted) offerings, and they will sell justice by accepting bribes.[18]

What is presupposed in this text is the importance of purity in the priesthood—not only moral purity, but purity in lineage. The fact that 6:2 mentions the wanton king, "who will not be of a priestly family," indicates the importance to the author of the priest-kingly lineage begun with the Maccabean Jonathan (160-143).[19] In addition the Messiah-like figure Taxo, who will warn the people bringing about the end times and divine vengeance (9:1-10:1), comes from the tribe of Levi.

Clearly this polemic against the priesthood serves to subvert allegiance to the dominant priestly authority. The faction represented by the author is strengthened and legitimized by deprecating the priests in power. The fact that the author's contemporary priests were illegitimate according to the law disqualified them from the office and from fulfilling the duties of the office. Their offerings were polluted and their service was compromised.

---

[17] Though still debated the likely date of this text is between 4 BC and the fall of Jerusalem in AD 70. Chapter 6 almost certainly describes Herod the Great (37–4 BC), with the reference to the king who ruled for 34 years, not of the priestly family. Since his death is mentioned in that chapter, the earliest the document could have been written would be about 4 BC. The fact that it was written before AD 70 is demonstrated by the reference to the temple still standing in 1:17. See J. Priest, "Testament of Moses," in *The Old Testament Pseudepigrapha* 2 vols, ed. James H. Charlesworth; (Garden City, N. Y.: Doubleday, 1983) 1:920.

[18] *T. Mos.* 5.5-6. All quotations from the Pseudepigraphical writings are taken from James H. Charlesworth, ed., *The Old Testament Pseudepigrapha*, 2 vols. (Garden City, N.Y.: Doubleday, 1983). Josephus describes John Hyracanus in *Ant.* 13.105 as receiving gifts and honors from King Ptolemy.

[19] H. W. Hoehner, "Hasmoneans," in *ISBE* 2:622–23.

Psalms of Solomon

Another important work that criticizes the Levitical priesthood is the *Psalms of Solomon*.[20] It is dated from about 63 BC to AD 70[21] and represents a response first to what it considered an illegitimate uprising of fellow Jews. But after this group was overthrown by non-Jews, the Psalms respond to the even graver desecration brought about by Gentile invaders. Since there seems to be no earthly hope in regaining power, the group turns to apocalyptic messianism as its only solution.[22]

The Psalms describe their loss of hope in the cultic institutions because of the corruption and compromise of the priests, "their lawless actions surpassed the gentiles before them; they completely profaned the sanctuary of the Lord."[23] Who were these priests? Very likely, they were the Hasmonean priests who ruled and presided over the cult after the revolt of the Maccabees. These priests are described as living in sin, "Because the sons of Jerusalem defiled the sanctuary of the Lord, they were profaning the offerings of God with lawless acts; because of these things he said, 'remove them far from me; they are not sweet-smelling.'"[24]

Not only is there a direct charge of corruption and defilement in the priesthood, but there is also an indication that God himself would remove these wicked priests, who were simply vying for political power and influence. Later in 8:16, the author describes Jewish leaders receiving the foreign invader, "the leaders of the country met him with joy. They said to him, 'may your way be blessed. Come, enter in peace.'" This seems to be an allusion to Hyrcanus and Aristobulus each wanting Pompey's help against the other in order to secure personal position and power.[25]

---

[20] The foreign conqueror described in the text is most likely Pompey. He is described as one who comes from the west (17:12), was at first welcomed into Jerusalem (8:16-18), but after he entered met resistance, requiring extra troops and a siege machine (2:1). Once the city fell, he entered the Temple desecrating it (2:2); and when he was assassinated, his body was left unburied (2:26f.-27).

[21] The earliest direct allusion in the *Psalms of Solomon* to a historical event is the invasion of Pompey in 63 BC. The latest is Pompey's death in 48 BC. The fact that Jerusalem is described as desecrated and not destroyed argues for a date of the final form before AD 70. Therefore, the general limits for the date would be from 63 BC to AD 70. See R. B. Wright, "Psalms of Solomon," in *The Old Testament Pseudepigrapha*, ed. James H. Charlesworth, 2 vols. (Garden City, N.Y.: Doubleday, 1983) 2:641.

[22] See Wright, "Psalms of Solomon," 2:642–43.

[23] *Pss. Sol.* 1:8.

[24] *Pss. Sol.* 2:3-4.

[25] See Josephus *Ant.* 14.29-33.

Not only does this writing seek to subvert allegiance to the priests in authority, but it also establishes an alternative structure in which the people put their hope in a Messiah to come. The legitimacy of this faction comes at the cost of deprecating the priesthood. The fact that God is described as displeased with these priests and their offerings further strengthens the author's position. The author and his faction are on God's side, while the wicked priests are out of God's favor. Their improper motives and corruption render them useless for their appointed task in regulating the people's relationship with God.

Testament of Levi

The *Testament of Levi*[26] is just one part of the *Testaments of the Twelve Patriarchs*. These testaments take the form of the final words of each of the twelve sons of Jacob,[27] and look forward to the arrival of a king from the tribe of Judah and a priest from the tribe of Levi, who will together bring about redemption.[28] This "dyarchic messianism" was fueled by a disappointment with the current Jewish leadership. Though the office and calling of the priests are highly exalted throughout the *Testament of the Twelve Patriarchs*,[29] the *Testament of Levi* portrays the priesthood as becoming corrupt. Levi is described speaking to his children saying,

> . . . you plunder the Lord's offerings; from his share you steal choice parts, contemptuously eating them with whores. You teach the Lord's commands out of greed for gain; married women you profane; you have intercourse with whores and adulteresses. You take gentile women for your wives and your sexual relations will become like Sodom and Gomorrah. You will be inflated with pride over your priesthood, exalting yourselves not merely by human

---

[26] Many scholars believe the *Testament of Levi* was written during the reign of John Hyrcanus (137–107 BC). Others believe it had Essene origins and was thus written sometime after 150 BC. Regardless, it is commonly understood to have been written by a Hellenized Jew, though there may have been some Christian interpolations. See H. C. Kee, "Testament of the Twelve Patriarchs," *The Old Testament Pseudepigrapha*, ed. James H. Charlesworth, 2 vols.; (Garden City, New York: Doubleday, 1983) 1:777–8.

[27] Kee, "Testament of the Twelve Patriarchs," 1:775.

[28] See *T. Dan.* 5:10; *T. Gad.* 8:1; *T. Benj.* 4:2; *T. Levi* 18:1-11; and Kee, "Testament of the Twelve Patriarchs," 1:778.

[29] See *T. Reu.* 6:5-12; *T. Sim.* 7:1-2; *T. Jos.* 19:11; *T. Naph.* 5:1-5; *T. Jud.* 21:1-6; *T. Iss.* 5:7-8.

standards but contrary to the commands of God. With contempt and laughter you will deride the sacred things.[30]

The *Testament of Levi* continues by describing the eventual corruption of the priesthood in seven cycles using the imagery of seventy weeks from Daniel 9.[31] The corruption will bring about the final judgment of God and the rise of a new eschatological priest,

> When vengeance will have come upon them from the Lord, the priesthood will lapse. And then the Lord will raise up a new priest to whom all the words of the Lord will be revealed. He shall effect the judgment of truth over the earth for many days. And his star shall rise in heaven like a king; kindling the light of knowledge as day is illumined by the sun.[32]

It is this priest who will bring about an end to sin and the opening of paradise.[33] Though there is no explicit reference to the tribe from which he will come, the context seems to presume that he will arise from the tribe of Levi.

Similar to the *Psalms of Solomon*, the *Testament of Levi* criticizes the contemporary priesthood in order to persuade the readers to look for a messianic figure. In this case, it is the eschatological priest, who will faithfully fulfill God's intention for the office. The polemic in this writing also seeks to subvert allegiance to the priests in power and legitimize the faction or sect represented by the author. It is the moral weakness of the contemporary priests that render them disqualified for the office. The superiority of the eschatological priest is found in his ability to reveal God's words and execute true judgment.

Dead Sea Scrolls

Careful attention shall be made to the view of the Levitical priesthood put forth by the Qumran writings.[34] These writings are important for our study not only because there are many common themes found in these writings

---

[30] *T. Levi* 14:5-8. Though some parts of this chapter are suspected to be later Christian interpolations, it is likely that the priests mentioned in this passage refer to the secularized Maccabean priests.

[31] *T. Levi* 15:1-2; 16:1; 17:1.

[32] *T. Levi* 18:1-3.

[33] *T. Levi* 18:9-10.

[34] The general scholarly consensus dates the scrolls from between 200 BC to AD 70. See Geza Vermes, *The Complete Dead Sea Scrolls in English* (London: Penguin, 1997) 13; all quotations from the scrolls are from this volume.

and the epistle to the Hebrews—though it is unlikely that there is a direct dependence[35]—but also because the social situation of the Qumran community is similar to that of the Hebrews community. Both can be considered sectarian movements employing counter-cultural rhetoric. It is understood that the Qumran community separated itself from the larger dominant Jewish society precisely because of concerns over the priesthood. In our examination of these writings, we shall see that there is both a high regard for the Levitical priesthood and a stinging critique of how the priests of their day were carrying out their priestly functions.[36]

THE RULE OF THE COMMUNITY (1QS)

The importance of the Levitical priesthood is demonstrated by the prominent leadership role priests played in the sectarian community. The council of the community, who are to "preserve the faith in the Land" and generally function as the leaders of the community are to be made up of "twelve men and three Priests" (1QS 8.1-4). Furthermore,

> wherever there are ten men of the Council of the Community there shall not lack a Priest among them. And they shall all sit before him according to their rank and shall be asked their counsel in all things in that order. And when the table has been prepared for eating, and the new wine for drinking, the Priest shall be the first to stretch out his hand to bless the first fruits of the bread and new wine (1QS 6.3-9).[37]

The priests had jurisdiction over matters of justice, property, and doctrine in that they were to interpret and apply the law carrying both legislative and judicial powers.

---

[35] Though there are some linguistic parallels between Qumran's view of the priesthood and that of Hebrews, the theological interest and historical occasion for the writings are very different. See F. F. Bruce, "To the Hebrews or to the Essenes?" *NTS* 9 (1963) 217–32; Cf. Elisabeth Schüssler Fiorenza, "Cultic Language in Qumran and in the NT," *CBQ* 38 (1976) 159–77. Others have argued for a closer connection between the epistle and the Qumran community. See Yigael Yadin, "The Dead Sea Scrolls and the Epistle to the Hebrews," *ScrHier* 4 (1958) 36–55; and H. Kosmala, *Hebräer, Essener, Christen: Studien zur Vorgeschichte der frühchristlichen Verkündigung* (Leiden: Brill, 1959). Our analysis will primarily focus on how the Levitical priesthood was viewed and criticized by the Qumran community.

[36] See Scholer, *Proleptic Priests*, 35–36.

[37] See also 1QSa 2.11-12, 19, 20 and CD 12.22—14.12, which describe the role of the priest as the teacher, shepherd, the ruler, the guardian, and generally the leader in the community.

> They shall separate from the congregation of the men of injustice and shall unite, with respect to the Law and possessions, under the authority of the sons of Zadok, the Priests who keep the Covenant, and of the multitude of the men of the Community who hold fast to the Covenant. Every decision concerning doctrine, property, and justice shall be determined by them (1QS 5.1-3).[38]

Though they were leaders, what is important to note is the fact that they did not participate in any sacrificial cultic activities. Because the law specifically mandated that sacrifices and other cultic rituals were to be performed in the temple alone, they were relegated to spiritualizing the cultic functions prescribed in the law. The Qumran priests would "atone" for the people not with bloody sacrifices, but through prayer.

> When these become members of the Community in Israel according to all these rules, they shall establish the spirit of holiness according to everlasting truth. They shall atone for guilty rebellion and for sins of unfaithfulness, that they may obtain lovingkindness for the Land without the flesh of holocausts and the fat of sacrifice. And prayer rightly offered shall be as an acceptable fragrance of righteousness, and perfection of way as a delectable free-will offering (1QS 9.3-6).[39]

Though the community was quite averse to participating in the cult of their day, they were not against the idea of the Levitical priesthood in general. In fact they believed that the Temple and its cult would be brought back in the eschatological age.[40] Scholer writes, "No passage suggests hostility toward ritual sacrifice, but only an antipathy to the contemporary practice in Jerusalem."[41]

Damascus Document (CD)

The critique of what was presumably the current practice of the priesthood in Jerusalem at the time is seen in several passages in the *Damascus Document*. CD 2.12-20 is an indictment of the "anointed" priests who have fallen by the "stubbornness of their hearts." They did not follow pre-

---

[38] See also 1QS 6.2-8; 9.7; CD 10.5-6; 11QT 54.1-9.

[39] See also 1QS 2.26—3.12, 5.1-7; 8.1-10; CD 3.21—4.4; 4QFlor 1.6-7.

[40] According to the *War Scroll* (1QM 2.1-6), after a decisive battle against Belial and the angels of his kingdom, the priests and the Levites will be reinstated to offer sacrifices to the Lord perpetually.

[41] Scholer, *Proleptic Priests*, 48.

cisely in the ways of the Lord. In contrast, CD 6.12-17 describes the heart and attitude priests should have,

> None of those brought into the Covenant shall enter the Temple to light His altar in vain. They shall bar the door, forasmuch as God said, who among you will bar its door? And, you shall not light my altar in vain (Mal 1:10). They shall take care to act according to the exact interpretation of the Law during the age of wickedness. They shall separate from the sons of the Pit, and shall keep away from the unclean riches of wickedness acquired by vow or anathema or from the Temple treasure; they shall not rob the poor of His people, to make of widows their prey and of the fatherless their victim (Isa 10:2). They shall distinguish between clean and unclean, and shall proclaim the difference between holy and profane.[42]

Not only is the critique focused on the improper attitude and morals of the Jerusalem priests, but also on their improper lineage. Bertil Gärtner writes, "an important element in the profanation of the temple was that a family other than that from which the high priest could traditionally be drawn had taken over the office, thereby 'defiling' the cultus."[43] It is possible that the founders of the Qumran community came from the temple and were perhaps the "sons of Zadok." Therefore they would have thought of themselves as the legitimate heirs to the priesthood.[44]

In addition to profaning the temple cult, the Jerusalem priests were not following the proper cultic calendar according to those in the Qumran community. In speaking of what the priests in the covenant ought to do the author of the *Damascus Document* writes,

> They shall keep the Sabbath day according to its exact interpretation, and the feasts and the day of fasting according to the finding of the members of the New Covenant in the land of Damascus.

---

[42] CD 4.18-19 and 5.6-8 also describe a profaning of the temple by not distinguishing between the clean and unclean. 1QpHab 8.8-13 describes the wicked priest betraying the laws of God for riches and living in uncleanness. The reference to the contemporary priests in Jerusalem as those who defraud the people for money is made clear in 1QpHab 9.4-5, cf. 11.4-15, 12.1-10.

[43] Bertil E. Gärtner, *The Temple and the Community in Qumran and the New Testament*, SNTSMS 1 (Cambridge: Cambridge University Press, 1965) 14.

[44] See CD 4.1-2, where the author interprets Ezekiel 44:15 as allowing only the sons of Zadok to serve in the new temple. Cf. CD 5.5; 4Q171 3.15, 1QpHab 1.10ff.; 8.15—9.12; 11.10-16; 12.1-9.

They shall set aside the holy things according to the exact teaching concerning them (CD 6.18-20).[45]

The counter-cultural rhetoric in these writings functions to subvert allegiance to the Jerusalem priesthood and legitimize the alternative sectarian community. The rhetoric here seeks to confirm the decision to remain for those already in the community and to persuade those who may be thinking of leaving to stay. By criticizing the Jerusalem cult, the identity of the Qumran sect is further strengthened and distinguished. Those who submit to the priests at Qumran are on the inside of the community, while those who submit to the leadership of the Jerusalem priests are excluded.

Temple Scroll (11QT)

The *Temple Scroll* is thought to be the community's law book not only for their present state, but also for their future, when the true Zadokian priesthood would be reestablished.[46] Some scholars believe this writing was a polemic against the wicked priest in the time of John Hyrcanus.[47] The community saw itself as a temporary solution to the current defilement in the Jerusalem cult. However, their ultimate solution to the corruption was eschatological. God would have to come down, bringing judgment toward the wicked and vindication for the righteous by the establishment of a renewed Temple with the sons of Zadok as its priests.[48]

Klinzing argues that the Temple was seen as a realized eschatological means of salvation, "Wie im Neuen Testament ist dieser Tempel ein sich schon verwirklichendes, eschatologisches Heilsgut."[49] But he does not argue against a future fulfillment of the Temple in the last days.[50] Burrows also argues that the Qumran community held on to eschatological hopes of renewal and restoration, "Presumably, the sect, like many other Jews,

---

[45] See Gärtner, *The Temple and the Community*, 14.

[46] Most scholars agree that the *Temple Scroll* was composed by the Qumran community because: 1) it was found in a cave in the Qumran region; 2) it follows the solar calendar of 364 days, which was used by the Qumran community, and 3) it shares the same apocalyptic thought that there will be a restored temple in the future. For a contrary view see Hans Burgmann, "11QT: The Sadducean Torah," in *Temple Scroll Studies*, ed. George J. Brooke, JSPSS 7 (Sheffield: Sheffield Academic, 1989) 257–63.

[47] See Scholer, *Proleptic Priests*, 60; Y. Yadin, *The Temple Scroll*, 3 vols. (Jerusalem: Israel Exploration Society, 1983) 1.389.

[48] Cf. G. Klinzing, *Die Umdeutung des Kultus in der Qumrangemeinde und im Neuen Testament*, SUNT 7 (Göttingen: Vandenhoeck & Ruprecht, 1971) 217.

[49] Klinzing, *Die Umdeutung des Kultus*, 224.

[50] Ibid., 224.

expected the New Jerusalem with its Temple to be built on earth, but on earth miraculously renewed,"[51] (cf. 1QS 4.25).

Gärtner notes that there are both extreme criticisms of the temple institution as well as positive comments. He attributes this to the fact that the Qumran community, though critical of the Maccabean priesthood, had their hope in a future restored temple and the complete fulfillment of the law.[52] The future hope brought about the positive attitude, while the current practice of the Maccabean priests brought out the criticisms.

Géza Xeravitis also notes the important role the priests played in the community, not only as leaders, but also as forerunners of the eschatological priest.

> These two reasons at least explain why the Community considered the presence of the (high) priestly figures in the eschatological *scène* to be so important: 1. As opposed to the contemporary high priesthood of Jerusalem, which was considered by the Qumranites as corrupt, they expected the appearance of a future righteous high priestly figure. 2. According to the actual system of the Community, they expected the eschatological continuation of their present priestly leadership.[53]

The superiority of the present priestly leadership in the community is strengthened by the idea that they prefigure the future eschatological high priest. The rhetoric here further legitimizes the community and its leadership as the faithful remnant that alone finds favor with God. The fulfillment of God's intention for the priesthood would be realized in their community, when the end time comes. The socio-rhetorical goal of these writings is to solidify allegiance to the sectarian community.

Philo

As we look to the Alexandrian Jewish author Judaeus Philo,[54] we must note that his rhetorical goals were different from most of the Jewish writings previously surveyed. He wants to make Judaism more palatable to a broader Gentile audience, rather than to set up boundaries around Judaism. In his writings, he defends Judaism by demonstrating its compatibility with

---

[51] M. Burrows, *More Light on the Dead Sea Scrolls* (New York: Viking, 1958) 351.

[52] Gärtner, *The Temple and the Community*, 18–19.

[53] Géza G. Xeravitis, *King, Priest, Prophet: Positive Eschatological Protagonists of the Qumran Library* (Leiden: Brill, 2003) 166.

[54] Philo is thought to have lived from 20 BC to AD 50. See Samuel Sandmel, *Philo of Alexandria: An Introduction* (New York: Oxford University Press, 1979) 3.

Greek philosophy. Therefore we do not see in his writings the kind of critique and polemic found in many of the writings above. Rather, we find a very sincere respect for the Levitical priesthood and the prescriptions of the Law and a creative reinterpretation of the priesthood.

Philo writes in *Spec. Laws* 1.79, "The nation has twelve tribes, but one out of these was selected on its special merits for the priestly office, a reward granted to them for their gallantry and godly zeal on an occasion when the multitude was seen to have fallen into sin…"[55] Philo goes on in the subsequent sections to discuss the qualifications required of priests, and the regulations prescribed to them in their service.[56] He describes the priest as someone who has been "dedicated to God and has been made captain of the sacred regiment."[57] Philo also states that if a king is unable to render judgment on a case that he is to "send them up to more discerning judges. And who should these be but the priests, and the head of the leader of the priests?"[58] Clearly the role and prominence of the Levitical priesthood even in the Diaspora was significant according to Philo.

Even with such veneration for the Levitical priesthood, Philo is perhaps the most creative in reinterpreting the priesthood through his Middle Platonic philosophy. He allegorizes the high priest as the *logos*. Williamson writes, "… in Exodus, he [Philo] sees in the figure of the high priest entering the Holy of Holies a symbol of the Logos as a means of access for the human mind into the world of ideas."[59] What is notable for our purposes is not the precise formulation of the priesthood, but the freedom Philo has in reinterpreting the visible rituals with spiritual meaning.[60]

The importance and significance of the priesthood is demonstrated by Philo's lengthy discussion on it. And yet, he is not hindered in thinking about the priesthood in creative, non-traditional ways. His spiritualizing

---

[55] All quotations of Philo are taken from *Philo,* trans. F. H. Colson et al., 12 vols., LCL (Cambridge: Harvard University Press, 1929–1953).

[56] See *Spec. Laws* 1.80-298.

[57] *Spec. Laws* 1.114.

[58] *Spec. Laws* 4.190.

[59] R. Williamson, *Philo and the Epistle to the Hebrews,* ALGHJ 4 (Leiden: Brill, 1970) 419. See also Sidney G. Sowers, *The Hermeneutics of Philo and Hebrews: A Comparison of the Interpretation of the Old Testament in Philo Judaeus and the Epistle to the Hebrews,* Basel Studies of Theology 1 (Zürich: EVZ, 1965) 58–63; *Heir* 84, *Dreams* 2.189, 231; *Giants* 52–53, *Migration* 174.

[60] We must note that Philo does not believe his allegorical interpretations render the visible cult superfluous. For Philo, "the cult observances are the medium by which the loyal and observant Jew can be united with the Divine Logos" (Sandmel 1979, 96).

of the priesthood in no way diminishes its importance and role in the community.

Perhaps the reason why there is not a critique of the Jerusalem priesthood in Philo is because he was removed from the capitol, having presumably only visited once.[61] Or perhaps it is because a critique of the priesthood would have done little to further his own rhetorical goals in making Judaism more appealing to his Gentile audience.[62]

Josephus

As we begin to examine the writings of the first century Jewish historian Flavius Josephus, we must note that he too was writing presumably to a Gentile audience and perhaps to Jews who opposed him.[63] Therefore his writings are colored not only by his own personal convictions and views, but also by his audience. Many of his writings can be seen as an introduction of Judaism to a non-Jewish world, forming an apologetic of sorts.

Josephus' Positive Testimony of the Priesthood

Clemens Thoma argues "the high priesthood, according to Josephus Flavius' judgment, was the most important institution of Early Judaism with regard to the cult, prophecy, salvation, and worldly policy."[64] Josephus himself was an aristocratic chief priest as well as a politician.

Josephus has in view a global extension of the temple worship and the role of the high priest. In his retelling of King Solomon's prayer (cf. 1 Kgs 8:27-53; 2 Chron 6:14-40), Josephus writes, "And this help I ask of Thee not alone for the Hebrews who may fall into error, but also if any come even from the ends of the earth or from wherever it may be and turn to Thee, imploring to receive some kindness, do Thou hearken and give it to them."[65] With this world-embracing focus, Josephus argues for

---

[61] *Providence* 2.64.

[62] R.M. Wilson, "Philo Judaeus," in *ISBE* 3:847.

[63] Flavius Josephus was born around AD 37/39 and died probably around AD 100. See H. Schreckenberg, "Josephus, Flavius," in *ISBE* 2.1132–33.

[64] Clemens Thoma, "The High Priesthood in the Judgment of Josephus," in *Josephus, the Bible, and History*, ed. Louis H. Feldman and Gohei Hata (Detroit: Wayne State University Press, 1989) 196. See also Seth Schwartz, *Josephus and Judaean Politics* (Leiden: Brill, 1990) 61–67; Josephus, *Ant.* 18.1-3.

[65] Josephus, *Ant.* 8.116-117. All Josephus quotations are taken from *Josephus*, trans. H. St. J. Thackeray et al., 10 vols., LCL (Cambridge: Harvard University Press, 1926–1965). See also *J.W.* 4.324, *Ant.* 11.85.

the practice of offering and accepting gifts and sacrifices from the Roman authorities, contrary to the Zealots.[66]

Josephus portrays the office of the high priest as one of great prestige and power.[67] The role of priests went beyond the cult and into politics.[68] The high priest, "with his colleagues will sacrifice to God, guard the laws, adjudicate in cases of dispute, punish those convicted of crime."[69] It is important to note not only what Josephus says about the priesthood, but also what he does not say. In his descriptions of the priests before and after the Hasmonean period, he ". . . never objects to any extensions of the high priestly power, except for the case of Pinchas from Chafta."[70]

Josephus also shows great pride in the priesthood and its legitimacy in the records that were kept of the priests. He writes,

---

[66] See *J.W.* 2.409, 414.

[67] Josephus even quotes the Greek historian Hecataeus of Abdera, c. 300 BC and his positive testimony of the Levitical priesthood (*Ag.Ap.* 1.183-205). The authenticity of Hecataeus' testimony is challenged for the following reasons: 1) the extreme language of voluntary martyrdom seems to fit the time of Antiochus Epiphanes' persecution; 2) the high priest, Ezechias is not found in the list of high priests given by Josephus in *Ant* 12.43f.; 3) the language of priests receiving tithes reflects a Maccabean practice (Judith 11:13, Jubilees 32:15), while earlier documents indicate tithes are to be given to Levites; 4) the fact that Judea and Jerusalem were praised indicates a Jewish authorship; and 5) the favorable words toward Ptolemy are likely an apologetic for the Jews to show that from the beginning Jews were in good relations with the Ptolemies. These challenges are countered by: 1) the phrases describing the willingness to suffer than transgress the law are applicable to earlier times as well as during the Antiochus Epiphanes' persecution, i.e., Jews received harassment under Artaxerxes (Josephus, *Ant* 11.297); 2) the term *archiereus* may not have been used technically, but loosely to indicate a very prominent priest (there is some evidence from the excavations at Beth-Zur of a Jewish coin with Ezechias' name stamped on it); 3) the change in tithing practice could have occurred earlier during the fourth and second century BC or Hecataeus may not have distinguished between Levites and priests; and 4) the final two arguments only make sense in a context where a document is proven inauthentic on other grounds. Thus it is likely that this document is authentic. See Robert Doran, "Pseudo-Hecataeus," in *The Old Testament Pseudepigrapha*, ed. James H. Charlesworth, 2 vols. (Garden City, N.Y.: Doubleday, 1983) 2:914–16.

[68] Knowing that he would be denied the high priesthood if he married a foreigner, "Manasses went to his father-in-law Sanaballetes and said that while he loved his daughter Nikaso, nevertheless the priestly office was the highest in the nation and had always belonged to his family, and that therefore he did not wish to be deprived of it on her account" (*Ant.* 11.309-310).

[69] *Ag.Ap.* 2.194.

[70] Thoma, "The High Priesthood in the Judgment of Josephus," 201. See also Schwartz, *Josephus and Judaean Politics*, 92–93.

> But the most convincing proof of our accuracy in this matter is that our records contain the names of our high priests, with the succession from father to son for the last two thousand years. And whoever violates any of the above rules is forbidden to minister at the altars or take any other part in divine worship.[71]

The list of high priests and Josephus' mention of the list indicate that this priestly institution was very much a part of the living history of the Jews.

Unlike the Qumran community, Josephus is not as critical of the Hasmonean high-priestly lineage. He follows the author of 1 Maccabees in accepting the new lineage on a pragmatic level. These priests proved themselves to be efficient leaders who delivered their nation.[72] Thoma argues that Josephus believed that the high priest should do all that he can in order to build relations with non-Jews.

> Moreover, he (Josephus) is firmly convinced – this is shown in no other case so distinctly as with John Hyrcanus – that the high priests must be prepared to make all possible concession to the non-Jewish nations, even if this would result in uncertain expectations of meeting the non-Jewish powers halfway.[73]

Josephus' Polemic

Interestingly enough, Josephus writes against the last high priest of the second temple. He criticizes the zealots for choosing by lot Pinchas from Chafta. Josephus describes him as "…a man who not only was not descended from high priests, but was such a clown that he scarcely knew what the high priesthood meant."[74] What Josephus fails to mention is the fact that Pinchas was actually a descendent from the "sons of Zadok", the original lineage of the high priests of Israel before the Hasmonean priesthood. Clearly these words are guided by his disapproval of the Zealot movement in favor of a more open engagement with non-Jewish powers.

Though generally positive in his view of the priesthood, Josephus does include some unseemly characteristics and criticisms of other high priests. John ben Jaddus is described as murdering his brother in the tem-

---

[71] *Ag.Ap.* 1.36.

[72] See *Ant.* 13.197-99; Thoma, "The High Priesthood in the Judgment of Josephus," 207.

[73] Thoma, "The High Priesthood in the Judgment of Josephus," 208. Josephus praises John Hyrcanus in *J.W.* 1.68-69 and *Ant.* 13.299-300.

[74] *J.W.* 4.154-56.

ple.[75] Onias II is called "small-minded and addicted to money."[76] Jason, Menelaus, and Alcimus are criticized harshly.[77] Aristobulus I is described as bloodthirsty and cruel.[78] Finally, Josephus was also critical of the priests appointed by Herod. He states in *Ant.* 20.247, that Herod "assigned the office to certain insignificant people of merely priestly descent."[79]

These criticisms seem to be motivated by personal and/or political reasons. On the whole, Josephus' rhetoric is more in line with the dominant culture's rhetoric. By painting the priesthood in a positive light, he seeks to persuade his Gentile readers to be more sympathetic to the Jewish leadership. What is communicated clearly in his portrayal of Judaism is the importance and significance of the priesthood for the Jewish people.

Conclusion

What is clear from the survey of Second Temple Jewish writings is the fact that the Levitical priesthood played a prominent role in the social, political and religious life of the people. It was very much a part of the identity of the Jewish people because God himself had ordained it and established it as the institution that regulated his relationship with his people. And because God established it, the institution itself is never criticized. However, the high priests who abused or disgraced the office are the subject of intense polemic. Much of this polemic against the priests stems from issues of descent and legitimacy. The legitimacy of the priests was determined by how faithful they were in keeping to the prescriptions of the law. What seems to be at the core of the argument is that illegitimate priests could not faithfully fulfill the intent of God for the office.

Therefore if the priests are illegitimate, so also is the community in which the priest serves. The legitimacy of the community is tied to the legitimacy of its priestly leadership. Thus the polemic functions to maintain allegiance to the contra or counter-cultural group, while seeking to dissuade the readers from following the dominant culture's leadership. For example, the Qumran community criticized the Jerusalem priests not only to subvert allegiance to the dominant Jewish culture, but also to legitimize their own community and priestly leadership.

---

[75] *Ant.* 11.297-301.
[76] *Ant.* 12.158.
[77] *Ant.* 12.237-41, 383-5, 391, 393-401.
[78] *Ant.* 13.301-17. See also Schwartz, *Josephus and Judaean Politics*, 92 n. 128.
[79] See Schwartz, *Josephus and Judaean Politics*, 93.

Analysis of Hebrews 7:1-19

As we turn to Hebrews 7:1-19, what becomes immediately clear is how radical the polemic against the Levitical priesthood must have sounded to Jewish ears. The author of Hebrews does not simply criticize individual priests, but the entire priestly institution and law.[80] He argues that the institution could not fulfill its intended function (7:11) and has been changed or rather replaced (7:12). Furthermore, the law upon which the priesthood was founded is described as weak and useless (7:18-19). Clearly the polemic in this chapter goes further than the polemic found in the Second Temple Jewish writings surveyed above.

At the same time, we recognize that the author's use of polemical rhetoric functions similarly to that of the other Jewish writers. By criticizing the Levitical priesthood, he seeks to subvert allegiance to the dominant Jewish community and legitimize his own sectarian community. The legitimacy and superiority of Jesus' priesthood is intimately connected to the legitimacy and superiority of the author's community. Furthermore, the polemic against the priesthood in chapter 7 functions to confirm and strengthen the allegiance of those already in the community as well as persuade those who may be thinking of reverting back to the dominant Jewish faith. What is underlying the author's argument is the conviction that Jesus is the messianic high priest, who fulfills perfectly God's intention for the priesthood.

Overview of the Argument

After introducing the concept of Jesus as a high priest in Hebrews 2:17 and 3:1 the author does not pick up the thought again until 4:14. In chapter 5:1 he states, "For every high priest taken from among men is appointed [καθίσταται] on behalf of men in things pertaining to God, in order to offer [προσφέρῃ] both gifts and sacrifices for sins."[81] The two concepts introduced here, namely the appointment of the priest and the offering for sin, are further unraveled in Hebrews 7-10. In fact, the author

---

[80] The author's polemic against high priests in 7:23, 27 refers to high priests in general. No individual priests are named and the critique applies to all the high priests throughout Israel's history (all died, and all had to offer sacrifices for their own sins). However, the contrast between Jesus as "holy, innocent, undefiled, separated from sinners," and the priests who need to offer sacrifices for their own sins would have resounded to Jews who were disillusioned with their contemporary Jerusalem priests.

[81] All New Testament quotations are taken from the New American Standard Version unless otherwise noted.

begins to discuss the idea of Jesus' appointment as high priest in 5:2-10, but then digresses with a warning against falling away from the faith, only to pick up the idea again in chapter 7. The discussion of Jesus' appointment as high priest ends in 7:28 where a contrast is made between the appointment of the Levitical priests and that of Christ. "For the Law appoints [καθίστησιν] men as high priests who are weak, but the word of the oath, which came after the Law, appoints a Son, made perfect forever." The idea of Jesus offering his body as a priestly sacrifice is then discussed beginning in chapter 8 through chapter 10. Chapter 8:3 states, "For every high priest is appointed to offer both gifts and sacrifices; so it is necessary that this high priest also have something to offer [προσενέγκῃ]."[82]

Chapter 7 as a whole primarily addresses the legitimacy of Jesus' priesthood in light of his descent from the tribe of Judah rather than the tribe of Levi. The need for this argument should be clear in light of the discussion above regarding the importance of the high priestly appointments. And yet the rhetorical goal of this passage moves beyond simply legitimizing Jesus' priesthood to arguing for the superiority of his priesthood. The author does not see Jesus' priesthood simply as one alternative to the Levitical priesthood, but rather the eschatological fulfillment of the Levitical priesthood.

Melchizedek (7:1-10)

In Hebrews 7:1-10 Abraham's interaction with Melchizedek is described,[83] creating a seamless transition from the author's previous discussion at the end of chapter 6. The author sets up his extended reflection on Melchizedek by discussing the promise made by oath to Abraham, "I will surely bless you and I will surely multiply you" (6:14; cf. Gen 22:17). The oath theme will later be picked up to show by analogy the steadfastness of Jesus' appointment as a priest by the oath of God (7:20-21, 28). Frey makes this same connection in his discussion of Hebrews 7:28,

> Bereits in Heb 6,13ff. hatte der Autor die Bedeutung des Eides thematisiert und—unter Bezugnahme auf den göttlichen Eid in der Abrahamverheissung Gen 22,16f.,—die Unwiderruflichkeit und Rechtsgültigkeit der eidlich bekräftigten Zusage Gottes herausgestellt.[84]

---

[82] Προσενέγκῃ is the aorist active subjunctive form of προσφέρω.

[83] Cf. Gen 14:18-20.

[84] Jörg Frey, "Die alte und die neue diatheke nach dem Hebräerbrief," in *Bund und Tora*, ed. Friedrich Avemarie and Hermann Lichtenberger, WUNT 92 (Tübingen: Mohr/Sie-

The author of Hebrews draws from a story that is deeply embedded within the Jewish culture to support his argument. He is well acquainted with the Jewish community and understands the radical implications that Jesus' priesthood would have for that community. And so he appeals to an authoritative tradition that they would immediately recognize.

Without denigrating Abraham, the author argues for the superiority of Melchizedek, the priest-king of Salem. The first three verses set out the necessary facts that will be used to prove the author's particular point:[85] 1) Melchizedek blesses Abraham (7:1); 2) Abraham gives Melchizedek a tithe (7:2); and 3) Melchizedek is like the Son of God and remains a priest perpetually (7:3).[86] With these premises stated, the author proceeds with his argument: 1) the one who receives the tithes is greater than the one who gives (7:4-5); 2) the one who blesses is greater than the one who is blessed (7:6); 3) the one who lives perpetually is greater than the one who is mortal (7:8).[87]

It is important to note that in verse 5, the author acknowledges that the Levitical priests did indeed have a position of honor, by pointing out that they received tithes from the people.[88] What is presupposed then is that those who received tithes were to be highly esteemed. Keeping with this principle, the author argues that since Melchizedek received tithes from the Levites' forefather (Abraham), Melchizedek's priesthood is greater than the Levitical priesthood. He concludes this particular section with

---

beck, 1996) 273.

[85] "In providing the necessary information about Melchizedek, Hebrews does not repeat Gen 14,18-20 but has provided us only with the data relevant for the argument"; James Kurianal, *Jesus our High Priest: Ps. 110,4 as the Substructure of Heb 5,1—7,28*, EUS 693 (Frankfurt: Lang, 2000) 88.

[86] According to Kurianal what is unique to the exegesis in Hebrews is the Christological perspective. "In Hebrews, the interest in the figure of Melchizedek lies in the fact that Melchizedek is the *typos* of Christ; Christ is declared High Priest according to the order of Melchizedek (Heb 5,10), and Melchizedek has been likened to the Son of God (Heb 7,3)"; Kurianal, *Jesus our High Priest*, 192.

[87] Ibid., 97ff. See also Joseph A. Fitzmyer, "'Now this Melchizedek' (Heb 7:1)," *CBQ* 25 (1963) 305–21. Fitzmyer also identifies these three elements in the author of Hebrews' midrash of Genesis 14 arguing for the superiority of Jesus' priesthood.

[88] Kurianal argues that the superiority was not based on genealogy, but the privilege to receive tithes based on the law, "thus the basis of the superiority of the Levites over the people is limited to the fact that they had a commandment, ἐντολή, according to the Law. This indicates, though limited and not genealogical, a clear superiority over the people"; *Jesus our High Priest*, 100. For a discussion on why the author states that the priests receive a tithe, while Lev 18:21 describes the whole tribe receiving tithes, see William Horbury, "The Aaronic Priesthood in the Epistle to the Hebrews," *JSNT* 19 (1983) 50–52 [43-71].

the statement, "And so to speak, through Abraham even Levi, who received tithes paid tithes, for he was still in the loins of his father when Melchizedek met him."[89]

The general idea of 7:1-10 is the superiority of the Melchizedekian priesthood over the Levitical. The author is building his argument for the superiority of Jesus' priesthood over the Levitical priesthood. By identifying Jesus as a priest according to the order of Melchizedek (7:17), he implies that Jesus' priesthood is also superior to the Levitical priesthood. By using this superior/ inferior rhetoric, the author seeks to legitimize the priesthood of Jesus and the community that Jesus serves.

Perfection (7:11, 19, 28)

The author states in verse 11 that the Levitical priesthood failed to bring about perfection. "Now if perfection [τελείωσις] was through the Levitical priesthood (for on the basis of it the people received the Law)[90], what further need was there for another priest to arise according to the order of Melchizedek, and not be designated according to the order of Aaron?"

There seems to be two main trajectories for understanding the term τελείωσις mentioned in verses 11 and 19. One approach sees it in reference to moral perfection, i.e., expiating sins, cleansing one's conscience, sanctifying one's soul. For example, Moses Stuart understands "make complete" or τελείωσις to mean, "take away the burden of guilt, and to ren-

---

[89] Heb 7:9-10.

[90] There has been some debate on the precise translation of the phrase, ὁ λαὸς γὰρ ἐπί αὐτῆς νενομοθέτηται. The preposition ἐπί can take several different nuances; Richard Young, *Intermediate New Testament Greek* (Nashville: Broadman and Holman, 1994) 97; Daniel Wallace, *Greek Grammar Beyond the Basics* (Grand Rapids: Zondervan, 1996) 376. If taken temporally, then the verse would imply that the people received the law during the time of the priesthood. Yet this is not historically accurate, for the law established the priesthood (Heb 7:28). If taken with a referential nuance, it would be translated, "the people received the law concerning it (priesthood)." The problem with this translation is that it adds nothing to the argument, especially in light of the following verse, which intimately connects the priesthood with the law. The best alternative is to follow the NASB and translate ἐπί as "on the basis of," indicating that the foundation of the law was the priesthood. The priests applied the law and taught it to the people. Certainly this does not deny the fact that the priesthood also rested upon the law, but for the purposes of the author's argument the reverse needs to be emphasized. See Harold W. Attridge, *The Epistle to the Hebrews*, Hermeneia (Philadelphia: Fortress, 1989) 200.

der pure or holy the minds of the worshippers,"[91] based on the same use of the word in Hebrews 9:9, 14.[92]

The other approach, which does not necessarily exclude the first,[93] is to see perfection eschatologically, i.e., the fulfillment of God's design for his people.[94] This second approach broadens the idea of perfection and helps make sense of how Jesus was perfected (2:10; 5:9; 7:28). For example, William Lane sees τελείωσις as an eschatological term describing the fulfillment of the promises of the new covenant in granting a greater degree of access to God. Jesus himself gained this kind of access in his ascension.[95] And Otto Michel writes, "Es handelt sich vielleicht um die vollendete ‚Weihe', um die Eignung zum himmlischen Priesterdienst und Opferdienst, um die auch Herz und Gewissen umfassende Heiligung."[96]

David Peterson in his monograph *Hebrews and Perfection*, argues that the use of τελείωσις in verse 11 is certainly related to its use in verse

---

[91] Moses Stuart, *A Commentary on the Epistle to the Hebrews* (Andover: Flagg, Gould, and Newman, 1833) 401.

[92] Spicq defines perfection primarily in moral or ethical terms. He comments, "L'impuissance de la Loi à purifier la conscience, à préserver du péché, à favoriser le bien, en un mot à ne rien porter à la consommation"; C. Spicq, *L'Epitre aux Hebreux*, Sources Bibliques (Paris: Gabalda, 1977) 126. See also Simon J. Kistemaker, *Exposition of the Epistle to the Hebrews*, NTC 19 (Grand Rapids: Baker, 1984) 197–98.

[93] Attridge starts with the idea that perfection refers to the cleansing of conscience and removal of sin, but connects this with the idea that this cleansing brings about a renewed relationship with God (Attridge, 1989, 200). See also Franz Delitzsch, *Commentary on the Epistle to the Hebrews*, 2 vols., trans. Thomas L. Kingsbury (1871; reprinted, Minneapolis: Klock & Klock, 1978) 350; A. B. Bruce, *The Epistle to the Hebrews* (Edinburgh: T. & T. Clark, 1899) 263; Hugh Montefiore, *A Commentary on the Epistle to the Hebrews* (New York: Harper & Row, 1964) 124.

[94] Craig R. Koester, *The Epistle to the Hebrews*, AB 36 (New York: Doubleday, 2001) 122–23.

[95] William Lane, *Hebrews 1–8*, WBC 47A (Dallas: Word, 1991) 181. See also F. F. Bruce, *The Epistle to the Hebrews*, rev. ed., NICNT (Grand Rapids: Eerdmans, 1990) 145, 149; Koester, *Hebrews*, 122–25. Contrary to Nairne, who believes that the Levitical system could not perfect in the sense that it could not make the worshiper clean enough to be able to approach God, Lane argues that Old Testament saints were able to approach God; cf. Alexander Nairne, *The Epistle of Priesthood* (Edinburgh: T. & T. Clark, 1913) 348. The contrast, according to Lane, is that the New Testament saints through Christ have a better hope by which they draw near to God. He goes on to state that the author was not implying that anything was wrong with the old system in and of itself, but rather it did not "complete" because it played the role of the shadow anticipating the fulfillment (Lane 1991a, 181). Lane does not, however, see the contradiction he makes in that if something does not complete, there is indeed something wrong with it.

[96] Otto Michel, *Der Brief an die Hebräer*, 13th ed., KEK (Göttingen: Vandenhoeck & Ruprecht, 1975) 269.

19.⁹⁷ In verse 19, the law, which makes nothing perfect, is contrasted with a better hope by which we draw near to God. Thus Peterson understands the use of τελείωσις in both 11 and 19 to refer to the consummation of humanity in an eternal relationship with God. He points to Luke 1:45, the only other place in the New Testament where the term is used, which describes Mary's belief that there would be "a fulfillment of what was spoken to her by the Lord."⁹⁸ Though this perfection certainly has a future element to it, there is a sense that believers are able to draw near to God even in the present (4:16; 7:19, 25; 10:22).⁹⁹

Adopting the eschatological definition of perfection, we then understand that the author is stating that the Levitical priesthood could not bring about the ultimate fulfillment of God's purposes for his people. Erich Grässer writes,

> In der christologischen Perspektive unseres Verfassers stellt es sich so dar, als sei das *alttestamentliche Priestertum* an seiner ureigensten Aufgabe gescheitert, nämlich die τελείωσις *Vollkommenheit* zu verleihen, also diejenigen kultischen Eigenschaften die nötig sind, um Gott zu nahen (7,19) und vor ihm zu stehen.¹⁰⁰

The Levitical priesthood served simply as a shadow or type of the eschatological priesthood, which would provide unprecedented access to the Father. The author uses this typological language to legitimize Jesus' priesthood over against the Levitical. Once the anti-type arrives, the shadowy predecessor is shown to be inadequate and imperfect. The result of such rhetoric leaves the reader with little choice but to align himself or herself with the priesthood that will bring about perfection or God's ultimate purposes for his people.

What is important to note, however, is the fact that the type provides the general framework upon which the anti-type is to be understood. In other words the author does not completely do away with the idea of "priesthood." In fact the Levitical priesthood informs the author's understanding of Jesus' priesthood. And yet the revelation of the final priesthood shows its superiority in meeting the ultimate goal of the Levitical priesthood, namely unadulterated access to God.

---

[97] David G. Peterson, *Hebrews and Perfection: An Examination of the Concept of Perfection in the 'Epistle to the Hebrews,'* SNTSMS 47 (Cambridge: Cambridge University Press, 1982) 127.

[98] Ibid.,128.

[99] Ibid., 129.

[100] Erich Grässer, *An die Hebräer*, 3 vols., EKK 17 (Zürich: Benziger, 1993) 2:36.

Priesthood and Law (7:11-19)

INTERCONNECTION OF PRIESTHOOD AND LAW (7:11-12)

The phrase, "for on the basis of it [priesthood] the people received the law," (7:11) describes the intimate relationship between the priesthood and the law. What does the author have in mind when he refers to the law? Is it just the cultic stipulations or the entire Mosaic legal code? From the immediate context, the cultic stipulations seem to be in view.[101] The issue at hand deals with the requirement that priests be descendants of Levi.[102] Two terms, which seem somewhat interchangeable, are used: νόμος in verses 12 and 19 and ἐντολή in verses 16 and 18. ἐντολή clearly refers to the cultic regulations for priests, i.e., "the law of physical requirement" and "former commandment." Verse 12 simply describes a "change" or μετάθεσις[103] in the νόμος, which seems to indicate that only a minor revision is needed. Verse 28 describes the imperfection of the law specifically in appointing weak priests. Therefore it seems that author is speaking only about the parts of the law dealing with the sacrificial system.[104]

Yet upon further reflection, we note that it may be a modern imposition to divide nicely the ethical elements of the law from the cultic. The whole system works together under the administration of the Mosaic covenant.[105] It is in this covenant relationship that the cult played a signifi-

---

[101] See Stuart, *Hebrews*, 402; Brooke Foss Westcott, *The Epistle to the Hebrews* (London: Macmillan, 1892) 181; Donald A. Hagner, *Hebrews*, NIBC 14 (Peabody, Mass: Hendrickson, 1990) 107; Philip Hughes, *A Commentary on the Epistle to the Hebrews* (Grand Rapids: Eerdmans, 1977) 256; Nairne, *The Epistle of Priesthood*, 348.

[102] Exodus 28:1; Lev 1:5-7; 8:1-3; 21:1; 22:1-4; Num 1:47-51; 3:5-9.

[103] Many scholars see this term referring to more than a few minor alterations, but an abrogation of the entire system. See Attridge, *Hebrews*, 200–201; Hagner, *Hebrews*, 107; Paul Ellingworth, *The Epistle to the Hebrews: A Commentary on the Greek Text*, NIGTC (Grand Rapids: Eerdmans, 1993) 374; Robert P. Gordon, *Hebrews*, Readings: A New Biblical Commentary (Sheffield: Sheffield Academic, 2000) 84.

[104] Charles Anderson argues vigorously that only the cultic elements of the Torah are in view. He takes the parenthetical phrase in 7:11 to read, "The people of Israel received regulations concerning the levitical priesthood"; Charles P. Anderson, "Who Are the Heirs of the New Age in the Epistle to the Hebrews?" in *Apocalyptic and the New Testament: Essays in Honor of J. Louis Martyn*, ed. Joel Marcus and Marion L. Soards, JSNTSS 24 (Sheffield: JSOT Press, 1989) 269. Therefore, according to Anderson, the change in law in verse 12 refers to the priestly law. He then uses contextual clues to limit the change to matters of cultic regulation (255–77).

[105] The argument in 8:13 that the first covenant is becoming obsolete also argues for an entirely different system by which one approaches God. If the old covenant is abrogated, then the entire law associated with it must also be abrogated (not merely a part of the law).

cant role in assuring not only cultic purity, but also ethical purity. There seems to be no nice divide.[106] Therefore it is likely that the term νόμος refers to the entire legal system within the Mosaic covenant.[107] This is a larger category, which includes the law of physical requirements, or former commandments (ἐντολή).[108] But because of the weakness and uselessness of these commandments, the entire law fails in perfecting anything (vs. 19). It is precisely the weakness of the cultic administration of the law in achieving God's intended goal that renders the entire law useless.[109]

The basic idea then, is that the law and the Levitical priesthood are intimately intertwined.[110] Westcott writes, "The efficacy of the Law may justly be represented by the efficacy of the priesthood, for the people, called to be the people of God (v. 5), hath received the Law, resting on it (the priesthood) as its foundation . . . ."[111] If one changes, then by necessity the other changes. If one fails to bring about perfection, then the other also fails to bring about perfection (7:11,19).[112] The failure of both the law and priesthood implies a need for change.

Montefiore essentially equates the law with the old covenant (Montefiore 1964, 124). Anderson, though admitting that 'covenant' includes the 'entire sweep of Mosaic legislation,' argues that the author has primarily in mind the regulations concerning the sacrificial ritual (Anderson 1989, 271). He then states that there is one Torah, but two covenants. Therefore even though the covenant is completely replaced, the Law simply needs to be changed, not replaced (Anderson 1989, 272). What he fails to consider, however, is the fact that covenant is the broader framework under which laws have their significance. If you completely replace the framework, you must necessarily replace the law.

[106] See Koester, *The Epistle to the Hebrews*, 114.

[107] See Delitzsch, *Hebrews*, 352; Montefiore, *Hebrews*, 126; F.F. Bruce, *Hebrews*, 145.

[108] See Lane, *Hebrews 1–8*, 185.

[109] Certainly this does not mean that the ethical statements in the law do not still reflect God's ethical standard of righteousness. One can still deduce from the ethical commandments in the law what the Lord desires of his people.

[110] See also Stuart, *Hebrews*, 401; Hagner, *Hebrews*, 103–4; Ellingworth, *Hebrews*, 372; Hughes, *Hebrews*, 256; James Moffatt, *A Critical and Exegetical Commentary on the Epistle to the Hebrews*, ICC (Edinburgh: T. & T. Clark, 1924) 96; Kistemaker, *Hebrews*, 71.

[111] Westcott, *Hebrews*, 181. See also Delitzsch, *Hebrews*, 351.

[112] Grässer notes the interconnection between the law and priesthood, but also expresses how the claim that they failed would have been shocking to Jewish ears. He writes concerning the law and priesthood, "Sie stehen und fallen miteinander—für jüdisches Verständnis mehr als anstößig, da der Tora ewige Dauer und Gültigkeit eignen"; Grässer, *Hebräer*, 2:39.

Jesus' Lineage (7:13-16)

What seems to be driving the author's fairly radical statement that a change in the priesthood necessitates a change in the law is the obvious fact the Jesus did not descend from Levi, the tribe that the law explicitly mentions as the priestly tribe. It is this most obvious contradiction to the idea that Jesus is high priest that needs to be addressed.

> For the one concerning whom these things are spoken belongs to a different tribe, from which no one has officiated at the altar. For it is evident that our Lord was descended from Judah, a tribe with reference to which Moses spoke nothing concerning priests (7:13-14).

The author anticipates this objection and yet instead of apologizing for Jesus' lack of genealogical credentials according to the law, he argues that Jesus' appointment is based on a more superior credential, namely his indestructible life (7:16). And because Jesus' life is indestructible, the logical implication is that his priesthood is also indestructible. Grässer writes,

> Das macht, daß Jesus selbst das Leben ist, das kein Tod zerbricht, das wahrhaft Heilige, das keine Macht der Finsternis entweiht, das wahrhaft Wirksame, dessen Reichtum sich nie erschöpft und dessen Kraft nie erlahmt. Darum ist das Priestertum Jesu unvergänglich.[113]

The change in the law is grounded upon two arguments. First is the fact that Jesus did not descend from the tribe of Levi (7:13-14). Thus there is somewhat of a circular argument used here.[114] He presupposes that Jesus is a high priest. But because he is not a descendant of Levi—which is required by the law—the law itself must be changed.[115] The second is

---

[113] Grässer, *Hebräer*, 2:46.

[114] Graham Hughes notes "what is to be 'proved' is already assumed: the function of the scriptures is not to 'prove' but to communicate the 'encouraging word', which in the nature of things can only, for this author, be a Christian logos"; *Hebrews and Hermeneutics: The Epistle to the Hebrews as a New Testament Example of Biblical Interpretation*, SNTSMS 36 (Cambridge: Cambridge University Press, 1979) 57.

[115] It seems clear from verses 13-14 that the author began with the idea that Jesus is the final high priest and because of this revelation, deduced other necessary implications (i.e., the Levitical priesthood did not perfect, the law must be changed, etc.). This is in contrast to the idea that the author began by noting the failure of the Levitical priesthood and the prophecy of another priesthood from a different order. So when Jesus came he simply filled a role previously constructed. Rather, it is more likely that the revelation of Jesus as high priest initiated the theologizing that resulted in this epistle.

the fact that another priest arose according to the likeness of Melchizedek (7:15).

The author must convince his readers that the law has indeed been changed in order to legitimize Jesus' priesthood. The legitimacy of Jesus' priesthood is tied to the legitimacy of his community. Therefore in order to prove his point, he appeals to an authority well accepted by his Jewish readers, the Holy Scriptures.

Use of Psalm 110:4 (7:17)

Midrash Pesher

The author's use of Scripture betrays an intimate understanding of the Jewish culture and faith. Simon Kistemaker argues that the author of Hebrews follows the hermeneutical method of the Midrash pesher which is found in 1QpHab.[116] Some of the principles of this approach are: 1) everything has a veiled eschatological meaning; 2) the veiled meaning may be revealed through abnormal or forced constructions of the text; 3) the application of a text can be determined by allegory.[117] Kistemaker notes, "These early *Midrashim,* in the application of Scripture passages, reveal a more or less creative freedom in the manipulation of the scriptural text."[118]

James Kurianal, however, clarifies the similarities and differences between Hebrews' exegetical methods and that of the Qumran pesherim. He concludes, "though Hebrews shares with the Qumran documents some common perspectives about the eschatological fulfillment of the Scriptures, . . . Heb 7 does not have the form of a Qumran *pesher.*"[119] Nevertheless, Kurianal does admit that the author uses widespread Jewish exegetical principles, such as "argument from silence" and *gezêrâ šawâ*. Yet these do not prove a direct dependence upon a specific Jewish exegetical tradition.[120] What really distinguishes Hebrews' approach according to Kurianal is its Messianism and its unique realized eschatological perspective.[121]

---

[116] Simon Kistemaker, *The Psalm Citations in the Epistle to the Hebrews* (Amsterdam: Van Soest, 1961) 11. See also Donald Hagner, "Interpreting the Epistle to the Hebrews," in *The Literature and Meaning of Scripture,* ed. Morris A. Inch and C. Hassell Bullock (Grand Rapids: Baker, 1981) 226.

[117] Kistemaker, *Psalm Citations,* 66–67.

[118] Ibid., 67.

[119] Kurianal, *Jesus our High Priest,* 193–94.

[120] Ibid., 196.

[121] Ibid., 197. Deborah W. Rooke argues that the author of Hebrews' portrayal of Jesus as

Even though there may not be a direct dependence, the use of these Jewish exegetical principles indicates a very intimate acquaintance with the Jewish community. The author knows his audience and seeks to employ exegetical principles that would be easily accepted by his Jewish readers. Donald Hagner writes, "It is very typical of our author's style to quote a passage and then to proceed to comment on the clauses most appropriate to his argument (see especially 3:12-4:10; 7:11-28; 10:8-18). This approach is reminiscent of a Jewish method of interpretation called 'Midrash.'"[122] At the same time, the author's uniquely Christological readings also function to socialize his community members in how to read and appropriate Scripture. Not only are they to agree with his interpretation, but also his Christological hermeneutical method.

In Lillian Freudmann's critique of the epistle of Hebrews as an anti-Semitic tract, she bases much of her argument on the idea that the author of Hebrews twisted or manipulated Scripture in his exegesis.[123] Freudmann seems to assume the author was alone in his eschatological, messianic approach to Scripture. What we have found, however, is that the exegetical method the author uses is in fact quite similar to his contemporary Jewish writers.[124] Even though his own Jewish contemporaries may not have agreed with his conclusions, they would not have had difficulty with his interpretive methods.

Perpetual Priesthood (7:17)

Much of the author's argument concerning Jesus' priesthood is based on his interpretation of Psalm 110:4. The initial quote of Psalm 110:4 is found in 5:5-6 and yet its fuller exposition is not dealt with until chapter 7. Though it is quoted again only in 7:17 and 21, it is clearly in the background of the entire chapter.[125]

---

a high priest according to the order of Melchizedek follows traditional Messianic categories, ". . . inasmuch as Hebrews has shown Jesus to be an exalted figure of sacral monarchy, it has depicted him as a truly messianic figure, in whose person the lines of both priesthood and monarchy converge"; "Jesus as Royal Priest: Reflections on the Interpretation of the Melchizedek Tradition in Heb 7," *Bib* 81 (2000) 94.

[122] Hagner, "Interpreting the Epistle to the Hebrews," 229.

[123] Lillian C. Freudmann, *Antisemitism in the New Testament* (Lanham, Md.: University Press of America, 1994) 150.

[124] See Kurianal, *Jesus our High Priest*, 196.

[125] Kistemaker argues that chapter 7 is actually a midrash on Psalm 110:4, where verses 1-12 expound the words, "priest after the order of Melchizedek," and verses 13-25 expound the words, "thou art a priest forever" (Kistemaker, *Psalm Citations*, 118). This suggestion, however, is hampered by making an unnatural divide between verses 12 and 13.

The basis of Jesus' priesthood according to the order of Melchizedek is his indestructible life, which is perhaps a reference to his resurrection.[126] Because Jesus will never die again, he is uniquely qualified to be a priest according to the order of Melchizedek, who "remains a priest perpetually" (7:3). In order to bring these two ideas together, the author quotes Psalm 110:4 and applies it directly to Jesus.[127] He quotes it as if God himself were speaking to Jesus, "You are a priest forever, according to the order of Melchizedek."[128] Now certainly this new meaning takes on a significance that the original author could have never understood.[129] It is the "forever" quality of this priesthood that requires one to have an indestructible life. This use of Scripture follows a distinctly messianic, eschatological hermeneutic.[130]

By appealing to Scripture, the author further establishes the legitimacy of Jesus' priesthood.[131] God himself is the one who establishes Jesus' priesthood. He is the one who initiated the change (7:11-12) in priesthood and law. Michel writes, "Die ἀθέτησις geschieht durch das Psalmwort: Gott erklärt das vorangehende Gebot (προάγων auch in 1 Tim 1 18 524) für ungültig, schwach und nutzlos. Die Konstruktion ἀθέτησις γίνεται ist hier also eine Umschreibung des göttlichen Handelns."[132] Because the change is part of God's will, the readers have no other choice but to accept the change. The implication is that if they don't accept the change in

---

[126] Walter Edward Brooks, "Perpetuity of Christ's Sacrifice in the Epistle to the Hebrews," *JBL* 89 (1970) 206–7.

[127] Hughes writes "for the author, all understanding of God's declaration of his word now has its meaning in terms of Christ as the fullest form of that Word. That is why no scripture text is left bare and uninterpreted but is gathered up into the new Christian situation, in which synthesis both the old *logion* and the new situation are each indispensable elements" (Hughes 1979, 62–3).

[128] Ellingworth argues that the term τάξιν translated "order" in 7:17 does not necessarily refer to priestly succession, rather it simply communicates that Christ is just like Melchizedek, who can never lose his priesthood. See Paul Ellingworth, "The Unshakable Priesthood: Hebrews 7:24," *JSNT* 23 (1985)125–26; "Just Like Melchizedek," *BT* 28 (1977) 236–39.

[129] Hughes, *Hebrews and Hermeneutics*, 59.

[130] See M. J. Paul, "The Order of Melchizedek (Ps 110:4 and Heb 7:3)," *WTJ* 49 (1987) 195–211, esp. 210–11.

[131] The author again quotes Psalm 110:4 in verse 21, but this time to emphasize the oath nature of the appointment. "The Lord has sworn and will not change his mind, you are a priest forever." The use of this quotation helps confirm and strengthen the commitment of those in his community by emphasizing the security of Jesus' priesthood based on God's own oath.

[132] Michel, *Der Brief an die Hebräer*, 273.

priesthood or if they revert back to the Levitical priesthood, they will be rejecting God's will or desire for them.

Annulment and Fulfillment (7:18-19)

Verses 18 and 19 reveal perhaps the most radical statement of the passage. "For, on the one hand, there is a setting aside (ἀθέτησις)[133] of a former commandment because of its weakness and uselessness (for the Law made nothing perfect), and on the other hand there is a bringing in of a better hope, through which we draw near to God." The author sets two contrasting ways of drawing near to God. The first is through the "former commandment," or the sacrificial law and implicitly the cult.[134] The second, from the context, is obviously the priesthood of Jesus. The priesthood of Jesus is the better hope, by which "we draw near to God" (7:19). The change in priesthood implies a comprehensive change in the entire system by which God's goals and intentions are realized. Neither the Levitical priesthood, nor the law can guarantee a secure hope, which is found only in the new covenant. Michel writes, "Der νόμος könnte ein trügerische Hoffnung erwecken, dagegen schenkt der Neue Bund eine ‚bessere', d.h. eine verbürgte, gewisse und zum Ziel führende."[135]

What is clear from the argument is that there can be only one priesthood in the Jewish religious system.[136] Because of this presupposition, once the final, more superior priesthood came, the former priesthood and law no longer had any use. Before then, the former cultic system served as a shadow or type of what was to come. This language is clearly eschatological language indicating that Jesus' priesthood is the fulfillment of the Levitical priesthood. It was the better hope through which the original goal and intent of the Levitical priesthood was fully realized.

The author uses this comparative rhetoric to indicate the superiority of Jesus' priesthood and thereby secure allegiance to his community. The legitimacy of Jesus' priesthood is key in establishing the legitimacy of his

---

[133] The word ἀθέτησις is used in early papyri as a technical legal term. See Raphael Taubenschlag, *The Law of Greco-Roman Egypt in the Light of the Papyri 332 B.C.—A.D. 640* (New York: Herald Square, 1944) 318.

[134] The implication of course is that the entire Law is also set aside or annulled because of its inability to carry forward God's purposes for his people, i.e., drawing humanity near to himself.

[135] Michel, *Hebräer*, 273.

[136] Koester, *Hebrews*, 359.

sectarian community. He does not want his members to revert back to the inferior, annulled, and set aside way of drawing near to God.

In order to further support his radical statement of the fulfillment of the Levitical priesthood, the author catalogues other reasons for the superiority of Jesus' priesthood: 1) it was based on an oath of God (7:21); 2) Jesus holds his priesthood permanently, securing our access to God and his intercession forever (7:23-25); and 3) Jesus as high priest was without sin (7:26-27).[137]

Socio-Rhetorical Function

From our analysis it is clear that the author is employing counter-cultural rhetoric. He questions the dominant culture's priestly institution and offers an alternative priestly institution. The author wants to persuade those who were tempted to revert back to the Jewish sacrificial cult to remain faithful to Jesus as their high priest. The polemic functions to subvert allegiance to the dominant culture's priesthood and legitimize and maintain allegiance to Jesus as high priest.

The legitimacy of Jesus' priesthood is demonstrated using a superior/inferior dialectic, a Christological interpretation of Scripture, and type/anti-type rhetoric. These rhetorical devices work in concert to: 1) persuade those tempted to revert back to Judaism to remain connected to the community; 2) confirm and strengthen the faith of those in the community; and 3) socialize the community members.

Anti-Semitism, Anti-Judaism, Supersessionism in Hebrews 7:1-19

As we evaluate the degree to which Hebrews 7:1-28 can be considered anti-Semitic, anti-Judaic or supersessionist, we must keep in mind the Jewish context in which the author of Hebrews wrote. The term "anti-Semitism" is clearly not an adequate description of the passage. It is inadequate because the term itself emerged in the 19th century and has to do more with ethnic or racial differences.[138] The picture that has been painted from our analysis more aptly describes the situation as a theological disagreement

---

[137] It is interesting to note that a subtle change occurs in verse 26. Jesus is no longer described as a priest, but here he is called a high priest. It seems that the author first wants his readers to get used to the idea that Jesus is qualified to be a priest, and then without much explanation or justification, indicates that he was indeed a high priest.

[138] See above "Introduction," pages 2-3. See also Clark M. Williamson, "Anti-Judaism in Hebrews?," *Int* 57 (2003) 276–77.

among Jews. This is shown by the fact that: 1) Abraham is described as the patriarch, presumably of the readers (7:4); 2) the author bases his arguments on Hebrew Scripture using Jewish hermeneutical principles (7:17, 21); and 3) the intimate knowledge of Jewish law and practices in the text (7:13-14).

Anti-Judaism

However, it does seem that we can speak of the text as anti-Judaic; but some distinctions need to be made. We start with Douglas Hare's three different kinds of "anti-Judaism." As we have already seen, he speaks of: 1) prophetic anti-Judaism, which describes internal critiques of Judaism by Jews; 2) Jewish-Christian anti-Judaism, which are criticisms of Judaism by Jews who believe Jesus is Messiah; and 3) Gentilizing anti-Judaism, which rejects Israel emphasizing the Gentile character of Christianity.[139]

The context in the epistle is that the Jewish –Christian community in Hebrews, though originally part of the larger Jewish society, was seeking to separate and distinguish itself from its parent group. The epistle clearly calls its readers to separate themselves from the old covenant practices, rituals, and life.[140] Therefore it seems clear that the author was indeed speaking as a Jew against the Levitical priesthood, in order to establish the legitimacy of Jesus' priesthood.

The discontinuity between the larger Jewish society and the community addressed in Hebrews rules out the approach to the question of anti-Semitism/ anti-Judaism that ignores the sociological context assumed in the epistle.[141] William Lane, for instance, argues:

> The pejorative statements that there has been a change in the law (Heb 7:12) and that the law that regulated the priesthood has been annulled (Heb 7:18) are not intentionally polemical. They occur as reflections on a prophetic oracle announcing a startling departure from Israel's priestly tradition. They are put forth not as anti-Judaic

---

[139] See page 4, footnote 18 in the "Introduction."

[140] Hebrews 9:11-14; 10:1-2; 13:9-10.

[141] See Robert W. Wall and William Lane, "Polemic in Hebrews and the Catholic Epistles," in *Anti-Semitism and Early Christianity*, ed. Craig Evans and Donald Hagner (Minneapolis: Fortress, 1993) 173; D. Sänger, "Neues Testament und Antijudaismus: Versuch einer exegetischen und hermeneutischen Vergewisserung im innerchristlichen Gespräch," *KD 34* (1988) 210–31; and William Klassen, "To the Hebrews or against the Hebrews? Anti-Judaism and the Epistle to the Hebrews," in *Anti-Judaism in Early Christianity*, Vol. 2 of *Separation and Polemic*, ed. Stephen G. Wilson (Waterloo, Ont.: Wilfred Laurier University Press, 1986) 1–16.

polemic but as deductions from the biblical text, which draw their support from the formulation of the oracle.[142]

Lane fails to acknowledge that the community addressed in Hebrews was a distinct social entity from the dominant Jewish society and that there was a real threat of reversion. The rhetoric in Hebrews 7 is clearly polemical for the purpose of legitimizing Jesus' priesthood over against the Levitical and subverting allegiance to the dominant Jewish society.

The real question at hand, however, is whether the author's polemic against the Levitical priesthood necessarily equates to polemic against the Jewish people as a whole? Certainly there was a close connection of identity between the Jewish people and the Levitical priesthood. Yet this identity was not a mechanical identity. There was nothing in the Levitical priesthood itself that uniquely qualified it as the defining identity marker for the Jews. It was only because God himself established it as the means by which his people should worship and draw near to him that it had its significance. What truly forged the identity of the Jews was their relationship and worship of God. The Levitical priesthood was simply the means by which that relationship was nurtured.

Many of the authors of the Second Temple Jewish writings surveyed above felt obligated to criticize those priests who failed to fulfill God's intention for the office. The author of Hebrews seems to follow this pattern, but argues that the priesthood itself—not simply individual priests—fails in fulfilling God's intention for the priesthood.

Furthermore, there is an effort by the author of Hebrews to retain the history and legacy of the Jewish faith by painting his community as the true heirs or righteous remnant of the Israelite community. He is not speaking against the Jewish people, but what he considers an inadequate, imperfect institution to carry out God's intended goal. By using Psalm 110:4, the author argues that God himself calls for a replacement of the old priesthood by the new priesthood of Jesus. What is not implied is a replacement of the people themselves.

In this light, it is difficult to characterize Hebrews 7:1-19 as that which promotes hatred toward Jews or the destruction of the Jewish people. On the contrary, it promotes what the author understands as God's true intention for the Jewish nation in drawing near to God in worship. If the author were to be faithful to his understanding of God's eschatological revelation in Jesus Christ, he must exhort his Jewish brothers and sisters

---

[142] Lane, *Hebrews 1–8*, cxxxi.

to abandon the old means and cling to the new means, which he believes God himself had intended and established.

Supersessionism

Does Hebrews 7:1-28 argue for the abandonment by God of Israel and Israel's replacement with the church? Clearly, we can speak of the passage as describing the supersession of the Levitical priesthood. But does this necessitate the supersession of the Jewish people?

Though the Levitical priesthood is a very important cultural symbol for the Jews, it did not completely encompass the totality of the Jewish identity. In fact, the inauguration of the Levitical priesthood itself marked a major change in how the people sacrificed and related to God. It was the establishment of the Levitical priesthood that also necessitated a change (or establishment) of the law and yet the identity of the Jewish people remained the same.[143]

Furthermore, we must note that the idea of a priesthood that is distinctively Jewish remains in the author of Hebrews' formulation. Indeed, it is the Old Testament priesthood that informs the author's understanding of the priesthood of Jesus.[144] Therefore we are to see the supersession of the Levitical priesthood as not damaging the identity of God's people as God's people. It is a supersession within a Jewish framework, in which the eschatological goal of the Levitical priesthood is reached in Jesus Christ.[145]

---

[143] Peter J. Leithart, "The Priests of Culture," *First Things* 27 (1992) 11. Leithart notes other examples in Israel's history where a change in the priesthood necessitated changes in the law.

[144] Ronald Williamson argues that there is a probable influence of Jewish *Merkabah*-Mysticism in the background of Hebrews. See Ronald Williamson, "Background of the Epistle to the Hebrews," *ExpTim* 87 (1976) 232–37. Shinya Nomoto argues that early Christian tradition, by and large, lies behind the high priestly thought in Hebrews, "So ergibt sich, dass die Hohepriestervorstellung des Hebr. vom Verfasser aufgrund urchristlicher Traditionen weitgehend eigenständig mit Hilfe der typologischen Betrachtungsweise entworfen wurde"; "Herkunft und Struktur der Hohenpriestervorstellung im Hebräerbrief," *NovT* 10 (1968) 23. William Horbury, however, argues most convincingly that the priestly thought in the epistle to the Hebrews has its foundation in the Penteteuch, "the antecedents of the priestly thought characteristic of Hebrews should be sought neither in Christianity, nor in sectarian or visionary Judaism, but in the pervasive influence upon Jewry of the Pentateuchal theocracy"; "The Aaronic Priesthood in the Epistle to the Hebrews," *JSNT* 19 (1983) 68.

[145] Donald Hagner argues that the law played its role before the coming of Christ, but after Jesus came and fulfilled the law, there was no longer any need for it; *Hebrews*, 109. See also Ellingworth, *Hebrews*, 381; Gordon, *Hebrews*, 27–28; Hughes, *Hebrews*, 258; Delitzsch, *Hebrews*, 359; A. B. Bruce, *Hebrews*, 264; Spicq, *Hebreux*, 125; Lane, *Hebrews 1–8*,

Perhaps a better way of describing the relationship between the Levitical priesthood and Jesus' priesthood is in terms of fulfillment. Supersession gives the impression that something completely new has done away with the old. But here in our text, a more organic relationship between the Levitical priesthood and Jesus' priesthood is described. It is a relationship of shadow and reality, type and anti-type. Donald Hagner prefers the term "fulfillment" and argues that it balances well both the continuity and discontinuity of Christianity with Judaism. Hagner writes:

> The point I wish to make here is that all of this cannot mean that the Christian church is a new religion, or the replacement of Judaism. It is of the greatest importance to understand that theologically the church is the *fulfillment* of Judaism. On this point the Jewish remnant of believers in Jesus have always been rightly adamant. The church does not represent a non-Judaism; it is instead the *true Judaism*.[146]

What seems clear from our analysis is the fact that the priesthood of Jesus is in fact described as the fulfillment of the Levitical priesthood.

Conclusion

In conclusion, we assert that Hebrews 7:1-19 does indeed call its readers to distance themselves from the dominant Jewish culture. The polemic against the priesthood functions to legitimize the sectarian community represented by the author and to subvert allegiance to the Levitical priesthood. What was motivating this rhetoric is the belief that Jesus is the eschatological high priest who has fulfilled the Levitical priesthood. It is this belief that obligates the author to speak of the annulment of the older priesthood and law.

Though this polemic can be considered anti-Judaic, it does not promote hatred or hostility toward the Jewish people. Nor does it argue for the complete abandonment of the Jewish people by God. Rather it speaks of the fulfillment of God's purposes for the Jewish people. If the author were to be faithful to the revelation he received, he must disclose the radical implications of Jesus' priesthood to his Jewish brothers and sisters. The words that he pens are not against the Hebrews, but for the Hebrews.

185.

[146] Donald Hagner, "A Positive Theology of Judaism from the New Testament," *SEÅ* 69 (2004) 14. Donald G. Bloesch writes, ". . . Christianity represents not the annulment of the heritage of Israel but its fulfillment even in the midst of negation"; "'All Israel Will Be Saved': Supersessionism and the Biblical Witness," *Int* 43 (1989) 139.

5

Covenant and Polemic in Hebrews 8:1-13

ERICH Grässer writes, "Bis in unsere Gegenwart nimmt die antijüdische Polemik ihre Argumente vor allem aus 8,7.13."[1] He identifies the author's strong words against the old covenant as the most well established springboard for anti-Jewish polemic in our day. Our examination of this passage will be crucial in determining whether the epistle to the Hebrews itself is anti-Semitic, anti-Judaic, or supersessionistic.

As we analyze the rhetoric in Hebrews 8:1-13, we will ask, "Was the author of Hebrews attacking the Jewish people? Was he calling for the destruction of the Jewish faith?" In order to answer these questions, we need to determine how this passage functions in the social context in which it was given.

As in chapter 4, there will be three major sections to this chapter. In the first section, we will seek to determine the importance of Mosaic covenant to the life and identity of the Jewish people and how Second Temple Jewish authors used covenant language to further their own rhetorical goals. In the second section we will examine in great detail Hebrews 8:1-13, seeking to determine its socio-rhetorical function or goal within the Jewish-Christian community. In the final section we will discuss whether the author of Hebrews' rhetoric in 8:1-13 promotes negative attitudes toward the Jewish people.

Mosaic Covenant in the Second Temple Period

How important was the Mosaic covenant to the identity and culture of the Jewish people? Was the Mosaic covenant so intimately tied to their identity that if one were to speak of its abrogation, they would in essence be speaking of the destruction of the Jewish people? These are the questions we need to address in this section. In addition, we shall examine how vari-

---

[1] Erich Grässer, *An die Hebräer,* 3 vols., EKK 17 (Zürich: Benziger, 1993) 2:106.

ous Jewish authors use covenant rhetoric to further their own goals and objectives. This will help us determine how the author of Hebrews uses covenant rhetoric in his own social setting.

As we survey several different Second Temple Jewish writings,[2] we shall see that for the most part, they confirm that the Mosaic covenant was extremely important in the life of the community.[3] However, there are some writings (Josephus and Philo) that seem to downplay the concept of covenant and covenant language. The reason for this may be explained by the sociological context in which these writings were written.

Apocrypha and Pseudepigrapha

What seems to be a common theme throughout the apocryphal and pseudepigraphical works considered in this chapter is a desire to rally together Jews in their commitment to their Jewish heritage and identity. For most of these writings, what is motivating this nationalistic call is the political, social, and cultural threat posed by the Gentile world. The call to covenant faithfulness is intimately connected with a desire to maintain the unique Jewish identity, culture, and faith.

Jubilees

The importance of the Mosaic covenant is clearly demonstrated in the Pseudepigraphical writing *Jubilees*.[4] Ellen Juhl Christiansen suggests that this writing addresses two threats to the Jews. The first is that foreign powers will impose non-Jewish laws and regulations upon them and the second is that "less strict interpretations of traditional laws are suggested and adopted as a new life-style, with the danger that traditional Jewish identity is lost."[5] Thus the author of *Jubilees* retells the Genesis 1:1- Exodus 15:22

---

[2] As mentioned in chapter 4, page 62, n. 1, we will exclude rabbinic literature in our discussion because of the difficulty in determining the precise date of certain ideas or traditions in the literature.

[3] Bruce W. Longenecker writes, ". . . the best starting point for the study of Early Judaism is the recognition of the importance of the covenant for Jewish reflection and practice"; *Eschatology and the Covenant: A Comparison of 4 Ezra and Romans 1–11*, JSNTSS 57 (Sheffield: JSOT Press, 1991) 19.

[4] This text is clearly dated before 100 BC based on the dating of the earliest fragment of the text found at Qumran. If one assumes that the author of *Jubilees* was a spiritual parent of the Qumran community, then the dating of the writing can be set from 161 -140 BC. See O. S. Wintermute, "Jubilees," in *The Old Testament Pseudepigrapha*, 2 vols., ed. James H. Charlesworth (Garden City, New York: Doubleday, 1983) 2:43-44.

[5] Ellen Juhl Christiansen, *The Covenant in Judaism and Paul: A Study of Ritual Boundaries*

account, "recording the establishment and renewal of the covenant."[6] It is the covenant that establishes the identity of the people according to *Jubilees*.

One literary technique used by the author of *Jubilees* to communicate the need for his own community to keep faithfully the law of the covenant is to correlate certain Mosaic commandments with events in Israel's history.[7] For example, in his description of the creation of Adam and Eve, the author gives a justification for certain purity rules contained in the Mosaic Law.

> In the first week Adam was created and also the rib, his wife. And in the second week he showed her to him. And therefore the commandment was given to observe seven days for a male, but for a female twice seven days in their impurity...And therefore the command was written in the heavenly tablets for one who bears, "If she bears a male, she shall remain seven days in her impurity like the first seven days. And thirty-three days she shall remain in the blood of her purity. And she shall not touch anything holy. And she shall not enter the sanctuary until she has completed these days which are in accord with (the rule for) a male (child). And that which is in accord with (the rule for) a female is two weeks—like the two first weeks—in her impurity. And sixty-six days she shall remain in the blood of her purity. And their total will be eighty days."[8]

By tying these ordinances to the Biblical history, a demand for greater fidelity to them is communicated. In other words, the implication for the readers is that they should remain faithful in keeping the Mosaic Law. They are to keep all the liturgical, dietary, moral, and civil commandments contained in the covenant writings. The writer is using the traditional stories of the past to forge the present identity of the community and the need for covenant renewal and faithfulness.

What is also clear in *Jubilees* is a strong sense of continuity among the different covenants (Noahic, Abrahamic, Mosaic, etc.). Subsequent covenants are seen as renewals of previous covenants (*Jub.* 6:17, 19; 14:20). The festival associated with the renewal of the covenant is described as being valid for all subsequent generations (*Jub.* 6:20, 24, 28, 35). Jacques

---

as Identity Markers, AGAJU 27 (Leiden: Brill, 1995) 68.

[6] Ibid., 68.

[7] See *Jub.* 2:25-33; 3:8-11; 4:31-32; 6:4-38; 15:25-34; 20:1-10; 23:16-21; 30:7-17, 21-23; 33:18-20; Betsy Halpern-Amaru, *Rewriting the Bible: Land and Covenant in Post-Biblical Jewish Literature* (Valley Forge, Pa.: Trinity, 1994) 30.

[8] *Jubilees* 3:8-11. Cf. Lev 12:2-5.

Van Ruiten argues that the author of *Jubilees* sees the Noahic covenant as the prototype of all subsequent biblical covenants.[9] Or conversely, that the Mosaic covenant was an outworking of the Noahic covenant. Van Ruiten goes into great detail showing how the author attempts to forge a close relationship between the Noahic and Mosaic covenants.[10] The effect of such a connection highlights the importance of the Mosaic covenant in light of its unity, not only with the Noahic covenant, but also with all biblical covenants.[11]

Christiansen also notes that the adherence to specific covenantal laws and rituals functions as an identity marker for those in the community, separating them from those on the outside. "In this way the annual celebration of the covenant becomes an *identity mark for all Israel* (cf. 6:11), a unifying factor."[12] She sees these obligations setting up boundaries and establishing a social identity for those addressed in *Jubilees*. The present identity of the people is tied to the promise of land and the existence of the community. Therefore, the author of Jubilees calls for separation from pagan society.

> By urging the readers to be conscious of what belonging to the people meant in the past, the author of *Jubilees* sanctions the call for separation for the sake of preserving Israel's present national status. To the individuals as well as to the people as a whole this status is marked by concrete observances, which guard the religious and social identity of Israel.[13]

Finally, strong warnings against neglect and betrayal of the covenant are found in *Jubilees*. "And many will be destroyed and seized and will fall into the hand of the enemy because they have forsaken my ordinances and my commandments and the feasts of my covenant . . ." (*Jub* 1:10). This warning indicates that the very existence of the nation is at stake if the covenant is neglected.[14] There is also, however, the hope of a perfect future relationship with God without sin, evil, or curse.[15] This future covenant

---

[9] Jacques Van Ruiten, "The Covenant of Noah in *Jubilees* 6.1-38," in *The Concept of Covenant in the Second Temple Period*, ed. Stanley E. Porter and Jacqueline C. R. de Roo (Leiden: Brill, 2003) 167–90.

[10] Ibid., 177–89.

[11] Ibid., 190.

[12] Christiansen, *The Covenant in Judaism and Paul*, 79.

[13] Ibid., 85.

[14] Ibid., 86.

[15] *Jubilees* 1:15-17, 23, 25-26; 23:29.

will not be a new covenant, a new law, or a new order, but an acceptance of the existing covenant and law by all of Israel.[16]

The use of covenant language serves to bind the community together as those who share the same covenant history. The author seeks to forge the unique identity of the people by his use of covenant rhetoric.

Sirach/Ecclesiasticus

The work of Ecclesiasticus or Sirach is thought to be a response to the influence of Hellenism in the Jewish community.[17] It follows the traditions of Proverbs and Ecclesiastes. Larry Helyer writes, "Hellenism, with all that it entailed, presented a grave threat to the well-being of the ancestral faith. Ben Sira is deeply concerned to preserve the Hebrew traditions based upon the sacred Scriptures of Israel."[18]

Several passages in Sirach speak of the covenant.[19] It seems that the author has one covenant in mind that stretches throughout Israel's history. Though this one covenant was uniquely established with individuals, there seems to be a sense that the same law is implicit in all of them. In 17:1-12, Ben Sira describes God making a covenant with man at creation and the concomitant statues associated with it. "The Lord created man out of earth, and turned him back to it again. . . . He bestowed knowledge upon them, and allotted to them the law of life. He established with them an eternal covenant, and showed them his judgments" (Sir 17:1-12).

In reference to the covenant made with Abraham, Ben Sira writes, "Abraham was the great father of a multitude of nations, and no one has been found like him in glory; he kept the law of the Most High, and was taken into covenant with him; he established the covenant in his flesh, and when he was tested he was found faithful" (44:19-20). What is communicated in this passage is the idea that the covenant law was revealed to Abraham, even before Sinai.

After personifying wisdom and speaking of all its benefits, Ben Sira writes, "All this is the book of the covenant of the Most High God, the law which Moses commanded us as an inheritance for the congregations

---

[16] Christiansen, *The Covenant in Judaism and Paul*, 87.

[17] For dating, see page 66, footnote 15 in Chapter 4.

[18] Larry R. Helyer, *Exploring Jewish Literature of the Second Temple Period: A Guide for New Testament Students* (Downers, Grove, Ill.: InterVarsity, 2002) 96.

[19] Some passages that speak of covenants other than the Mosaic covenant are: Sir 17:12; 44:18, 19-21, 23; 45:6-7, 15, 24, 25; 46:11.

of Jacob" (24:23).[20] The passage continues to describe this book of the covenant as giving wisdom, understanding, instruction, etc. In essence, Ben Sira is arguing that Torah is the foundation of wisdom and implicitly that all his (Jewish) readers should adhere to these covenant stipulations. Clearly then, the covenant and its Torah were intimately connected with the identity of the Jewish people according to Ben Sira. The use of covenant rhetoric served to tie the community together as those who share the same covenant history.

Tobit and Additions to Daniel

The apocryphal books, Tobit[21] and the Additions to Daniel: Prayer of Azariah,[22] Susanna,[23] Bel and the Dragon,[24] and the Song of the Three Young Men[25] communicate to their readers a need to remain faithful to the covenant while living in the midst of a pagan society. Susanna and Daniel are described as faithful Jews committed to the requirements of Torah (Sus 3, 23, 62). The three young men are also described as those who keep covenant (Sg Three 18).[26] Helyer writes,

> These stories all share a deeply felt concern: they are designed to reinforce Jewish identity in the midst of pagan culture. The intention of the authors, therefore, was to instill hope in the God of Israel and pride in their heritage as his chosen people. In spite of their lowly estate and loss of political autonomy, they must never forget this lesson: if Jews are faithful to the covenant, God will at last reward and restore them.[27]

---

[20] See also Sir 28:7; 39:8; 41:19; 42:2; 45:1-5.

[21] Tobit is thought to be dated around 250 to 175 BC. Early fragments of the writing were found at Qumran and there is no mention of the Maccabean revolt. See deSilva, *Introducing the Apocrypha: Message, Context, and Significance* (Grand Rapids: Baker, 2002) 68.

[22] The Prayer of Azariah is difficult to date. One important clue, however, is that Pr. Azar 9 mentions the pious being handed over to apostates and a wicked king. This seems to reflect the Hellenization crisis from 175–164 BC. See ibid., 227.

[23] It is difficult to date this work because it seems to fit well with the conditions of the Jews throughout most of the Persian and Hellenistic periods. See ibid., 233.

[24] Some have argued that this work was composed during the persecution under Antiochus VII Sidetes. Yet deSilva gives evidence that Antiochus was not necessarily an enemy of the Jewish religion and that a precise date is difficult to ascertain. See ibid., 239.

[25] This work is thought to be dated no later than the approximate date of its translation into Greek in the Septuagint (about 100 BC). See ibid., 227.

[26] See also Sus 44-45, 64; Bel 4-5, 25, 41; Tob 4:6, 19, 21.

[27] Helyer, *Exploring Jewish Literature*, 55.

The danger posed in these texts is the assimilation of the minority Jews into the majority culture. What this involves is not only adopting the values of the larger society, but "turning away from the distinctive lifestyle called for by the Mosaic covenant . . ."[28] Therefore the covenant rhetoric found in these writings functions to encourage the Jewish readers to maintain their unique identity in a pagan society.

First Maccabees

First Maccabees[29] also communicates a strong message to Jews to remain faithful to the covenant of God in the face of great threats from Gentiles. First Maccabees 1:11-15 describes a group of "lawless" Jews who urged their brothers to adopt the ways of the Gentiles and forsake the holy covenant. Clearly the author speaks out against those who would compromise their covenant identity, even removing the sign of circumcision (1:15), for the false hope of prosperity and security. It is in this context that the author of 1 Maccabees extols those who resisted the Gentile customs—even to death—in order not to profane the holy covenant (1:62-3).[30] The clear implication to the reader is to cling to the covenant and reject Gentile customs and practices. In this way, covenant rhetoric draws clear boundaries with those on the outside and seeks to unify those on the inside.

Judith

The book of Judith[31] seems to indicate that the Jewish people were still in covenant with God, even though they were subject to the military aggression of the Assyrians. In her prayer to the Lord before she goes to beguile Holofernes, the commander of the Assyrian army, Judith states, "Make my deceitful words to be their wound and stripe, for they have planned cruel things against thy covenant, and against thy consecrated house, and against the top of Zion, and against the house possessed by thy children" (9:13). Though this is the only explicit mention of covenant in the book

---

[28] Ibid., 55. *Pss. Sol.* 17:15 also reflects the concern that the Jewish people had given themselves over to Gentile idolatrous practices, "And the children of the covenant (living) among the gentile rabble adopted these (practices)."

[29] For dating see page 64, footnote 6 in chapter 4.

[30] See also 1 Macc 2:15-28, 50; 2 Macc 6:10-11; 6:18-7:42; 8:1-36.

[31] The date of this book is thought to be after the Maccabean revolt (164–163 BC). Parallels between Holofernes and Antiochus IV are fairly clear. The power of the high priest as a military commander also indicates a dating during the Hasmonean period. See deSilva, *Introducing the Apocrypha*, 91–92.

of Judith, the author seems to presuppose the covenant relationship with God still stands.

In her deception to Holofernes, Judith states that the downfall of the Jewish people will ultimately be brought about by their sins.

> Now as for the things Achior said in your council, we have heard his words, for the men of Bethulia spared him and he told them all he had said to you. Therefore, my lord and master, do not disregard what he said, but keep it in your mind, for it is true: our nation cannot be punished, nor can the sword prevail against them, unless they sin against their God.[32]

Judith goes on to describe the particular sin of eating the first fruits of the grain and the tithes of wine and oil, which were consecrated and set aside for the priests.[33]

What seems clear from this passage is the idea that disobedience to the laws of the covenant would reap God's wrath and chastisement. Though this text comes in the context of deceiving Holofernes, it seems to reflect the author of Judith's own theological understanding of Israel's covenant relationship with God. Therefore, the importance of the covenant and keeping covenant with God is demonstrated. The writing as a whole serves to inspire the Jewish readers to remain faithful to the covenant in the face of Gentile threats. It serves to strengthen the unique identity of the Jews as God's people.

Liber Antiquitatum Biblicarum (Pseudo-Philo)

Another set of pseudepigraphical writings seem to speak to communities that feel God's covenant with them has been irreparably broken. In order to encourage these communities, these writings speak of the eternal, indestructible nature of the covenant with the hope that the readers would renew their commitment to God and the covenant community.

Pseudo-Philo's *Biblical Antiquities* or *Liber Antiquitatum Biblicarum*[34] highlights the gracious aspect of the covenant relationship Israel has with God through its retelling of the history of Israel from Adam to David. Bruce Longenecker writes, "Throughout, Pseudo-Philo is animated by this

---

[32] Judith 11:9-10.
[33] Judith 11:12-13.
[34] The text is dated around the time of Jesus, but has its lower and upper limits from 135 BC to AD 100. See Daniel J. Harrington, "Pseudo-Philo," in *The Old Testament Pseudepigrapha*, 2 vols., ed. James H. Charlesworth (Garden City, N.Y.: Doubleday, 1983) 2:299.

notion of the unique covenant relationship between God and Israel. One can turn to almost any page of the text and find the fundamental concern of its author to be the preservation of the covenant."[35]

Frederick Murphy argues along similar lines. He notes that the idea of repentance or calling upon God for help is virtually absent in the text. His point is that God's restoration of his people is not based on their response or repentance, but on God's promises and the indestructibility of his covenant.[36] He argues that Pseudo-Philo describes the law as eternal specifically because it is established by an eternal covenant.

> God tells Moses that he will give him "an everlasting Law (*legem sempiternam*)" (11.2). It is not just the Law that is eternal, but also the *giving* of the Law to Israel, i.e. the covenant: on Sinai God establishes "the Law of his eternal covenant (*legem testamenti sempiterni*) with the sons of Israel" and gives "his eternal commandments that will not pass away (*precepta eternal, que non transient*)" (11.5).[37]

John Levinson argues that Pseudo-Philo describes the Sinai covenant as playing a prominent role in the history of Israel. "The *telos* of the covenant of Noah and Abraham ('his fathers'), therefore, is the covenant established through Moses. The long shadow of Sinai does not encompass the past alone but casts its influence as well over future covenants."[38] There is a phrase in Pseudo-Philo 21:10 that describes Joshua's blessing to Israel and his desire for the permanence of the covenant.

> And Joshua blessed them and said, "The Lord grant that your heart may abide in him all the days and you do not depart from his name. May the covenant of the Lord remain with you and not be broken, but may there be built among you a dwelling place for God, as he said when he sent you into his inheritance with joy and gladness."[39]

The author of *Liber antiquitatum biblicarum* seems to believe that the Mosaic covenant was still intact and sought to convince his readers to keep

---

[35] Longenecker, *Eschatology and the Covenant*, 24. See also Halpern-Amaru, *Rewriting the Bible*, 87–88.

[36] Frederick J. Murphy, "The Eternal Covenant in Pseudo-Philo," *JSP* 3 (1988) 43–57.

[37] Murphy, "Eternal Covenant," 46. Cf. *L.A.B.* 10:4-6; 19:9; 23:10.

[38] John R. Levinson, "Torah and Covenant in Pseudo Philo's *Liber Antiquitatum Biblicarum*," in *Bund und Tora,* ed. Friedrich Avemarie and Hermann Lichtenberger, WUNT 92 (Tübingen: Mohr/Siebeck, 1996) 113–14.

[39] *L.A.B.* 21:10.

covenant with God. The obvious concern would be a departure from this covenant relationship, either because of apathy or thoughts that God had rejected his people. Though there does not seem to be any direct Gentile threat addressed in this writing, the more general threat of abandoning the covenant, i.e., their Jewish identity is apparent. Thus we see that the use of covenant rhetoric here is to forge and maintain Jewish identity in response to crisis.

Testament of Moses

The *Testament of Moses*[40] also emphasizes the unconditional and eternal nature of the Mosaic covenant. Betsy Halpern-Amaru notes that the author of the *Testament of Moses* does not stress the conditional nature of the Sinai covenant, but rather "the primary purpose of the work is to demonstrate that, regardless of historical circumstance, the covenant through which the Israelites acquired the Land from God is permanent and eternal."[41] The author describes the covenant in association with God's oath[42] and calls upon God to "remember" his covenant with his people.[43] Therefore, what is most emphasized in the use of covenant language is that Israel's final hope is grounded upon God keeping his covenant promises.[44] It is this idea that is to inspire the readers to put their hope in this covenant and remain connected to this covenant community.

4 Ezra (2 Esdras)

One work that highlights the importance of the law and its keeping is *4 Ezra*.[45] In contrast to the writings above, the conditional element of the covenant is stressed. The book of *4 Ezra* indicates that at least some Jews believed their salvation was wholly and completely dependent upon their faithfulness to the law. In this writing, the importance of the covenant is

---

[40] For dating, see page 67, footnote 17 in chapter 4.

[41] Halpern-Amaru, *Rewriting the Bible*, 59.

[42] *T.Mos.* 1:9; 2:7; 3:9; 11:17; 12:13.

[43] *T.Mos.* 3:9, 11:17. We see the same kind of covenant language in *Pss. Sol.* 9:10; 10:4.

[44] Halpern-Amaru, *Rewriting the Bible*, 56.

[45] Most scholars believe this writing was composed around AD 100. The reference to the "destruction of our city," (3:1) is thought to be an allusion to the destruction of the temple in AD 70. See Bruce M. Metzger, "The Fourth Book of Ezra," in *The Old Testament Pseudepigrapha*, 2 vols., ed. James H. Charlesworth (Garden City, N.Y.: Doubleday, 1983) 1:520. Though this writing may fall outside the boundaries of the Second Temple Period, the ideas it contains may reflect the sentiment of that time.

expressed by stating that those who deny or neglect its stipulations deserve God's punishment and rejection. Uriel expresses to Ezra how it would be better for the disobedient to perish than for God's laws to be disregarded. He explains how the people have rejected God's covenant, "they scorned his Law, and denied his covenants; they have been unfaithful to his statutes and have not performed his works."[46]

Longenecker states that Uriel "makes the point that the observance of the law is the only corrective to the anthropological condition of sin. God's law is the bridge from this world to the next, and those who have disobeyed God's commandments will not arrive at his salvation."[47] It seems that the author of *4 Ezra* is responding to a crisis event, namely the destruction of the temple in AD 70.[48] The reason why Israel is experiencing calamity is because she did not keep the law and remain in covenant with God.[49] The obvious implication for the readers is to keep the law and remain in covenant with God.

Regardless of whether the conditional or unconditional aspect of the covenant is stressed, what is clear is that the Mosaic covenant was important in forming the unique identity of the Jewish people. All these writings seek to rally the Jews back to God and his covenant either by pulling (emphasizing the unconditional, gracious aspect of the covenant), or by pushing (emphasizing the conditional, judgment aspect).

Dead Sea Scrolls

As mentioned in chapter 4, the Dead Sea Scrolls[50] are particularly important for our study. Not only because of the use of "new covenant" language found in these writings, but also because the community addressed in these writings had clearly separated from the larger Jewish community. Therefore much of the rhetoric used by the authors of the Scrolls can be considered counter-cultural sectarian rhetoric, similar to the rhetoric used in Hebrews.[51] And so we shall see how the covenant rhetoric in

---

[46] *4 Ezra* 7:24, cf. 2:5-7, 5:29.

[47] Longenecker, *Eschatology and the Covenant*, 80.

[48] Ibid., 268.

[49] 2 Baruch, which also seems to be responding to the crisis in AD 70 calls upon its readers to "remember Zion and the Law and the holy land and your brothers and the covenant and your fathers, and do not forget the festivals and the Sabbaths" (84:8). This indicates that the idea of covenant, or keeping the covenant law should evoke the same kind of nostalgic feeling as the ideas of brotherhood, paternity, and the inheritance.

[50] For dating see page 70, footnote 34 in chapter 4.

[51] Counterculture rhetoric speaks against the dominant culture. It promotes separation

the Qumran writings functions to legitimize the community, socialize its members, and subvert allegiance to the dominant Jewish culture.

Certainly, the concept of covenant was very important to the Dead Sea Community. The term *berît* occurs more than 200 times in the Scrolls.[52] But how does the covenant language found in these writings relate to the Mosaic Covenant? What is the "new covenant" described in these writings?[53] Most scholars argue that the language of the "new covenant" in the Dead Sea Scrolls, echoing Jeremiah 31:31 refers to a renewal rather than a replacement of the Mosaic covenant.[54] Craig Evans argues that the Sinai covenant and its renewal are primarily in view and are for the most part the reason why the community existed.[55] Therefore as we examine the covenant language found in these writings, we must keep in mind that the authors did not envision the abrogation of an old covenant, but simply a renewal of a broken covenant.[56]

---

from the dominant society by advocating new institutions that would facilitate independence. See Vernon K. Robbins, *Exploring the Texture of Texts: A Guide to Socio-Rhetorical Interpretation* (Valley Forge, Pa.: Trinity, 1996) 87.

[52] Craig A. Evans, "Covenant in the Qumran Literature," in *The Concept of Covenant in the Second Temple Period*, ed. Stanley E. Porter and Jacqueline C. R. de Roo (Leiden: Brill, 2003) 55.

[53] The phrase, "new covenant" occurs in CD 6:19; 8:21; 19:33-34; 20:12; and possibly in 1 QpHab 2:3.

[54] See Evans, "Covenant in the Qumran Literature," 59; Shemaryahu Talmon, "The Community of the Renewed Covenant: Between Judaism and Christianity," in *The Community of the Renewed Covenant: The Notre Dame Symposium on the Dead Sea Scrolls*, ed. Eugene C. Ulrich and James C. VanderKam (Notre Dame, Ind.: University of Notre Dame Press, 1994) 12–13; Christiansen, *The Covenant in Judaism and Paul*, 56; Martin Abegg, "The Covenant of the Qumran Sectarians," in *The Concept of Covenant in the Second Temple Period*, 84–85; Craig R. Koester, *The Epistle to the Hebrews*, AB 36 (New York: Doubleday, 2001) 113. CD qualifies this new covenant as the new covenant of the land of Damascus (6.19; 8.21).

[55] Evans, "Covenant in the Qumran Literature," 55. In several places CD describes God's covenant with all of Israel (3.13; 15.5, 16.1, cf. 15.8-9). This expression shows "an awareness of continuity, particularly with Sinai, the event in which the people was born"; Christiansen, *The Covenant in Judaism and Paul*, 109.

[56] Christiansen, *The Covenant in Judaism and Paul*, 129. Also confirming the idea that a renewal is in mind is the *Liturgical Prayer* (1Q34 and 1Q34bis).

> But in the time of Thy goodwill Thou didst choose for Thyself a people. Thou didst remember Thy Covenant and [granted] that they should be set apart for Thyself from among all the peoples as a holy thing. And Thou didst renew for them Thy Covenant (founded) on a glorious vision and the words of Thy Holy [Spirit], on the works of Thy hands and the writing

Damascus Document (CD)

In the *Damascus Document* covenant language was used to define who was on the inside of the community and who was on the outside. The community viewed itself as the righteous remnant with whom God would reestablish his covenant.[57] "But with the remnant which held fast to the commandments of God He made His covenant with Israel for ever, revealing to them the hidden things in which all Israel had gone astray" (CD 3.13-14). Christiansen notes two things, "one, that because the covenant is established by God, it has eternal validity, and two, that God's covenant is with those who have kept the commandments."[58] The determining factor then of those who remain in covenant with God according to the *Damascus Document* is obedience to the law.[59] Those who do not keep the law were considered outside the chosen remnant.[60] CD 15.7-10 states,

> On the day that he speaks to the Guardian of the congregation, they shall enroll him with the oath of the Covenant which Moses made with Israel, the Covenant to return to the Law of Moses with a whole heart and soul, to whatever is found should be done at the time.

Therefore, keeping the stipulations of the covenant according to the interpretation of the community was the identity marker for those who comprised the faithful remnant of God. These alone would not bear God's wrath (cf. CD 1.5).[61]

---

of Thy Right Hand, that they might know the foundations of glory and the steps towards eternity… (1Q34bis 2.5-7).

Clearly the imagery described here is a reference to the Sinai covenant. The choosing of a people refers to the birth of Israel at Sinai. The glorious vision is a reference to the theophany described in Exodus 19:16, 18-20. The writing of "Thy Right Hand" alludes to the writing of God's laws given to Moses. Thus we conclude that the author understood their present covenant as a renewal of the Sinai covenant.

[57] In her discussion of the Dead Sea Scrolls, Susan Lehne argues that the Qumran community viewed itself as living in the last days waiting for a cosmic battle to ensue. The community understood that the new covenant was made with them as the uniquely chosen people of God. Cf. CD 6:18-19; 8:20-21; 19:34; 20:11-13; 1QpHab 1:16—2:10a. See Susan Lehne, *The New Covenant in Hebrews*, JSNTSS 44 (Sheffield: JSOT, 1990) 44–46.

[58] Christiansen, *The Covenant in Judaism and Paul*, 110.

[59] CD 3.12-16; 10.14-12.22.

[60] CD 2.6-7; 3.1-12.

[61] The importance of the covenant is also found in the warnings given to the readers in the *Damascus Document* not to reject God's covenant. See CD 2.2, 14-15; 3.3-5, 9-11; 8.1-4, 21-24.

This covenant language functions to legitimize the community and to separate it from the larger Jewish society. By claiming the exclusive identity as the faithful remnant, the community implies that all others, who do not follow their covenant laws, are on the outside. The boundaries have changed from being based on birth and election, to being based on commitment and choice.[62] Christiansen argues that a change in self-identity occurs when one enters into a new particularistic covenant relationship,

> When symbolic acts, like the oath, are seen as boundary marks and means for attaining a state of perfection demanded by the law, a *change* in self-understanding is evident. What emerges is a relatively *closed community* whose self-image is that of a remnant, called to preserve priestly purity by demanding ritual and ethical obedience and faithfulness. Because the focal point is obedience, mirrored in keeping concrete prescriptions, and based on the theological principle of holiness, there is *a change both of identity and boundaries*, from an ethnic covenant to a particularistic covenant. Eventually, there is a change in the relationship between God and Israel, or God and humanity.[63]

By more narrowly defining those who comprise the new covenant community, the author of this document seeks to subvert allegiance to the dominant Jewish religious leaders and their community.

Rule of the Community (1QS)

Much of the covenant language found in the *Rule of the Community* is used to socialize its members. It is an instruction manual. And one important part of this instruction is to "admit into the covenant of grace all those who have freely devoted themselves to the observance of God's precepts . . . ."[64] The community's understanding of the covenant involved various laws and traditions dealing with how to keep the Sabbath, purity, sacrifice, and calendar events.[65] By emphasizing the need to enter into the covenant, the author presupposes that the covenant relationship was broken. Part of the entrance rites included an acknowledgement of personal sins and the collective sins of their fathers.[66] What is implied is that all those who do

---

[62] Christiansen, *The Covenant in Judaism and Paul*, 131–32. See CD 1.18-19; 2.15; 3.2-11; 8.8; 19:20.
[63] Christiansen, *The Covenant in Judaism and Paul*, 143–44.
[64] 1QS 1.7-8.
[65] Evans, "Covenant in the Qumran Literature," 62.
[66] 1QS 1.24-26.

not acknowledge their sins and do not enter into the covenant relationship remain on the outside.

The author of the *Rule of the Community* connects entering into and maintaining a covenant relationship with God with salvation. "On entering the Covenant, the Priests and Levites shall bless the God of salvation and all His faithfulness, and all those entering the covenant shall say after them, 'Amen, Amen!'"[67] Evans makes the statement, "Israelites who repent and commit themselves to the Covenant and to the Community that teaches the way of the Covenant correctly will be saved; those who do not will be damned."[68] By highlighting the very grave implications of not entering and maintaining the covenant relationship, the author of this writing leaves the readers with no alternative but to follow the *Rule of the Community*.

This document also makes clear the connection between covenant practices within the community and those stipulated in the Mosaic covenant.[69] The renewed covenant is in essence the same as the covenant established at Sinai with the same rules and regulations.

> Whoever approaches the Council of the Community shall enter the Covenant of God in the presence of all who have freely pledged themselves. He shall undertake by a binding oath to return with all his heart and soul to every commandment of the Law of Moses in accordance with all that has been revealed of it to the sons of Zadok, the priests, Keepers of the Covenant and Seekers of His will . . . .[70]

By describing the community's present covenant as renewal of the Sinai covenant, the author evokes a greater sense of legitimacy and continuity with Israel's past. According to the author, the problem here is not with

---

[67] 1QS 1.19-20.

[68] Evans, "Covenant in the Qumran Literature," 79.

[69] Christiansen argues that the idea of "covenant" in this writing is not connected to any historical covenants, but rather stands alone as a "timeless principle." She points out the intentional absence of terms and phrases that would connect the present covenant with those in the past. Her point in this discussion is that the author was focusing on how "covenant" was valid for the present community in its present form rather than arguing its validity from past events; Christiansen, *The Covenant in Judaism and Paul*, 147–51. Her observations are noted and yet, it seems that she too would agree that 1QS presents the covenant essentially as the Sinai covenant. Moses is described as the mediator of the law in 1QS 1.3; 8.5.

[70] 1QS 5.7-9.

the covenant itself, but with the people and their propensity to sin or break covenant with God.

The enduring quality of the covenant is described in the *Rule of the Blessings* (1QSb), a fragment that was originally attached to the Scroll containing the *Rule of the Community* (1QS) and the *Rule of the Congregation* (1QSa).[71] This incomplete document describes the covenant as "everlasting."

> Words of blessing. The Master shall bless them that fear [God and do] His will, that keep His commandments, and hold fast to His holy [Covenant], and walk perfectly [in all the ways of] His [truth], whom He has chosen for an eternal Covenant which shall endure for ever.[72]

By emphasizing the eternal nature of the covenant, the author provides a sense of security and stability for those who align themselves with it. In this way, the author encourages the readers to also endure in their fidelity to the covenant.

Other Dead Sea Writings

The *Thanksgiving Hymns* demonstrate how covenant rhetoric functions to solidify the community's commitment and identity. The way one related to God and to others in the community was in the framework of the covenant.[73] Those who are in covenant will be embraced, but those outside the covenant will be despised. One hymnist declares that he will hate those whom God removes from his presence and reject "those who have turned [from] Thy [Co]venant."[74]

Loyalty to the covenant is also stressed in these hymns. This translates to suffering for the sake of the covenant, which would also imply suffering in order to stay connected to the community and to God. One hymnist writes, "Violent men have sought after my life because I have clung to Thy Covenant."[75] He confesses that even though "my heart melted like water,

---

[71] This fragment is thought to be dated around 100 BC. See Vermes, *Complete Dead Sea Scrolls*, 374.

[72] 1QSb 1.1-3, cf. 3.22-25, 27.

[73] See 1QH 12.17-19, 22-25, 33-36; 4Q175 l.17; 1QpHab 2.2-10. See also Michael O. Wise, "The Concept of a New Covenant in the Teacher Hymns from Qumran (1QHa X-XVII)," in *The Concept of Covenant in the Second Temple Period*, 111, 121.

[74] 1QH 6.22.

[75] 1QH 10.22.

my soul held fast to Thy Covenant."[76] His willingness to endure suffering in order to remain faithful to the covenant is a challenge for the readers to do the same.[77] This rhetoric functions to inspire the readers to reject alternative communities and ideologies and remain firmly connected to their covenant community.

The *War Scroll* (1QM) also uses covenant rhetoric to solidify the identity of the people. It describes the constituents of the community as the "people of the saints of the Covenant."[78] Mention is made more than once of God's faithfulness in keeping covenant with his people, indicating that he will maintain it through the ages.[79] By highlighting the permanence of the covenant relationship, the author seeks to create confidence in the community's longevity and security.

One aspect that is often overlooked is the fact that the covenant and its laws regulated the community's food production, distribution, preparation, and consumption. Remaining in covenant with God required them to abide by his dietary regulations. And so the Qumran community, in zeal for the covenant, ordered their eating habits accordingly. Stephen Reed goes at great length to demonstrate the strict adherence of the community to the food regulations prescribed in the Law and their application in the community.[80] He notes that the food laws for the community took on a strictness equivalent to that required in the Temple.[81] He concludes,

> Careful attention to practicing strictly the food laws of the Bible and the particular interpretations of these food laws was seen as essential for living as the covenant people of God . . . Writers of Qumran texts knew that issues related to food were important for their identity as a people.[82]

The covenant regulations themselves functioned to create a unique identity for the people. Those who were in and those who were out could have easily been determined by how and what they ate. The idea then of

---

[76] 1QH 10.28.

[77] See also Wise, "The Concept of a New Covenant," 111–13.

[78] 1QM 10.10, cf. 17.9.

[79] 1QM 13.7-8; 14.8-10; 18.5-7.

[80] Stephen A. Reed, "The Role of Food as Related to the Covenant in Qumran Literature," in *The Concept of Covenant in the Second Temple Period*, 129–64. He refers especially to 1QS and part of CD in describing the appropriate behavior related to food for those in the community.

[81] Ibid., 137.

[82] Ibid., 163.

annulling or making obsolete this covenant would have had great implications on the culture and identity of the people.

Philo and Josephus

In contrast to the authors above, Philo and Josephus are rather tacit in their appropriation of covenant language and rhetoric. They are not antagonistic toward the covenant, but simply do not speak about it in theological terms.

Philo

Philo's[83] treatment of "covenant" is occasional and seems to be guided primarily out of necessity. The term διαθήκη happens to turn up in the biblical account; and therefore, Philo must comment on it in his interpretation of biblical texts. Lester Grabbe argues that since Philo did not likely know Hebrew, he depended exclusively on the Septuagint version of the Old Testament.[84] Grabbe then notes that the Greek term διαθήκη was understood by Philo to refer to a testament or will. Thus, in typical allegorical fashion, Philo understands διαθήκη as referring to a complex of closely related phenomena that may be summarized as follows:

- The wise man—the person of virtue (without implying perfection)—as God's heir (Mut. 51-53; Her. 313; QG 3.60).
- God's gift of grace, freely given without compulsion or necessity (Sacr. 57; Mut. 51-53), because God is eternal and will not pass on his inheritance at death (QG 2.10).
- God's law (Somn. 2.223).
- God's word (Somn. 2.223, 2.237).
- Divine justice (Somn. 2.224).
- The entirety of the intelligible world (in the Platonic sense) (QG 3.40; 3.42).
- God's gift of himself (Mut. 57-59).[85]

What is absent is the idea that covenant forms the structure by which one relates to God and the community. Covenant rhetoric is used by Philo

---

[83] For dating, see page 75, footnote 54 in chapter 4.

[84] Lester L. Grabbe, "Did All Jews Think Alike? 'Covenant' in Philo and Josephus in the Context of Second Temple Judaic Religion," in *The Concept of Covenant in the Second Temple Period*, 252.

[85] Ibid., 257.

neither to solidify the identity of the Jews nor to promote the separation of the Jews from Gentiles or apostates.

Perhaps the neglect of the concept of covenant could be attributed to the fact that Philo was speaking to a broader audience of Jews and Gentiles. The idea of covenant presupposes a unique relationship between God and a certain group of people. It seems that Philo, in seeking to make Judaism appeal to a more universal audience, sought to avoid the concept altogether. Instead of placing the Law of Moses in the context of God's covenant with Israel, he seeks to show how the Law of Moses is in harmony with the Law of Nature. Sidney Sowers describes Philo's connection between the Law of Nature and the Law of Moses, "The Law of Nature itself was engraved on the souls of the patriarchs, and it is also the basis of the O.T. legislation, since the latter is a written copy of the words and deeds of the 'living and vocal laws,' the patriarchs, who lived according to Nature (*Migr.* 127-128)."[86]

Because Philo was not intent on calling his fellow Jews to separate themselves from the larger pagan community, but was rather trying to bring these communities into harmony, he did not use language that implicitly set up boundaries. For this reason, it seems that "covenant" was not very significant to Philo.[87]

Josephus

Josephus[88] also does not use the term "covenant," in a theological, worldview forming sense.[89] The occurrences of the term διαθήκη almost exclusively refers to Herod's will.[90] Grabbe suggests that Josephus' lack of usage of the term "covenant" was due to his predominantly Gentile readership. Certainly he would have occasion to speak of the covenant as he discussed various Biblical passages, and yet he deliberately does not. And so Grabbe

---

[86] Sidney G. Sowers, *The Hermeneutics of Philo and Hebrews: A Comparison of the Interpretation of the Old Testament in Philo Judaeus and the Epistle to the Hebrews*, BST 1 (Zurich: EVZ, 1965) 46. See also *Mos.* 2.14, 51, 52; *Spec.* 3.189; *QE* 2.42; *Opif.* 143; *Prob.* 47; *Ios.* 31.

[87] Grabbe, "Did All Jews Think Alike?," 266.

[88] For dating, see page 77, footnote 63 in chapter 4.

[89] Halpern-Amaru notes that the term διαθήκη does not appear in the sections of the *Jewish Antiquities* that parallel the Scriptural narratives. There seems to be a conscious suppression of the term and concept in this writing. See Halpern-Amaru, *Rewriting the Bible*, 95–96.

[90] Grabbe, "Did All Jews Think Alike?" 257.

concludes that the idea of covenant was not important to Josephus either.[91]

Halpern-Amaru notes that though Josephus speaks about Jewish laws and regulations, these are not put in the context of God's covenant with Israel. She writes,

> He does maintain a connection between adherence to the laws, maintenance of national sovereignty, and retention of the Land. However, that connection involves neither a covenantal past nor a notion of particular sanctity adhering to the Land. It is rather a commitment to virtue expressed in adherence to the laws and the stability of established national institutions.[92]

Perhaps for both Philo and Josephus, who were writing to broader audiences (not exclusively to Jews), the idea of covenant sounded too exclusive and boundary forming. And so it would make sense for those writing to commandeer the favorable opinion of Gentiles to exclude terms or concepts that would be somewhat offensive. The fact that they do not emphasize the covenant in their social context indirectly argues that the covenant was important in forging the unique identity of God's people in distinguishing them from the larger dominant society.

Conclusion

From our survey above, it is apparent that for a large segment of the Jewish community the Mosaic covenant was important. To speak of its annulment or obsolescence would have radical implications for the life and identity of the Jewish people.[93] God's relationship with Israel can best be understood

---

[91] Ibid., 266. André Paul argues that the deliberate omission of covenant from Josephus' recounting of the Biblical narratives was an intentional polemic against Christianity. The covenant concept he argues was replete in the Septuagint, or the Christian's Bible, and thus Josephus wanted to eradicate it in the history of the Biblical account. See André Paul, "Flavius Josephus' *Antiquities of the Jews*: An Anti-Christian Manifesto," *NTS* 31 (1985) 473–80. Paul's argument seems a bit weak in light of the fact that there is little explicit polemic in Josephus' *Jewish Antiquities* against Christianity. In fact, *Ant.* 18 or the *Testimonium Flavianum* records a very positive witness to Jesus. Even if one were to purge suspect Christian interpolations from the *Testimonium*, there would still be a neutral witness to Jesus.

[92] Halpern-Amaru, *Rewriting the Bible*, 108. Cf. *Ant.* 4.294-295. See also Yehoshua Amir, "Josephus on the Mosaic 'Constitution,'" in *Politics and Theopolitics in the Bible and Postbiblical Literature,* ed. Henning Reventlow and Yair Hoffman, JSOTSS 171 (Sheffield: JSOT Press, 1994) 13–27, esp. 13, 18–19.

[93] E. A. C. Pretorius writes, "The *berith* with Yahweh was one of the most remarkable and vital realities of the religion of Israel. It not only constituted the very existence of Israel as

in relation to the covenant. It was on Mount Sinai that the nation of Israel was given its distinct identity from all the other nations (Exod 19:16-25; 20:17-26). Furthermore, the covenant stipulations governed not only the religious life of the community, but also the civil. Israel under the Mosaic covenant was a theocracy; God's laws governed all of life.[94] Meredith Kline has shown that the form of the legal document produced at Mount Sinai has the form and function of other ancient Near Eastern treaties.[95] This treaty functions as the "canonical foundation of Israel's life in relationship to himself [God]."[96]

Christiansen describes the Jewish identity as "covenantal." She sees it involving not only the people's relationship with God, but with one another.

> As agreement the covenant is never a term for a mere *vertical* relationship between the individual and God. There is always a *horizontal*, a social/political dimension, since the blessings, the promise of land, dynasty, and descendants concern the existence of the nation and the future of God's people.[97]

J. M. Lundquist argues for the intimate relationship between the temple, covenant, and the law. He states, "The temple founds (legitimizes) the state; covenant binds the foundation; law underlies the covenant."[98] Buchanan acknowledges this relationship and unravels some of the social

---

a separate, dedicated nation, but it encompassed all religious thought and activities and even made itself felt in every day matters"; E.A.C. Pretorius, "*Diatheke* in the Epistle to the Hebrews," *Neot* 5 (1971) 38.

[94] A close identification between the Law and the covenant is found in Sir 45:3-5. See also Christiansen, *The Covenant in Judaism and Paul*, 46–47.

[95] Meredith G. Kline, "Canon and Covenant," *WTJ* 32 (1970) 49–67, 179–200. George Wesley Buchanan also notes the legal nature of the idea of covenant. See George W. Buchanan, "The Covenant in Legal Context," in *The Concept of Covenant in the Second Temple Period*, 27–52.

[96] Kline, "Canon and Covenant," 29.

[97] Christiansen, *The Covenant in Judaism and Paul*, 61. Christiansen makes the interesting point that unlike other covenants, the Sinai covenant "emphasizes obligations and sanctions; blessings and promises result from obedience. Keeping the law should first of all be seen as a social factor identifying who belonged to the community. Israel's existence is based on the idea that divine obligations mark the people's identity and boundaries" (52). Thus, according to Christiansen, the decisive identity marker for those under the Mosaic covenant is keeping the law.

[98] J. M. Lundquist, "Temple, Covenant, and Law in the Ancient Near East and in the Old Testament," in *Israel's Apostasy and Restoration*, ed. A. Gileadi (Grand Rapids: Baker, 1988) 293.

consequences of the contract or covenant. He notes that those in the contract consider themselves alone to be holy, segregating the rest as unholy. It is the contract that holds the community together as a corporation, binding them to each other and to God by law.[99] The implication of course is that if the covenant is broken or annulled then the whole fabric that binds the community together is also torn asunder. The identity of the people is put in flux.

Because the covenant played such a vital role in shaping the identity of the people, the use of it rhetorically had great power and force. Covenant rhetoric was used to legitimize a particular community. We have seen from many of the apocryphal and pseudepigraphical writings that covenant language was used to distinguish the Jews from Gentiles. The Dead Sea Scrolls used covenant language to distinguish their community from those who have allegedly compromised their faith. The new covenant language was applied to a minority group seeking to distinguish and separate itself from the majority group. This rhetoric necessarily excludes certain groups and seeks to solicit allegiance to the community.

The use of covenant rhetoric for this purpose is implicitly supported by the fact that Josephus and Philo did not use it in their writings to a broader audience. Their rhetorical goals were primarily to present Judaism positively to the Greco-Roman world. Since the idea of covenant was necessarily exclusive, it did not play a role in their writings.

From our survey then, we can conclude that for the majority of the Jews in the Second Temple Period, the idea of "covenant" was very important, indeed, a vital part of their self identity. In fact, the authors that urged their readers to covenant fidelity did so in order to solidify the unique identity of the Jewish people in terms of the covenant. In other words, the covenant functioned as a unifying framework, in which social, religious, and cultural boundaries were formed. These writers were concerned about outside influences jeopardizing the social and religious cohesiveness of those in the covenant. And so by calling the readers to covenant fidelity, the authors were in essence challenging their audience to distance themselves from those on the outside and retain the norms, values, and ethics of those on the inside. This covenant rhetoric functions, then, to confirm and legitimize the existing community, and subvert the influence of competing communities.

---

[99] Buchanan, "The Covenant in Legal Context," 50–51.

Analysis of Hebrews 8:1-13

As we transition into our discussion of Hebrews 8:1-13, two competing thoughts are brought to the fore. First, in light of the discussion above, the language of annulment and obsolescence of the old (Mosaic) covenant found in verse 13 must have certainly sounded alarming to Jewish ears.[100] The social, cultural, religious implications of the abrogation of the Mosaic covenant to a Jewish community would have been devastating. The very identity of the people would have been threatened. Second, what also becomes clear is the fact that the author of Hebrews uses new covenant language for the purpose of shaping the identity of his community. In other words, he uses covenant rhetoric for the same purpose as many of the other Jewish authors previously discussed, namely securing the commitment of his members in the face of external threats.[101]

We must also note that what replaces the old covenant is a new covenant cast in essentially the same mold as the old. Certainly there are differences in these covenants, but the same basic framework exists. The author does not do away with basic covenant categories, but simply argues that the new covenant has superior covenant institutions and elements. For example, the priesthood of Christ in the new covenant is superior to the Levitical priesthood in the old covenant (5:1-10; 7:11-28). The once-for-all sacrifice of Christ is superior to the sacrifices of the old covenant (9:12-14; 10:1-10). And the heavenly tabernacle is superior to the old covenant tabernacle (9:1-11, 23-28). The author does not do away with the basic covenant institutions—he too conceives of a priesthood, a sacrifice, a tabernacle—but he simply argues that the new covenant institutions fulfill the old covenant institutions.

As we shall see, the technique the author employs in his covenant rhetoric is a superior/inferior dialectic. By painting the new covenant, which regulates his community, as superior to the old, he persuades his readers to remain committed to his group and not revert back to Judaism. And yet what is motivating the sociological need to commit and remain in the new covenant community is the theological conviction that they are living in the last days and that Jesus Christ has achieved the final goal of the old covenant by his once-for-all sacrifice.

---

[100] Unlike the Dead Sea Scrolls, Hebrews describes the new covenant not as a renewal of the old, but a replacement of it. See Grässer, *Hebräer*, 2:103.

[101] Jennifer L. Koosed writes, "Outside, the social pressure of the Jewish and Gentile world was threatening group identity and cohesion"; "Double Bind: Sacrifice in the Epistle to the Hebrews," in *A Shadow of Glory: Reading the New Testament after the Holocaust*, ed. Tod Linafelt (New York: Routledge, 2002) 91.

Our exegesis of this text will support the idea that the rhetoric in this passage is used to confirm and legitimize the Christian community as heirs of the new covenant as well as subvert commitment to the competing larger Jewish community. The author uses covenant rhetoric to solidify fidelity to his community and secure the boundaries of those who comprise his group.

Overview of the Argument

In Hebrews 8:1-6,[102] the author transitions in his argument from primarily discussing the legitimacy of Jesus' appointment as high priest to discussing Jesus' role in offering up gifts and sacrifices.[103] Verse 3 is key in understanding what will follow in his discussion, "For every high priest is appointed to offer both gifts and sacrifices."[104] The author is picking up the discussion he began in 5:1, where he stated, "For every high priest taken from among men is appointed on behalf of men in things pertaining to God, *in order to offer both gifts and sacrifices for sins*" (emphasis mine).[105] After fully discussing the legitimacy of Jesus' appointment as high priest (7:1-28), he shifts to the second aspect of the priestly ministry, namely the sacrifices. The author of Hebrews is drawing from the Old Testament conception of the priestly ministry. Koester writes, "given that Jesus is a high priest (5:1-10; 7:1-28), one can conclude that he must offer a sacrifice (8:3a)."[106]

How then is the author's discussion of a better covenant related to Jesus' sacrifice? The author of Hebrews understands Jesus' self-sacrifice as that which inaugurates the new covenant. He draws a parallel between the inauguration of the old covenant and the new covenant in that both required blood. Koester writes, "The Sinai covenant was inaugurated by a blood sacrifice offered by Moses (9:18-20), and the new covenant was

---

[102] Hebrews 8:1-6 sets up the discussion that is to follow through chapter 10. It introduces the topics that will be discussed in greater depth, namely, the heavenly tabernacle in comparison with the earthly (8:1-2, 5; cf. 9:1-28), the better gifts and sacrifices offered by Christ (8:3-4; cf. 10:1-18), and the new covenant (8:6; cf. 8:7-13).

[103] William Lane, *Hebrews 1–8*, WBC 47A (Dallas: Word, 1991) 202. See also Donald A. Hagner, *Hebrews*, NIBC 14 (Peabody, Mass: Hendrickson, 1990) 117.

[104] All New Testament quotations are taken from the NASB unless otherwise noted.

[105] Paul Ellingworth notes that this statement is virtually repeated in 8:3. And yet the phrase ὑπὲρ ἁμαρτιῶν is "kept in reserve for v. 12, the high point of the quotation from Je. 31"; *The Epistle to the Hebrews: A Commentary on the Greek Text*, NIGCNT (Grand Rapids: Eerdmans, 1993) 403.

[106] Koester, *Hebrews*, 382.

inaugurated by the once-for-all sacrifice of Christ (7:22, 8:6-13; 9:15-17; 10:12-18)."¹⁰⁷

Hebrews 8:7-13 functions very specifically to demonstrate why the covenant mediated by Jesus is better than the old and what the better promises of that new covenant are. There are three parts to this section: 1) the introductory claim of the imperfection of the first covenant (8:7-8a); 2) a proof text to support the claim (8:8b-12); 3) and a brief interpretation of the quotation supporting the initial statement (8:13).

Lane argues that the use of the Jeremiah quotation was mainly to expose the inadequacies of the first covenant. "In this setting, the citation of Jer 31:31-34 serves the fundamentally negative purpose of exposing the defective character of the old covenant."¹⁰⁸ Jörg Frey agrees and writes, "Anders als dem Jeremiatext kommt es dem Autor des Hebr zunächst nicht auf die Verheißung des Neuen an, sondern auf die Kritik an der alten διαθήκη, den er dieser Schriftstelle entnimmt."¹⁰⁹ It is precisely because of the negative tone of this section that we need to examine it carefully in our discussion of whether this epistle is anti-Semitic, anti-Judaic, or supersessionist.

The Imperfection of the First Covenant (8:7-8a)

The introductory statement in verse 7, "for if that first covenant had been faultless, there would have been no occasion sought for a second," sets the tone for the short discussion to follow. The type of argument found here is similar to that mentioned in 7:11 regarding the law and priesthood.¹¹⁰ The author uses a contra-factual conditional statement to communicate the inadequacies of the first covenant and the superiority of the second. Lehne sees the hermeneutical pattern of "correspondence, contrast, superiority" throughout Hebrews.¹¹¹ This pattern is certainly applied here in our text.

---

¹⁰⁷ Ibid., 112.

¹⁰⁸ Lane, *Hebrews 1–8*, 208. Cf. Ellingworth, *Hebrews*, 413; A. Vanhoye, "Le Dieu de la nouvelle alliance dans l'Epitre aux Hebreux," in *Le notion biblique de Dieu*, BETL 41 (Louvain: Louvain University Press, 1976) 325.

¹⁰⁹ Jörg Frey, "Die alte und die neue diatheke nach dem Hebräerbrief," in *Bund und Tora*, ed. Friedrich Avemarie and Hermann Lichtenberger, WUNT 92 (Tübingen: Mohr/Siebeck, 1996) 278.

¹¹⁰ Harold W. Attridge, *The Epistle to the Hebrews: A Commentary on the Epistle to the Hebrews*, Hermeneia (Philadelphia: Fortress, 1989) 226–27, n. 18. Cf. Philip E. Hughes, *A Commentary on the Epistle to the Hebrews* (Grand Rapids: Eerdmans, 1977) 297; Ellingworth, *Hebrews*, 411.

¹¹¹ Lehne, *The New Covenant in Hebrews*, 22.

FAULTY FIRST COVENANT (8:7)

In the Greek, the object of the adjective πρώτη is not made explicit, Εἰ γὰρ ἡ πρώτη ἐκείνη ἦν ἄμεμπτος, οὐκ ἂν δευτέρας ἐζητεῖτο τόπος.[112] What is the referent? Is it the λειτουργίας (ministry), ἐπαγγελίαις (promises), or διαθήκης (covenant)? All three are grammatically possible as feminine nouns. And yet the context seems clearly to argue for covenant rather than ministry or promises. What follows from verse 7 is a discussion of the new covenant in contrast to the Sinai covenant. Furthermore, the use of the same adjective πρώτην in verse 13 clearly has the old covenant in view in contrast to the καινήν, or new (covenant) described in the Jeremiah quotation (8:8).

What is quite alarming then is the fact that the author describes this first covenant as having fault. The clear implication of the contra-factual conditional statement, "if the first covenant had been faultless," is that the first covenant was not perfect. Now we must acknowledge that the new covenant language found in the Dead Sea Scrolls never implied any fault with the covenant itself, but rather the people.[113] Therefore the author of Hebrews' statement seems to reflect a greater degree of separation from mainstream Judaism than at Qumran.

The term ἄμεμπτος, or blameless, is used elsewhere in the NT to refer to individuals, usually in the context of being morally or ethically blameless.[114] But here it refers to the Sinai covenant. How are we to understand a covenant having blame or fault? It has fault in that it fails to fulfill God's intentions or goals for the people, namely heart obedience (8:10a), exclusive fidelity to God (8:10b), universal knowledge of God by its members (8:11), and the complete forgiveness of sins (8:12). Instead of placing the fault exclusively on the people, the author of Hebrews indicates that some fault belongs to the covenant itself.[115]

The author reasons that the mention of a new covenant implies that the old one was inadequate.[116] Why would you need a new covenant if the old one did its job properly? And so the author imagines that it was the inadequacies of the first covenant in achieving God's goals and intentions that led to the seeking of another covenant. But who was the one who sought out a second covenant? Clearly from the context, it was

---

[112] Hebrews 8:7.
[113] See above chapter 5, pages 112-115.
[114] See Luke 1:6; Phil 2:15, 3:6; 1 Thess. 3:13.
[115] Koester, *Hebrews*, 385.
[116] This argument is similar to his discussion of the priesthood (7:11) and "rest" (4:8-9).

God himself. Erich Grässer writes, "Die alte Ordnung hat das Verhältnis zu Gott nicht endgültig regeln können (7,19). Darum sucht Gott Raum für eine zweite."[117] The fact that God makes room for a second covenant will be important in answering the question, "how God could institute something that was imperfect?" This question will be addressed later in this chapter.[118]

Blameworthy People (8:8a)

In verse 8, the author shifts the blame from the covenant to the people, "for finding fault with them, he says . . . ."[119] The text here indicates that the problems with the first covenant not only involved the inadequacies of the covenant itself, but also with the people's failure to keep covenant with God. The author was keenly aware that the Jeremiah quotation itself focuses more on the failure of the people rather than the covenant. Therefore, he makes explicit in his introduction of the quotation that God found fault or blame with the people.

The intention of the author to subvert the foundation of the larger dominant Jewish society from which his community emerged is demonstrated in these verses. By pointing out the fault of the first covenant itself, the author leaves his readers no choice but to separate themselves from the community that embraced that covenant. If he were simply speaking about the fault of the people in keeping covenant, there would be some future hope of returning to the first covenant as other more righteous generations emerged (cf. the Qumran Community).

And yet to faithfully utilize the Scripture reference in Jeremiah 31:31-34, the author of Hebrews must temper his critique of the covenant itself to fit the context of the passage. It is this passage that will be used to legiti-

---

[117] Grässer, *Hebräer*, 2:97.

[118] See chapter 5, pages 128–29, 138–39 below.

[119] There is a textual variant here for the word, "them". In ℵ*, A, D*, I, K, P, Ψ, and others, the text has αὐτούς, but in P⁴⁶, ℵ², B, D², M, and others, the text reads αὐτοῖς. Most scholars in either case translate the word "them" as the object of the participle, referring specifically to the people, "Finding fault with them." A minority group, which argues for the dative case αὐτοῖς, understands the object of the participle to be implicitly the covenant and the pronoun to be associated with the verb λέγει. Thus the phrase would be rendered, "While finding fault with it (covenant), He says to them." See Lane, *Hebrews 1-8*, 199–202, esp. n. s; Hughes, *Hebrews*, 298–99, esp. n. 19. Koester, however, argues that this does not fit the author's style, noting that the author usually begins a quote of Scripture simply with a form of λέγειν without an indirect object. See Koester, *Hebrews*, 385. Cf. Attridge, *Hebrews*, 225.

mize his own community as the rightful heirs of the new covenant, which God himself had established.

Use of Jeremiah 31:31-34 (8:8b-12)

The quotation of the Jeremiah text can be broken up into three sections: 1) the introduction of the new covenant in the last days (8:8); 2) the failure of the old covenant (8:9); 3) and the superiority of the new covenant (8:10-11). The quotation itself follows the correspondence, contrast, and superiority pattern found in other parts of the epistle. The author uses this quotation to prove his statement that the covenant, which Jesus mediates, is better than the Sinai covenant.

MT, LXX, and Hebrews

The author of Hebrews quotes the LXX version of Jeremiah 31:31-34 (38:31-34 LXX). The LXX rendering of the MT is fairly faithful with few minor variations. The MT reads, אֶת-בְּרִיתִי הֵפֵרוּ, "they broke my covenant," in 31:32, while the LXX reads, αὐτοὶ οὐκ ἐνέμειναν ἐν τῇ διαθήκῃ μου, "they themselves did not remain in my covenant" in 38:32. In addition the MT reads, וְאָנֹכִי בָּעַלְתִּי בָם, "although I was a husband to them," in 31:32, while the LXX reads, ἐγὼ ἠμέλησα αὐτῶν, "I disregarded them" in 38:32. Another minor variation occurs in 31:33, where the MT uses תּוֹרָתִי, while the LXX in 38:33 uses the plural, νόμους μου. The MT also contains the phrase נְאֻם-יְהוָה in 31:34, though it is absent in the LXX.[120] These variations do not change the essential message of the original Hebrew.

The author of Hebrews' quotation of the LXX also has some minor variations.[121] These differences may be attributed to the author's freedom

---

[120] See Koester, *Hebrews*, 385; Ellingworth, *Hebrews*, 415–17.

[121] The main differences between the Jeremiah 38:31-33 LXX and Hebrews 8:8-10 are in bold print.

or different LXX versions.¹²² While most of these changes are minor stylistic differences, the change from διαθήσομαι (establish) to συντελέσω (complete) may have been intentional in order to further support his argument. The idea of completion is found in other parts of the letter (2:10; 5:9; 7:28).¹²³ Probably then, the author wanted to communicate a sense of finality, fullness, and perfection with the coming of the new covenant.

New Covenant in the Last Days (8:8b)

What seems to be driving the author's comparison between the old and new covenant is the theological understanding that his present community is living in the last days. It is his eschatological outlook that inspires and legitimizes his bold claims. His quotation of Jeremiah 31:31 begins with an understanding that the new covenant will be completed in the coming days (ἡμέραι ἔρχονται, "days are coming"). Otto Michel notes that this phrase, "ist eine bekannte eschatologische Formel und findet sich

Jeremiah 38:31-33 LXX:	Hebrews 8:8-10:
31 ἰδοὺ ἡμέραι ἔρχονται **φησὶν** κύριος καὶ **διαθήσομαι** τῷ οἴκῳ Ἰσραὴλ καὶ τῷ οἴκῳ Ἰούδα διαθήκην καινήν	8b Ἰδοὺ ἡμέραι ἔρχονται, **λέγει** κύριος, καὶ **συντελέσω ἐπὶ** τὸν οἶκον Ἰσραὴλ καὶ ἐπὶ τὸν οἶκον Ἰούδα διαθήκην καινήν,
32 οὐ κατὰ τὴν διαθήκην ἣν **διεθέμην** τοῖς πατράσιν αὐτῶν ἐν ἡμέρᾳ ἐπιλαβομένου μου τῆς χειρὸς αὐτῶν ἐξαγαγεῖν αὐτοὺς ἐκ γῆς Αἰγύπτου ὅτι αὐτοὶ οὐκ ἐνέμειναν ἐν τῇ διαθήκῃ μου καὶ ἐγὼ ἠμέλησα αὐτῶν **φησὶν** κύριος	9 οὐ κατὰ τὴν διαθήκην, ἣν **ἐποί**ησα τοῖς πατράσιν αὐτῶν ἐν ἡμέρᾳ ἐπιλαβομένου μου τῆς χειρὸς αὐτῶν ἐξαγαγεῖν αὐτοὺς ἐκ γῆς Αἰγύπτου, ὅτι αὐτοὶ οὐκ ἐνέμειναν ἐν τῇ διαθήκῃ μου, κἀγὼ ἠμέλησα αὐτῶν, **λέγει** κύριος
33 ὅτι αὕτη ἡ διαθήκη ἣν διαθήσομαι τῷ οἴκῳ Ἰσραὴλ μετὰ τὰς ἡμέρας ἐκείνας **φησὶν** κύριος **διδοὺς δώσω** νόμους μου εἰς τὴν διάνοιαν αὐτῶν καὶ ἐπὶ καρδίας αὐτῶν **γράψω** αὐτούς καὶ ἔσομαι αὐτοῖς εἰς θεόν καὶ αὐτοὶ ἔσονταί μοι εἰς λαόν.	10 ὅτι αὕτη ἡ διαθήκη, ἣν διαθήσομαι τῷ οἴκῳ Ἰσραὴλ μετὰ τὰς ἡμέρας ἐκείνας, **λέγει** κύριος **διδοὺς** νόμους μου εἰς τὴν διάνοιαν αὐτῶν, καὶ ἐπὶ καρδίας αὐτῶν **ἐπιγράψω** αὐτούς, καὶ ἔσομαι αὐτοῖς εἰς θεόν, καὶ αὐτοὶ ἔσονταί μοι εἰς λαόν.

---

122 Koester, *Hebrews*, 385–86. Lane argues against the notion that these changes have interpretive significance and simply attributes them to stylistic changes; *Hebrews 1–8*, 209.

123 See David A. deSilva, *Perseverance in Gratitude: A Socio-Rhetorical Commentary on the Epistle 'to the Hebrews'* (Grand Rapids: Eerdmans, 2000) 285. Attridge argues that this change may be recalling Christ's perfection and the perfection of the believer by the sacrifice of Christ; Attridge, *Hebrews*, 227.

besonders bei Jeremia."[124] For the author of Hebrews, the "coming days" have arrived. He refers to his own time as the "last days" (Heb 1:2; 9:26).[125] And yet there is a sense that the final consummation of all things is still in the future (4:9; 6:11; 10:26-30; 13:14).[126]

This eschatological mindset provides a context in which a radical change of the covenant makes sense. It enables the author to cast the old and new covenants in redemptive historical terms. The second or last will replace the first. There is a sense where the obsolescence of the first covenant is part of God's greater plan. It is in this framework that we can properly understand God's own annulment of the first covenant at the inauguration of the second.

By using this quotation, which describes God himself as the one who establishes the new covenant, the author further legitimizes the new covenant's place within God's redemptive history. This new covenant to which they belong is not independent of the history of Israel, but the climax of it. The author makes no effort to alter the thought that this new covenant will be made "with the house of Israel and with the house of Judah." He sees his present community as those intimately connected with the Jews of the past. The saints in the past as well as the present community are together members of God's house.[127]

FAILURE OF THE SINAI COVENANT (8:9)

Sinai Covenant

When the author writes, "not like the covenant that I made with their forefathers in the day when I took hold of their hand to lead them out of the land of Egypt" (8:9a), he unambiguously identifies the "old" covenant as the Sinai covenant, which was established after the Exodus event. The language used here stresses the discontinuity of the new covenant with the old. The new covenant is not like the old covenant. What was clear from our survey of Second Temple Judaism above is the fact that for the Jewish community, "covenant" essentially meant the Sinai covenant.[128] By pitting

---

[124] Otto Michel, *Der Brief an die Hebräer*, 13th ed., KEK (Göttingen: Vandenhoeck & Ruprecht, 1975) 295. Cf. Jer 7:32; 9:25; 16:14; 23:5,7.

[125] Attridge, *Hebrews*, 227.

[126] Koester, *Hebrews*, 385.

[127] See Heb 3:1-6.

[128] It is true that many Jews saw the Sinai covenant in close connection with the previous covenants, yet the prominent role of the Mosaic law in the community makes it clear that

the Sinai covenant against the new covenant, the author is implicitly distinguishing two separate communities: those who continue to remain in the Sinai covenant and those who enter into the new covenant.

Did Not Continue

The phrase, "For they did not continue in my covenant, and I did not care for them," (8:9b) speaks of the failure of the first covenant. It did not achieve God's intended goals. In fact, though Israel would renew their covenant with God, they eventually failed again and again. The change from the MT from "broke" to "did not continue" in the LXX, indicates the sense that the people continued to break covenant with God. The MT reading could refer to one specific event, perhaps the golden-calf incident in Exodus 32, while the LXX communicates an on-going rebellion.[129] "Not remaining" seems to characterize all things that belong to the old covenant. The Levitical priesthood will not remain, the earthly tabernacle will not remain, the Levitical sacrifices will not remain, the people did not remain in covenant, and here it seems that the old covenant itself will not remain. In contrast are Christ's priesthood (7:3), the heavenly sanctuary (9:11), Christ's sacrifice (9:12, 10:10-14), and implicitly this new covenant and its people.[130]

As a result of the people's continued disobedience, the Lord paid no attention to them. The idea is that he was unresponsive in continuing with his covenant responsibilities. Clearly these words are to cast the old covenant as inadequate and imperfect in achieving God's ultimate goals. The author seeks to diminish confidence, not only in the covenant, but in the community that remains in the old covenant.

Negative Example

The Sinai community functions in this epistle as a negative example for the present community. In 3:7-11, the author of Hebrews quotes Psalm 95:7-11, which warns the readers not to harden their hearts as those in the wilderness. He then exhorts his own readers to "take care, brethren, that there not be in any one of you an evil, unbelieving heart that falls away

---

Sinai covenant defined covenantal life for the Jews. See chapter 5, pages 100-121.

[129] Koester, *Hebrews*, 386. Attridge notes that the rest of the argument does not exploit this criticism of the people. Rather, the author of Hebrews goes on to criticize the institution itself. "The problem with the old covenant is seen to be not in its people, but in its institutions"; Attridge, *Hebrews*, 227; cf. Heb 9:9-10, 10:1-4.

[130] See Koester, *Hebrews*, 386.

from the living God" (3:12). The author clearly uses the Old Testament community as a negative example for his present community.[131]

And so perhaps even here in chapter 8, the author seeks to make a connection with his readers and the Sinai community. If God did not pay attention to those who did not remain in the old covenant, how much more will he not pay attention to those who do not remain in the new covenant? Here too, the Sinai community functions as a negative example for the present community. In this way, the quotation functions to call the present community to covenant faithfulness. It seeks to legitimize and solidify their unique identity as members of the new covenant by pointing out the failure of the old and the negative example of its members.

As much as the author seeks to differentiate the two covenants, he also sees continuity between his present community and the community in the past. The fact that he draws lessons from Israel's past implies that he sees his own community as heirs of this history. The connection between the "house of Israel and house of Judah" (8:8) is made with the author's contemporary hearers as he refers to them as belonging to the same house that Moses served (3:2-6). In addition, he assumes that it was with their "fathers" that the old covenant was made, indicating a genealogical connection with the saints in the past. There is continuity here with the people, but discontinuity with the covenant arrangement.[132]

Superiority of the New Covenant (8:10-12)

Two issues were implied in verse 9. The first was that the people were not able to remain in covenant with God. In other words, they broke his laws. The second was that he gave no heed or paid no attention to them. These issues are resolved in the new covenant. The new covenant will bring about: 1) heart obedience to God (8:10); 2) exclusive covenant fidelity to God (8:10); 3) universal knowledge of God within the new covenant (8:11); and 4) complete forgiveness of sins (8:12). These characteristics lead to the ultimate goal of God's people living in harmony and fellowship with him.[133]

---

[131] Cf. Heb 3:15-19; 4:11. See also Grässer, *Hebräer*, 2:100.

[132] See Koester, *Hebrews*, 389.

[133] In the new covenant they are able to enter into God's rest (4:9-11); approach his throne of grace "with confidence" (4:16); and "come to Mount Zion and the city of the living God, the heavenly Jerusalem . . ." (12:22).

HEART OBEDIENCE (8:10A) In the quotation, God promises, "I will put my laws into their minds, and I will write them on their hearts" (8:10b). There are two different ways in which scholars have taken the idea of having God's laws in one's mind and written on one's heart. The first is an internalization of the laws.[134] One might think of a conscience that is sensitive to God's laws or a desire to keep the intent and letter of the law, not merely external conformity. The second way is "completeness". What is in view here is that the result of having the laws etched in one's mind and heart is complete obedience. The heart and mind act in conformity to the law resulting in faithfulness. Koester understands complete obedience as the primary concern of the author of Hebrews.[135] "This new covenant not only offers forgiveness of past sins but also promises to change hearts and minds so people no longer fall into sin."[136]

Attridge nuances this idea by arguing that the writing of God's laws on their hearts is not demonstrated by the memorization of the law,[137] but by the "cleansing of one's conscience and in true spiritual worship."[138] These blessings of the new covenant are founded upon the sacrifice of Christ, which exemplifies the ultimate internal conformity to God's will or laws. It is this sacrifice that makes one's conscience clean and provides an example of what living with God's laws in one's mind and heart look like.[139]

Those in the new covenant will have a heart obedience to the laws of God that those under the old covenant have never known. The fact that God himself will write the laws on the hearts of the people places their hope and security on God himself. He will equip his people in the new covenant with what they need to keep covenant with him. This heart obedience secured by God's promise clearly places those in the new covenant in a superior position to those in the old covenant. The author makes the

---

[134] Koester, *Hebrews*, 386.

[135] Ibid., 386–87. See also deSilva, *Perseverance in Gratitude*, 285; and Lane, *Hebrews 1–8*, 209.

[136] Koester, *Hebrews*, 391. See also F. F. Bruce, *The Epistle to the Hebrews*, rev. ed., NICNT 58 (Grand Rapids: Eerdmans, 1990) 173; Hughes, *Hebrews*, 298; Hagner, *Hebrews*, 123; V. R. Gordon, "Studies in the Covenantal Theology of the Epistle to the Hebrews in Light of its Setting" (Ph.D. diss., Fuller Theological Seminary, 1979) 112. Other Biblical passages seem to describe the new covenant mentioned in Jer 31:31-34. Cf. Isa 55:3; 61:8; Ezek 11:19-20, 16:59-63; 34:25; 36:26-28, 37:26; Hos 2:18-23; Mal 3:1.

[137] See also Bruce, *Hebrews*, 172.

[138] Attridge, *Hebrews*, 227.

[139] Ibid., 227–28. Attridge wants to make more explicit the central role of the sacrifice of Christ in enabling and motivating the believer's obedience in the new covenant.

contrast in order to legitimize his community over against the dominant Jewish community.

EXCLUSIVE COVENANT FIDELITY TO GOD (8:10B) Second, the Lord promises, "And I will be their God and they shall be my people" (8:10c). This is not a new idea to the covenant relationship. In fact, this is the common thread that unites the major covenants made in the past.[140] And yet it was the failure of the people in remaining in covenant with God that prevented this formulaic declaration from being actually realized. God says, "I did not care for them" (9b). But in the new covenant, the covenant relationship intended in the former covenant will be established.

This particular characteristic was important in the context of the epistle. The wider culture was certainly having its influence on the community in Hebrews. There was a temptation to abandon the community, which in the author's perspective was equivalent to abandoning God and his new covenant.[141] The use of this familiar Jewish phrase, "I will be their God and they shall be my people," (8:10c) functioned to call the community together in their exclusive fidelity to God under the new covenant. Koester writes:

> Socially, identifying with one particular God sometimes led to conflict, and those who abandoned the covenant often did so to accommodate the wider culture. Like earlier generations, the listeners lived in tension with the wider society (10:32-34; 11:25-26; 13:13), but belonging to God's own people offers incentive to remain faithful, knowing that they have no earthly city, but are registered as citizens of God's city (12:22-23, 13:14).[142]

UNIVERSAL KNOWLEDGE OF GOD WITHIN THE NEW COVENANT (8:11) Third, the Lord promises, "and they shall not teach everyone his fellow citizen, and everyone his brother saying, 'know the Lord,' for all will know me, from the least to the greatest of them" (8:11). How are we to understand the fulfillment of this statement? The author of Hebrews himself is teaching his readers and they are told in 5:11-14 that they need teaching. Some have argued that the fulfillment of this aspect of the new covenant is re-

---

[140] Exod 6:7; 29:45; Lev 26:12; Deut 26:17-18; Jer 7:23; 24:7; 30:22; Ezek 11:20; 37:27; Hos 2:23; Zech 8:8; 13:9; 2 Cor 6:16; Rev 21:3. See Koester, *The Epistle to the Hebrews*, 387. Cf. Hughes, *A Commentary on the Epistle to the Hebrews*, 301; Hagner, *Hebrews*, 125.

[141] See Heb 10:23-27.

[142] Koester, *Hebrews*, 392.

served for the future.[143] Now it is certainly true that there is a future element to the complete fulfillment of this aspect of the prophecy. And yet there also seems to be a present fulfillment as well. The prophecy speaks specifically that "all will know me" (8:11). What seems to be in view here is a more comprehensive and universal knowledge of God in the new covenant.[144]

"All" in Jeremiah's context refers to all of Israel. From the perspective of the author of Hebrews, "all" would certainly refer to all in the new covenant. All from every class of people (least to the greatest) will know him beyond mere acknowledgement of his existence, but will trust him and remain loyal to him.[145] F. F. Bruce argues that this more intimate knowledge comes from the new heart God gives each of the members of the new covenant, resulting in a personal knowledge of God, similar to that of Jeremiah himself.[146]

Another aspect to their knowledge of God is their obedience to him. "Evidence that the people did not know the Lord was that they sinned (Isa 1:3-4; Jer 4:22; 9:3; Hos 4:1-3)."[147] The degree of obedience and fidelity to God in the new covenant seems to indicate the difference in knowledge between the old and new covenants. Hughes argues that knowledge of God by all the members of the community was hampered by sin. Thus precisely because of the removal of sin and forgiveness promised in the new covenant, all the people in the new covenant will know God and experience the blessings of his presence.[148]

By using this quotation that describes the members of the new covenant as "fellow citizens,"[149] the author draws upon the notion that they are all citizens of heaven.[150] In addition the fraternal language evokes a

---

[143] Koester argues, "this aspect of the new covenant remains unrealized"; ibid., 387.

[144] See deSilva, *Perseverance in Gratitude*, 286.

[145] Koester, *Hebrews*, 387–88.

[146] Bruce, *Hebrews*, 174–75.

[147] Koester, *Hebrews*, 387.

[148] Hughes, *Hebrews*, 302.

[149] A fellow citizen was a member of one's city. This does not mean, however, that they were all different ethnicities. All the members of a city could belong to the same ethnic group; Koester, *Hebrews*, 387; cf. 2 Macc 9:19; 14:8; 15:30). There is a variant reading πλησίον, "neighbor" that is not as well attested (P, 81, 104, 326, 436, 629 and others). This may have been the result of copyists who wanted to bring the text into greater conformity to a variant LXX text. Πολίτην is found in P^{46}, ℵ, A, B, D K, L and others; Lane, *Hebrews 1–8*, 202.

[150] Hebrews 12:22-23, 13:14.

sense of family and intimacy—all are members of one house (3:6). These terms help forge the identity of the community and the sense of responsibility toward those who remain in the group. How could someone leave or abandon his or her family? How could someone reject his or her citizenship?

The notion that all will know the Lord from the least to the greatest would have also appealed to those who were disappointed with the mainstream Jewish leadership. Those who may have felt marginalized or looked down upon by the religious elite in Judaism would have welcomed this vision of even the least having knowledge of God. This picture creates a sense of equality among the different classes. In addition, the picture of the greatest among those in the new covenant (namely the leaders) having (true) knowledge of God, would have been a comfort to those who have experienced abuse or unfaithfulness from leaders in their past.[151]

COMPLETE FORGIVENESS OF SINS (8:12) The final promise of the new covenant is that God "will be merciful to their iniquities" and will "remember their sins no more" (8:12). The basis of the greater, more extensive knowledge of God is the fact that there will be complete forgiveness of sins. It is this particular aspect of the promise that David deSilva identifies as most significant. The promise is again repeated in 10:17, where the author of Hebrews concludes the whole central section of his epistle (7:1-10:18).[152] Frey also notes the soteriological focus of the promise.

> Das sachliche Novum, das mit der neuen διαθήκη gesetzt ist, ist daher gerade die Wirklichkeit der Sündenvergebung. Die Verheissung ὅτι ἵλεως ἔσομαι ταῖς ἀδικίαις αὐτῶν καὶ τῶν ἁμαρτιῶν αὐτῶν οὐ μὴ μνησθῶ ἔτι (Jer 31 [38], 34b) bildet den Schluss des Zitats in Hebr 8,12 und wird in der verkürzten Reprise des Jeremiawortes, mit der die soteriologische Darlegung in 10,16f. endet, eigens herausgestellt.[153]

It is this particular promise of the new covenant that will set the stage for the lengthy discussion of Christ's once-for-all sacrifice. It is this sacrifice that inaugurates the new covenant (9:15-18) and brings about

---

[151] True knowledge of God seems to imply a fear of God and a desire to do what is right in his sight. In Heb 13:17, the author exhorts his readers to "obey your leaders and submit to them." He describes these leaders as those who must "give an account" to God.

[152] deSilva, *Perseverance in Gratitude*, 286. See also Attridge, *Hebrews*, 228.

[153] Frey, "Die alte und die neue diatheke nach dem Hebräerbrief," 279.

complete forgiveness of sins (10:11-18). In his discussion, the author of Hebrews draws a contrast between the on-going nature of the Levitical sacrifices and the once-for-all sacrifice of Christ.

The reader is left to believe that the ultimate goal of God can only be fulfilled through the new covenant. The old covenant with all its faults is not able to bring about the kind of relationship envisioned by God. And thus, these better promises outlined by this prophecy make it absolutely clear why the new covenant is superior to the old. Clearly the rhetorical intent is to persuade the readers to remain steadfast in their commitment to the present community and the new covenant.

Interpretation of the Jeremiah Quotation (8:13)

The author follows his quotation of the Jeremiah passage with perhaps the most radical statement in the epistle, "When He said, 'a new covenant,' He has made the first obsolete. But whatever is becoming obsolete and growing old is ready to disappear" (8:13). The author is concluding his argument, which began in 8:7, "For if that first covenant had been faultless, there would have been no occasion sought for a second." The fact that a second covenant was sought implies that there was something inadequate with the first. Michel writes, "Die Weissagung auf den ‚Neuen Bund' ist eine verhüllte Kritik am ersten."[154] And so it follows that once the second covenant has been inaugurated, there is no need for the first. What is implied is that the very purpose of the second covenant was to fulfill what the first covenant could not. There is no room or reason for the first covenant to continue, once the second has been established. In other words, the emergence of the second or new covenant renders the first old, null and void.[155] Lane writes, "The principle that a new act of God makes the old obsolete (cf. 7:11-12) reflects an eschatological outlook that perceives the Mosaic and Levitical institutions as fulfilled and superseded by Christ."[156] Ellingworth also notes a common principle in the author of Hebrews discussion of the law/priesthood, covenant, and sacrifice. Namely the rabbinic principle "that a new act of God supersedes the old."[157]

[154] Michel, *Hebräer*, 294.

[155] deSilva, *Perseverance in Gratitude*, 287. See also Attridge, *Hebrews*, 228; Hughes, *Hebrews*, 302; Ellingworth, *Hebrews*, 417.

[156] Lane, *Hebrews 1–8*, 210. See also Bruce, *Hebrews*, 179; Hagner, *Hebrews*, 124; H. W. Montefiore, *The Epistle to the Hebrews*, HNTC (New York: Harper & Row, 1964) 142; Ellingworth, *Hebrews*, 413; Homer A. Kent, "The New Covenant and the Church," GTJ 6 (1985) 295. All these authors use the language of supersession of the old covenant.

[157] Ellingworth, *Hebrews*, 418.

The meaning of πεπαλαίωκεν indicates the end of life, or to become powerless and unproductive.[158] The author uses the perfect tense of παλαιόω[159] to communicate that the old covenant had been declared or made obsolete by the declaration of the new covenant. The results of the obsolescence have their continuing effect even to the time of the author.[160] David deSilva writes, "The old covenant is likened to a law that is outdated and practically out of use. All that remains is to erase it from the books."[161] Thus this first covenant is associated with all things temporal, things that will eventually pass away.

The author states, "and that which is becoming obsolete (παλαιούμενον) and growing old (γηράσκον) is close to nullification" (translation mine). He does not directly state that the Sinai covenant is obsolete or old, but uses the two present participles, παλαιούμενον and γηράσκον[162] without indicating the subject explicitly. Clearly from the context, he refers to the Sinai covenant. And yet, by not explicitly mentioning the Sinai covenant, the author demonstrates a bit of caution as he voices such a radical statement.

The context clearly indicates that the author believed that the end of the Sinai covenant was at hand. He writes that the old covenant is close (ἐγγύς)[163] to being nullified (ἀφανισμοῦ).[164] And yet, this indicates that the covenant is not completely nullified. Why was the author exercising caution in his radical statements about the covenant? Why does he say that the old was *close* to nullification or *soon* to disappear?

---

[158] Koester, *Hebrews*, 388. See also Grässer, *Hebräer*, 2:104.

[159] Two other forms of this verb occur in Luke 12:33 and Heb 1:11. The Luke passage describes a bag that does not grow old. The Hebrews passage is a quote of Psalm 102:26 and contrasts God's creation with God himself. The heavens and the works of his hands will "become old (παλαιωθήσονται) like a garment," but his years "will not come to an end" (1:11). *BDAG* defines the active form of the verb as "to make old, declare/treat as obsolete." See J. H. M. Moulton and G. Milligan, "παλαιόω"; *BDAG* 751.

[160] See Ellingworth, *Hebrews*, 418.

[161] deSilva, *Perseverance in Gratitude*, 287. See also Attridge, *Hebrews*, 228–29, n. 47.

[162] Παλαιούμενον has the same root as πεπαλαίωκεν (παλαιόω). Γηράσκον simply means to grow old or age. See J. H. M. Moulton and G. Milligan, "γηράσκω"; *BDAG* 196. The only other occurrence of the verb γηράσῃς in the New Testament is found in John 21:18, describing Peter as growing old.

[163] The term ἐγγύς is also used in Heb 6:8 referring to the nearness of God's curse upon land that only produces thistles and thorns.

[164] The word, ἀφανισμοῦ, which can be translated "obliteration," in this context means nullification. This has radical implications for those identified with the Sinai covenant. See Koester, *Hebrews*, 388. Cf. Lane, *Hebrews 1–8*, 210.

There seems to be two different ways to understand this phrase. The first is to view the old covenant as being a valid and fully functional institution by which people can come to God, but will soon be made null. The second is to view the old covenant as all but useless at the inauguration of the new covenant, but having some remaining vestiges. What is close to happening then, is the complete nullification or disappearance of an already useless old covenant. The first view sees the transition from the old covenant to the new covenant happening at one time. The second view sees the transition as a process. There is an overlap between the old covenant and the new. From the context, it seems that the second view is correct.[165]

Donald Hagner suggests that the reason the author said that the old covenant was soon to disappear was perhaps because the Levitical rites were still continuing when the epistle was written. Even though they may have still been practiced, according to the author of Hebrews, they were pointless and would not remain. Hagner also suggests that the author may have had in mind Jesus' prophecy of the fall of Jerusalem in Mark 13:2.[166] Therefore, from the author's perspective the old covenant was as good as annulled.

Socio-Rhetorical Function

In order to persuade his audience to remain connected and faithful to his community, the author of Hebrews uses new covenant rhetoric. He identifies his present community as heirs of the new covenant, further solidifying their unique identity separate from the larger Jewish society. By describing the dominant Jewish society's social, cultural, and religious paradigm as obsolete, growing old, and near nullified, the author leaves the reader with no option of returning to the community from which he or she came. It will no longer be a viable option.

The careful formulation of his critique also demonstrates sensitivity to those who hold the Sinai covenant in high regard. By basing his argument upon God's own intention, the author of Hebrews avoids the impression that he is personally antagonistic toward older Jewish practices and traditions. The old covenant was not replaced simply because the people failed

---

[165] The author speaks of the "former commandment" in 7:18 as "set aside" and the Levitical sacrifices associated with the old covenant as "abolished." These strong statements indicate that from the author's perspective, the old covenant institutions are essentially obsolete.

[166] Hagner, *Hebrews*, 124.

to keep it, but because "a new unfolding of God's redemptive purpose had taken place."[167] Lane argues that the fact that God announced the coming of a new covenant in Jer 31:31-34 "indicates that he [God] fully intended the first covenant to be provisional."[168] In essence, the author of Hebrews reasons that God himself, by declaring a new covenant, renders the first obsolete. This particular rhetorical approach is powerful because potential opponents would not want to appear to be arguing against God.

Certainly it was understood by the audience that "legally, a person who made a covenant or testament (*diatheke*) could alter or annul it."[169] Therefore, since God himself made the Sinai covenant, he alone could alter it or render it obsolete. In this way, his strong statements are softened by placing God himself as the initiator of the change. The effect on the reader is that he or she would certainly want to be a part of what will remain, what is new, what has all but replaced the old.

Conclusion

Discontinuity and Continuity

As we reflect upon our analysis of this passage, the two competing ideas are verified. On the one hand there is a sharp discontinuity between the old covenant and the new covenant. The new covenant is "not like the covenant" made with their fathers (8:9). In addition the strong language in 8:7, 13 describes the old covenant as faulty, obsolete, growing old, and as good as annulled. What is implied is that those who continue to live under that covenant will not and cannot achieve the very goals of the covenant. The rhetoric is effective in subverting the religious and social framework of the dominant Jewish society.

On the other hand, there is a strong sense of continuity with the basic worldview of the Israelites. The whole new covenant framework is based and informed by the old. Susan Lehne writes:

> By an ingenious cultic reinterpretation of διαθήκη the writer makes the covenant motif the organizing principle in the text, and employs the same cultic categories to describe the contours of the old and the new orders. Their content, however, is depicted in strongly contrasting colors. But the argument moves beyond these

---

[167] Lane, *Hebrews 1–8*, 209.
[168] Ibid. See also deSilva, *Perseverance in Gratitude*, 283–84.
[169] Koester, *Hebrews*, 388.

contrasts and the main emphasis is placed, not on the shortcomings of the old, but on the superior and definitive nature of the new covenantal order and its priesthood.[170]

Koester writes, "Paradoxically the Day of Atonement ritual in the old covenant (Lev 16) enables Hebrews to present Christ's death as the sacrifice that fulfills the new covenant. In declaring that obsolescence of the old order, Hebrews uses its categories to speak of the new order."[171]

Though the author wants to distinguish his community from the larger Jewish society, he still wants to retain the rich history of his Jewish heritage. It is this historical continuity that legitimizes his community and is effective in persuading fellow Jews to remain committed to his new covenant community.

Also demonstrating the balance between forging the unique identity of the community and retaining the rich Jewish heritage, the author makes prudent use of Hebrew Scriptures. Victor Gordon admits that the passage in 8:13 speaks of the replacement of the old covenant by the new. And yet, the old covenant, though temporary, was not completely worthless as shown by the fact that the author of Hebrews uses the Scriptures of the old covenant as an authority to demonstrate its own replacement.[172]

New Covenant as the Fulfillment of the Old

What is guiding the author of Hebrews' argument is the idea that the new covenant is the eschatological fulfillment of the old covenant. William Lane writes, "The mediation of the new covenant demonstrates the eschatological superiority of Christ's ministry and the divine intention to replace the old arrangement with another that is eschatologically new."[173] In this way, the old covenant was not disparaged in and of itself, but only in the context of a type/anti-type formulation. The old covenant shadows do not compare with the new covenant realities.[174] Donald Hagner writes,

---

[170] Lehne, *The New Covenant in Hebrews*, 103.

[171] Koester, *Hebrews*, 390. Roger L. Omanson remarks, "Various interpreters have observed that the author is not logically consistent since he builds his own model of atonement on the sacrificial system which he rejects"; "A Superior Covenant: Hebrews 8:1—10:18," *RevExp* 82 (1985) 370.

[172] Gordon, "Studies in the Covenantal Theology," 134–35.

[173] Lane, *Hebrews 1–8*, 204.

[174] Though the author does not explicitly use type/anti-type or shadow/reality terms for the covenant, he does use them for various elements of the covenant. For example, the tabernacle and sanctuary, which belong to the first covenant, are described as copies and shad-

The author's courage in expressing to Jewish readers the transitory nature of the Mosaic covenant is notable. It is possible only because the discontinuity is counterbalanced by the underlying continuity of promise and fulfillment stressed by the author throughout the book.[175]

When seen in this redemptive historical framework, the old covenant played a very important role. Philip Hughes points out that the old covenant with its ritual "did more than cry out for the provision of an order that would be effective and abiding: it was also designed to teach that the way of atonement was the way of sacrifice and substitution…"[176] There was a positive function of the old covenant in presenting a framework in which to understand the new covenant. Hagner writes, "The new, the better, has come, but it was nothing other than this to which the old pointed and for which the old prepared the way."[177] Therefore, the old covenant is to be seen as simply playing its role in God's redemptive plan. And upon completion of its role, it is to fade off into the background. It is only in comparison with the new covenant that the old covenant is seen as obsolete.

The idea of fulfillment is very important in understanding the precise relationship between the new and old covenants. William G. Morrice writes, "These references to the covenant in the New Testament all look back to the old covenant; but in looking back they stress the fulfillment of the old order in the new."[178]

The reason why the sharp language of discontinuity with the old covenant was legitimate was because it was cast in this eschatological framework. The great eschatological act of God in the self-sacrifice of the Christ legitimizes the inauguration of a new covenant. Hagner argues that the extreme statements could only be made in the light of the extraordinary Christ event. "Only the eschatological event of Christ's cross and exaltation enable the author to draw his radical conclusion concerning discontinuity."[179]

The identity of the author's community is confirmed, legitimized, and solidified by his use of new covenant language. Their self-understanding as the eschatological community living under the new eschatological cov-

---

ows of heavenly things in 8:5. The tabernacle was a type (τύπον) of heavenly realities (8:5), cf. 9:9, 21-24. The law is also described as a "shadow of good things to come" in 10:1.

[175] Hagner, *Hebrews*, 124.
[176] Hughes, *Hebrews*, 280–81.
[177] Hagner, *Hebrews*, 124. See also Grässer, *Hebräer*, 2:106; Dunnill, *Covenant and Sacrifice*, 230.
[178] William G. Morrice, "New Wine in Old Wine-Skins, XI: Covenant," *ExpTim* 86 (1975) 134.
[179] Hagner, *Hebrews*, 126.

enant would have certainly brought about a greater sense of commitment and fidelity to the community. At the same time, it dissuades its members from forming an alliance with the dominant Jewish society, which was under an inferior covenant. Boundaries are formed by his rhetoric and the choice to stay connected to the new covenant is made obvious.

Anti-Semitism, Anti-Judaism, Supersessionism in Hebrews 8:1-13

As we evaluate the degree to which Hebrews 8:1-13 can be considered anti-Semitic, anti-Judaic or supersessionist, we must keep in mind the Jewish context in which the author of Hebrews wrote. The term "anti-Semitism" is clearly not an adequate description of the passage. As mentioned in chapter 4, the term itself emerged in the 19th century and has to do more with ethnic or racial differences.[180] The picture that has been painted from our analysis more aptly describes the situation as a theological disagreement among Jews. All are members of "one house," whose fathers received the old covenant (8:8-9).

Anti-Judaism

The polemic in this passage, however, could be described as anti-Judaic in the sense that it spoke against the old covenant and functioned to distinguish the author's community from the dominant Jewish society.[181] The epistle clearly calls its readers to separate themselves from the old covenant practices, rituals, and life.[182] Therefore it seems clear that the author was indeed speaking against the Sinai covenant. The real question at hand, however, is whether his polemic against the Sinai covenant necessarily equates to polemic against the Jewish people?

It is true that the Sinai covenant probably functioned more than anything else as an identity marker for the Jews, mainly because of its close association with the Law. To be a Jew in many communities meant to be in the Mosaic covenant. However, we must keep in mind that the significance of the Mosaic covenant was derived primarily from the fact that

---

[180] See above "Introduction," pages 2-3.

[181] Following Douglas Hare's distinctions, the polemic in this passage can best be described as "Jewish-Christian anti-Judaism, which are criticisms of Judaism by Jews who believe Jesus is Messiah." See Douglas R. A. Hare, "The Rejection of the Jews in the Synoptics and Acts," in *Anti-Semitism and the Foundations of Christianity,* ed. A. T. Davies (New York: Paulist, 1979) 28-32.

[182] Hebrews 9:11-14; 10:1-2; 13:9-10.

God himself established it as the means by which his people should relate to him. Therefore we can view the Mosaic covenant simply as a means to an end. What was truly significant for the identity of the people was their relationship with God. The Sinai covenant was simply the means by which that relationship was established and maintained.

Therefore, the polemic against the Mosaic covenant does not necessitate polemic against the Jewish people. The author of Hebrews is not speaking against Jews, but what he considers an older, outdated covenant. By using Jeremiah 31:31-34, the author argues that God himself calls for a replacement of the old covenant by the new covenant. Thus the identity of the Jews as God's people can be retained, while the means by which that relationship is governed can change.[183]

We conclude that Hebrews 8:1-13 does not promote hatred or the destruction of the Jewish people. Rather, it promotes what the author understands as God's true intention for the Jewish nation in entering the new covenant in the last days. The polemic against the old covenant can be seen then as that which is for the benefit of the Jewish nation. It is a declaration that God himself has provided a new and better way for his people to draw near to him.

Supersessionism

What has been argued in this paper is that the author of Hebrews was indeed supporting the supersession or perhaps better, the fulfillment of the Sinai covenant.[184] There are some scholars who have tried to limit or blunt the radical nature of the author of Hebrews' statements. For example, Steven L. McKenzie limits the supersessionism in Hebrews simply to the cultic elements of the law, rather than the entire Jewish system.[185] McKenzie writes, "Hence, as we have seen, the designation 'obsolete,' as Hebrews 8:13 uses it, is not appropriate for Judaism."[186] He notes that the New Testament and Christianity have at its base the heritage of Judaism and its several covenants. Certainly we would agree with McKenzie on this

---

[183] When the Mosaic covenant itself was inaugurated, there was a change in how God related to his people. And yet this change did not imply a rejection of the Jewish people. The identity of the people remained, while the means by which they were governed changed.

[184] Fulfillment better communicates both the continuity and discontinuity in the relationship between the old covenant and the new covenant. The new covenant is connected with the old covenant. However, like supersessionism, the term fulfillment also implies the obsolescence of the former at the arrival of the latter. See Donald Hagner, "A Positive Theology of Judaism from the New Testament," *SEÅ* 69 (2004) 14.

[185] Steven McKenzie, *Covenant* (St. Louis: Chalice, 2000) 118.

[186] Ibid., 120.

point. And yet, we cannot get around the language found in 8:13, which speaks of the obsolescence of the first covenant.[187]

McKenzie clearly wants to highlight the common heritage shared by contemporary Judaism and Christianity and the many lessons Christians can learn from the Jewish faith. And so he concludes, "Supersessionism, then, is unwarranted and is not endorsed by the New Testament. Judaism is not defunct."[188] This statement can only be affirmed if what he means is that the New Testament does not endorse the replacement or destruction of the Jewish people. But if McKenzie is speaking about the religious system regulated by the Sinai covenant, then he is clearly misreading Hebrews. The author of Hebrews was in essence arguing that the Sinai covenant as a means to approach God was obsolete at the revelation of the new and better way in Jesus Christ. This does not mean to say that ethnic Jews are somehow to be disparaged. The author of Hebrews is arguing theologically and pastorally about the means by which sins are forgiven and the covenant relationship is established and secured.

John Fischer, who also attempts to tame the strong language of discontinuity in the epistle, argues that the new covenant according to the author of Hebrews was not so much a different covenant, but a renewed covenant.[189] He writes, "The 'new covenant' is not really 'new'; it is only a true exegesis of Moses. The newness of the covenant is subjective and psychological: in Jeremiah's terms, it is the writing of the law on the heart."[190] Fischer does not disagree that Jesus does fulfill Judaism, but argues that fulfillment does not necessitate abrogation. He points to Matt 5:17 and shows that Jesus himself pits "abolish" and "fulfill" as opposites.[191] In the end, Fischer argues that the epistle to the Hebrews does not set aside Jewish identity and practice. Though it is true that fulfillment does not necessitate abrogation, the text in Heb 8:13 clearly makes this implication for the covenant. Fischer cannot get around the radical language found in the epistle.

John Dunnill agrees with McKenzie and Fischer and argues that the author of the epistle does not promote the new order by "denigrating or setting aside the old."[192] "A tactic more representative of the book, though,

---

[187] It is this covenant, which essentially defined the entire Jewish system.

[188] McKenzie, *Covenant*, 120–21.

[189] John Fischer, "Covenant Fulfillment and Judaism in Hebrews," *ERT* 13 (1989) 176.

[190] Ibid., 177.

[191] Ibid., 179; see also Roy A. Harrisville, "The Concept of Newness in the New Testament." *JBL* 74 (1955) 74.

[192] Dunnill, *Covenant and Sacrifice*, 229.

is to praise the new covenant and its agents, expressing moderated criticism of the old through the use of comparative formulae."[193] But does not the superior/inferior rhetorical approach automatically denigrate that which is old?

In his discussion of Heb 8:6-13, William Lane appeals to Jeremiah's understanding of these covenants as "dialectical" and not necessarily polemical. The old covenant is the shadow and example and though there are differences, there will also be continuity. He sees this comparison as a hermeneutical method highlighting the fulfillment of a promise that seemed to be questioned by the readers.[194] Certainly there is the aspect of shadow and fulfillment as was argued above. And yet this fact does not seem automatically to relieve the language of its polemical tone. The author of Hebrews sets up the quotation by describing the first covenant as having fault (8:7) and then speaking of its obsolescence and nullification (8:13). Verse 13 is the climax of his argument. The emphasis is clearly on the negative side. The author did not have to make this statement if he was simply trying to encourage his readers to remain committed to God. Clearly the author is speaking in a social context in which there is a real threat of retroversion back to the dominant Jewish faith.

It is much more reasonable to identify the language used in the epistle as polemical. The author clearly wants to cast the old covenant in a negative light in order to convince his readers to maintain their relationship in his community under the new covenant. Susan Lehne also argues that there is a polemical tone in this epistle.

> While many interpreters would deny the polemical intent of Heb. and think that the OT functions simply as a foil for the writer's theological exposition, we do not find such explanations adequate. It may not be possible to identify a particular group at which the author's treatise is aimed, but the whole tenor and tone of his work can be accounted for much better if one sees polemics at work.[195]

---

[193] Ibid.

[194] Robert Wall and William Lane, "Polemic in Hebrews and the Catholic Epistles," in *Anti-Semitism and Early Christianity: Issues of Polemic and Faith* (Minneapolis: Fortress, 1993) 180–81. Cf. Lane, *Hebrews 1–8*, cxxxiii. Grässer argues similarly. He writes, "Der Hebr polemisiert nicht gegen das nachchristliche Judentum. Seine Diastase lautet himmlisch/irdisch, nicht jüdisch/christlich. Er malt den himmlischen Kult vor dem Hintergrund des irdischen, um seinen überragenden Glanz deutlich werden zu lassen" (Grässer, *Hebräer*, 2:107). The author of Hebrews is not simply bringing up the old covenant to highlight the new, but he is also addressing a very real threat of reversion. Certainly he is not attacking individual Jews, but he does seek to highlight the superiority of the new covenant against the old covenant in order to maintain allegiance to his community.

[195] Lehne, *The New Covenant in Hebrews*, 103.

She concludes, "Paradoxically enough, it is the writer of Heb. who—while passionately arguing along Jewish lines—moves furthest in the direction of the breach with Judaism that was later to take place."[196]

Conclusion

From our analysis, we conclude that Hebrews 8:1-13 can be considered anti-Judaic in the sense that it was arguing against the Sinai covenant as the definitive means by which to commune with God. The author believed the old covenant was fulfilled by the new covenant. In his understanding of God's redemptive plan, the old and new covenants could not exist together for a prolonged period of time. His use of new covenant rhetoric did indeed seek to create boundaries between his community and the larger Jewish society from which he came. It also functioned to reinforce his community's unique identity as the eschatological community of God.

Even though his polemic struck at the very heart of the dominant Jewish religion and culture, it was replaced by an equally Jewish system. The author's conception of the new covenant was informed by the categories formed from the old covenant and intimately connected with the history of the Jewish people. Therefore his words in Hebrews 8:1-13 cannot be characterized as anti-Judaism that promotes hostility or hatred toward Jews; nor is the author arguing for the complete abandonment of the Jewish people by God. Rather Hebrews 8:1-13 simply reflects a Jewish theological and eschatological perspective for the benefit of the Jews in light of the revelation of Jesus Christ.

---

[196] Ibid., 124.

6

Sacrifice and Polemic in Hebrews 10:1-10

THE final passage that we will discuss is Hebrews 10:1-10. We will specifically examine the author's rhetoric against the Levitical sacrifices and how this rhetoric functions in the author's social context. Could this polemic be considered anti-Semitism, anti-Judaism? Does it advocate supersessionism?

Following the pattern established in chapters 4 and 5, there will be three major sections in this chapter. In the first section, we will seek to determine how the Levitical sacrifices functioned within the Jewish community and how important they were to the identity of the Jewish people. In the second section we will examine Heb 10:1-10, not only to determine the meaning of the text, but also to identify its socio-rhetorical function in the community. In the final section we will discuss whether the author's polemic against the Levitical sacrifices promotes hostile attitudes toward the Jewish people.

Levitical Sacrifices in the Second Temple Period

Our examination of Levitical sacrifices in Second Temple Jewish writings will help us understand how the author of Hebrews polemic against the sacrifices was understood in the Jewish context. Not only will we identify the importance of the Levitical sacrifices to the identity of the Jewish people, but we will also determine how other Jewish writers used sacrifice rhetoric. This will shed light on how the author of Hebrews uses sacrifice rhetoric.

In our survey of Second Temple Jewish literature, it will become clear that the Levitical sacrifices had a prominent place in the religious life of the Jewish people. Sacrifices were the means by which Jews were able to approach God. Many of the authors wrote zealously about the need to keep the Levitical sacrifices pure and acceptable to God. Included in this type of rhetoric was not only a desire to offer up sacrifices according to the Jewish law, but also a polemic against those Jews who would offer up sacrifices in an improper manner. As a result, one's view and practice of sacrifices functioned as an identity marker for those in the community. The rhetoric used by these authors rallied their communities to greater fidelity and faithfulness to their common set of beliefs, thereby strengthening the identity of the community within their larger social context.

There is also another strain of thought in some of these writings that argues against an *ex opere operato* view of sacrifice. These authors emphasize the need for piety and repentance when giving offerings. Some authors reinterpret or spiritualize sacrifice as praise, service, martyrdom, etc. Much of this rhetoric was a response either to a mechanical view of sacrifice or to some disappointment with the cult and its service. Many of these authors pick up these themes from the Hebrew Bible itself. E. E. Carpenter writes that there are several passages in the Old Testament that indicate "the rejection, condemnation, or fate of a corrupt Israelite system of sacrifices and offerings. Both the officiants and the worshipers themselves are involved in the guilt."[1] There are also passages in the Hebrew Bible that spiritualize sacrifices.[2] James Thompson writes, "There was an old Palestinian tradition extending to the psalms and prophets which had condemned any belief in the automatic efficacy of sacrifices, demanding in its place a 'sacrifice of thanksgiving' or deeds of mercy."[3]

Apocrypha and Pseudepigrapha

What runs throughout the pseudepigraphical and apocryphal writings examined in this chapter is the idea that the Levitical sacrifices functioned as an identity marker for the Jewish people. It was the Law-prescribed means by which the people in the community were able to approach God. Those on the inside of the community were to remain faithful to the Law and its sacrificial prescriptions. Unfaithfulness to these prescriptions resulted in God's disfavor and exclusion from the community.

---

[1] E. E. Carpenter, "Sacrifices and Offerings in the OT," in *ISBE* 4:270. See Amos 4:4; 5:21-25; Hos 8:11-13; 12:12; 13:2; Isa 1:10-15; 43:23-25; 57:6; 65:3-11; 66:3, 17; Jer 6:20; 7:21-31; 11:15; 14:12; 19:5; 32:25; Hab 1:16; Ezek 16:15-21; 20:25-31; 23:36-39; Mal 1:7-8; 3:8-9.

[2] See Ps 4:6; 26:6-7; 50:8-14; 51:17f–18.; 69:32; 107:22; 116:17; 119:108; 141:2.

[3] James W. Thompson, "Hebrews 9 and Hellenistic Concepts of Sacrifice," *JBL* 98 (1979) 567.

Jubilees

The pseudepigraphical writing, *Jubilees*[4] recounts the history of Israel as God himself disclosed it to Moses on Mount Sinai. This work was written to inspire its readers to maintain their allegiance to the Mosaic covenant and all its practices. Interspersed through this history are somewhat anachronistic elaborations or amplifications of Biblical accounts. There are descriptions of Adam, Enoch, Noah, Abraham, Isaac, Jacob, and Levi offering sacrifices in language that is taken from the Mosaic Law.

For example, Adam is described—after being covered by garments of skin—as "offering a sweet smelling sacrifice—frankincense, galbanum, stacte, and spices—in the morning with the rising of the sun from the day he covered his shame."[5] The author of *Jubilees* also describes Noah offering up sacrifices preceding the account of his drunkenness. "And on that day he made a feast with rejoicing. And he made a burnt offering to the Lord, one calf from the bulls, one ram, a lamb of seven years, and one kid of the goats in order that he might thereby seek atonement for himself and his sons."[6] In addition, *Jub.* 16:20-23 describes Abraham after the birth of Isaac celebrating the feast of booths:

> And he built an altar there to the Lord who delivered him and who made him rejoice in the land of his sojourn. And he celebrated a feast of rejoicing in this month, seven days, near the altar which he built by the Well of the Oath. And he built booths for himself and for his servants on that festival. And he first observed the feast of booths on the earth. And in these seven days he was making offering every day, day by day, on the altar a burnt offering to the Lord: two bulls, and two rams and seven lambs, one kid on behalf of sins so that he might atone thereby on behalf of himself and his seed. And a thank offering: seven rams and seven sheep and seven lambs and seven he-goats and their (fruit) offerings and their libations and all their fat he offered upon the altar as chosen burnt offering to the Lord for sweet-smelling odor.[7]

---

[4] For dating, see page 101, footnote 4 in chapter 5.

[5] *Jubilees* 3:27. Cf. Exod 30:34. There is of course no mention of sacrifice in the Genesis 3:21-24 account of God covering Adam and Eve with garments of skin.

[6] *Jubilees* 7:3. Cf. Num 29:2-5. The text in *Jubilees* continues to describe blood being placed on the altar, the fat and flesh of the animals placed on the altar, and the sprinkling of wine and frankincense (7.4-6). There is no account of this sacrifice in the Gen 9:20-29 account.

[7] *Jubilees* 16:20-23. Cf. Num 29:12-40; Deut 16:13-15. This is an amplification of the Gen 21:8 account.

The author of *Jubilees* wants to legitimize the Law and its practices by rewriting them back into the history of Israel.[8] He emphasizes the eternal nature of the Law and its regulations by demonstrating that they have always been a part of Israel's history. This association links the sacrificial language of the Mosaic Law to the very history and identity of God's people. The importance of keeping these regulations is thus emphasized.

Jubilees 22.16-17 describes Abraham's blessing of Jacob. In this blessing he explicitly warns Jacob of associating with Gentiles. Part of Abraham's tirade against Gentiles includes a deprecation of their sacrifices. "They slaughter their sacrifices to the dead, and to demons they bow down. And they eat in tombs."[9] This polemic against Gentiles and their sacrifices functions to set up boundaries for the existing community. Those who belong to the Jewish community worship through the Law-prescribed sacrifices. In this way, the Levitical sacrifices themselves function as identity markers for the Jews, separating them from the Gentile world.

Liber antiquitatum biblicarum (Pseudo-Philo)

The writing *Liber antiquitatum biblicarum* (Pseudo-Philo)[10] also recounts the history of Israel with some fanciful expansions and traditions. What is emphasized in this writing is the need for Israel to separate from Gentiles and pagan worship. D.J. Harrington argues that according to *Liber antiquitatum biblicarum* (*L.A.B.*), "Idolatry and mixed marriage are the most reprehensible sins against the law."[11]

Golden Calf Incident

The author of *L.A.B.* describes the law of the altar given to Moses in 13.2-3, directly following the account of the golden calf incident,[12]

> This is the law of the altar, according to which you will sacrifice to me and pray for your own souls. Now regarding what you will offer to me, from the cattle offer the calf and the sheep and the goat, but from the birds the turtledove and the dove. And if there be leprosy in your land and the leper be cleansed, they will take for the Lord two live chicks and cederwood and hyssop and scarlet;

---

[8] See also *Jub.* 4:25; 6:1-3; 21:7-9; 22:3-5; 32:4-15.
[9] *Jubilees* 22:17.
[10] For dating, see page 107, footnote 34 in chapter 5.
[11] Harrington, "Pseudo-Philo," 2:301.
[12] Cf. Exod. 32:1-14.

and he will approach the priest, and he will kill the one chick but keep the other alive.[13]

By placing this account directly after his rendering of the golden calf incident, the author forms a sharp contrast between unacceptable worship and acceptable worship. The author clearly wants to encourage his readers to follow closely the prescribed way to approach and worship God.

Covenant Renewal at Gilgal

In his description of Joshua's covenant renewal at Gilgal, the author of *L.A.B.* does not fail to mention the offering of sacrifices, a major element in the renewal ceremony. After writing the law of God on large stones, Joshua "came down with them and offered peace offerings on the altar; and all sang many praises."[14] Joshua is here described as a second Moses, further emphasizing the need to remain faithful to the Law.

Competing Altar Across the Jordan

The fact that the author of *L.A.B.* was speaking against unfaithfulness in offering up sacrifices according to the Law is also demonstrated in his retelling of the Joshua 22:10-34 account. The Old Testament account describes the sons of Reuben and the half-tribe of Manasseh building a competing altar on the other side of the Jordan River. Once the sons of Israel heard about this, they interpreted it as rebellion against the Lord and were ready to make war with them. The sons of Reuben and the half tribe of Manasseh responded by saying that the altar was simply a memorial signifying for the generations to come that they are indeed brothers and share the same inheritance.

> Therefore we said, "Let us build an altar, not for burnt offering or for sacrifice; rather it shall be a witness between us and you and between our generations after us, that we are to perform the service of the Lord before Him with our burnt offerings and with our sacrifices and with our peace offerings, so that your sons will not say to our sons in time to come, 'you have no portion in the Lord.'"[15]

---

[13] Ps.-Philo 13.2-3. Cf. Lev 1:1, 10, 14; 14:2-6.

[14] Ps.-Philo 21.8. Cf. 21.9; Jos 8:30-35. *Liber antiquitatum biblicarum* does not diverge very much from the Biblical account in its recounting of the offerings associated with this covenant renewal ceremony.

[15] Joshua 22:26-27. All Biblical quotations will be taken from the New American Standard Version unless otherwise stated.

The author of *L.A.B.* retells this story and describes the sons of Reuben and the half tribe of Manasseh's response differently. They claimed that they built the altar not out of wickedness,

> but rather for our posterity's sake so that their heart may not be separated from the Lord our God and that they may not say to us, "Behold our brothers who are across the Jordan have an altar and offer sacrifice on it, but we in this place do not have an altar and are far from the Lord our God; for our God is so far from our ways that we may not serve him." And on saying these words, we said among ourselves, "Let us make an altar for ourselves so that there may be zeal among us for seeking the Lord," For some of us who stand here did this.[16]

What is noticeably absent in the *L.A.B.* account is the clear statement that they were not planning on offering burnt offerings upon the altar and that it was simply a memorial. Joshua is then recorded as chiding his brothers and calling them to meditate more on the law of God so that they would not be led astray in making a man-made altar.[17] The people are then encouraged to dig up the altars and to teach their children the Law.[18] Afterward, Joshua offers up 1000 rams for their sins and destroys the competing altar.[19]

It seems that the author of Pseudo-Philo alters the Biblical account to better reflect the issues he seeks to address, namely, the practice of offering sacrifices contrary to the prescriptions of the Law. Thus the author uses pseudo-history to communicate the need to remain faithful to the Law in offering up sacrifices. He establishes a greater sense of legitimacy and authority for his argument by drawing upon the biblical account.

Psalms of Solomon

We read in the *Psalms of Solomon*[20] a sharp polemic against those who do not give proper reverence and respect to the sacrifices prescribed in the Law of Moses. These psalms describe the frustration of a group of devout Jews who are disappointed with the Jewish political and religious leader-

---

[16] Ps.-Philo 22.3-4.

[17] Ps.-Philo 22.5.

[18] Ps.-Philo 22.6.

[19] Ps.-Philo 22.7.

[20] For dating, see page 68, footnote 21 in chapter 4.

ship at the time of the capture of Jerusalem by the Romans.[21] In the eighth Psalm the author identifies the sins of the people as the underlying reason for the capture of Jerusalem. Aside from incestuous practices, sins relating to the sacrificial cult are identified.

> They stole from the sanctuary of God as if there were no redeeming heir. They walked on the place of sacrifice of the Lord, (coming) from all kinds of uncleanness; and (coming) with menstrual blood (on them), they defiled the sacrifices as if they were common meat. There was no sin they left undone in which they did not surpass the gentiles.[22]

One's attitude toward sacrifice defines one's inclusion or exclusion from this community of devout Jews. Those who treat these sacrifices lightly or impiously are those who are condemned and excluded. What is implied then, is that those who revere these sacrifices and remain faithful in offering them remain inside the community. The author seems to base his boundary-forming rhetoric on the fact that God himself excludes those who do not remain faithful to his cultic law.

JUDITH

In addition to the theme of remaining faithful to the prescriptions of the Law regarding sacrifice, the following apocryphal writings also emphasize the need for a proper attitude in bringing offerings to God. These writers reiterate the biblical contrast between obedience and sacrifice. Yet none of these writers argues for the complete replacement or annulment of the Levitical sacrifices.

The book of Judith[23] was written to inspire Jews to fear the Lord in the face of Gentile threats. Much of the sacrificial rhetoric functions to solidify commitment to the Jewish identity and faith.

Role, Function, and Importance of Sacrifice

The two explicit references to Levitical sacrifices occur at the beginning and at the end of the story. At the beginning of the narrative, sacrifices were offered at the Temple when the Assyrian army threatened the Jews. "The high priest Joakim and all the priests who stood before the Lord and ministered to the Lord, with sackcloth around their loins, offered the daily

---

[21] Wright, "Psalms of Solomon," 2:639.
[22] *Pss. Sol.* 8.11-13.
[23] For dating, see page 106, footnote 31 in chapter 5.

burnt offerings, the votive offerings, and freewill offerings of the people."[24] Concomitant with these sacrifices were prayers and fasting. Clearly the role of the sacrifices was to curry the favor of the Lord. They were signs of devotion and piety, which not only identified the people with their God but also functioned as the means by which they approached him with their petitions.

At the end of the story, after Judith leads the Jews to military victory over the Assyrian army, the people worship and celebrate at the temple by giving offerings and sacrifices. "When they arrived at Jerusalem, they worshiped God. As soon as the people were purified, they offered their burnt offerings, their freewill offerings, and their gifts" (16:18). Whether they were petitioning God or worshipping God with thanksgiving, the Jews came to God with sacrifices. The descriptions of faithfulness to these rites encourage the readers also to remain faithful to their identity as Jews in their appropriation of these sacrifices.

The importance of the sacrificial system is not only demonstrated in the explicit references to sacrifice, but implicitly in the story itself. One of the greatest concerns brought out in Judith is the need to preserve and protect the Jewish cultic system and sanctuary. The author describes the Assyrian army general's (Holofernes) practice of destroying the religious institutions of the land he conquered, "And he demolished all their shrines and cut down their sacred groves; for it had been given to him to destroy all the gods of the land, so that all nations should worship Nebuchadnezzar only, and all their tongues and tribes should call upon him as god."[25] When the Jews heard about these practices, they "were therefore very greatly terrified at his approach, and were alarmed both for Jerusalem and for the temple of the Lord their God."[26] The concern to preserve the existing religious institutions in the face of foreign threats was very relevant to the readers of this story. The positive outcome at the end only served to encourage the audience to continue in their zeal to maintain the purity and boundaries of their community in the face of Gentile threats.

In Judith's deception of Holofernes, she tells him that when the people sin against God by desecrating their tithes, then and only then will he be able to defeat them,

> Therefore, lord and master, do not disregard what he said, but keep it in your mind, for it is true. Indeed our nation cannot be

---

[24] Judith 4:14.
[25] Judith 3:8.
[26] Judith 4:2.

punished, nor can the sword prevail against them, unless they sin against their God. But now, in order that my lord may not be defeated and his purpose frustrated, death will fall upon them, for a sin has overtaken them by which they are about to provoke their God to anger when they do what is wrong. Since their food supply is exhausted and their water has almost given out, they have planned to kill their livestock and have determined to use all that God by his laws has forbidden them to eat. They have decided to consume the first fruits of the grain and the tithes of the wine and oil, which they had consecrated and set aside for the priests who minister in the presence of our God at Jerusalem—although it is not lawful for any of the people so much as to touch these things with their hands.[27]

The underlying assumption here is that God is in control and obedience or disobedience to him will determine the fate of the Jews. This is the worldview of the author, who also wants to communicate this point to the readers. Therefore, according to Judith, keeping the sacrificial law was very much a part of the identity and worldview of the Jewish people.

Sacrifices versus Fear of the Lord

There is also a subtle polemic against sacrifices in this writing. Judith 16:16 reads, "For every sacrifice as a fragrant offering is a small thing, and the fat of all whole burnt offerings to you is a very little thing; but whoever fears the Lord is great forever." The contrast is unmistakable. The leaders of Israel offered sacrifices, but did not demonstrate any genuine fear of the Lord. Judith on the other hand, because of her fear of the Lord, offered a better sacrifice—Holfernes' head.

Amy-Jill Levine makes the connection between Judith's slaying of Holofernes and the celebratory sacrifices that are given up to the Lord in Jerusalem.

> This celebration in Jerusalem (16:18-20) reappropriates the sacrifice in 13:6-9. The initial ritualized killing, which included the purification and festive garbing of the celebrant, her sexual abstinence, the painless slitting of the victim's throat (he being "overcome with wine" [13:2]), the aid of the assistant in disposing of the parts, the retention of a portion of the sacrifice for the community, and the efficacy that such an offering brings to Israel as a whole is given its full value only when the account—and the vessels, the

---

[27] Judith 11:10-13.

canopy, and the general's head—become part of the communal celebration.[28]

This subtle polemic against offerings without faith or reverence to God communicates to the readers that there is a proper way to approach God and an improper way. Judith's sacrifice was superior because it was grounded by a genuine faith. Those reading this story are persuaded to follow her example and reject simply offering sacrifices without faith or godly fear. What is important to note, however, is the fact that this subtle polemic in no way argues for an annulment or abandonment of the Levitical sacrifices.

The book of Judith clearly validates the premise that the Levitical sacrifices prescribed in the Law were very important to the identity and faith of the Jewish people. The sacrificial rhetoric in this writing serves to encourage the Jewish community to remain faithful to their Jewish identity and faith. The subtle polemic against the leaders also functions to promote and legitimize a very non-capitulating stance toward foreign powers and a definition of true sacrifice as that which is grounded by faith and godly reverence.

Prayer of Azariah / Song of the Three Young Men

The Prayer of Azariah[29] was written during a time when Jerusalem had been taken by foreign powers and there were, therefore, no sacrifices and offerings. "In our day we have no ruler, or prophet, or leader, no burnt offering, or sacrifice, or oblation, or incense, no place to make an offering before you and to find mercy."[30]

It is in this context that the prayer acknowledges the legitimacy of spiritualizing the sacrifices prescribed by the Law. The men thrown into the furnace, presumably as martyrs, hope that God would accept them as if they had given many sacrifices because of their devotion and piety. Azariah prays,

> Yet with a contrite heart and a humble spirit may we be accepted, as though it were with burnt offerings of rams and bulls, or with tens of thousands of fat lambs; such may our sacrifice be in your

---

[28] Amy-Jill Levine, "Sacrifice and Salvation: Otherness and Domestication in the Book of Judith," in *No One Spoke Ill of Her: Essays on Judith,* ed. James C. Vanderkam, SBLEJL 2 (Atlanta: Scholars, 1992) 26.

[29] For dating, see page 105, footnote 22 in chapter 5.

[30] Pr. Azar. 1:15.

sight today, and may we unreservedly follow you, for no shame will come to those who trust in you.³¹

Adrian Schenker points out that both the Prayer of Azariah and the Song of the Three Young Men³² compare martyrdom to sacrifices and offerings given in Jerusalem. He writes,

> Quant à la prière d'Azarias dans sa place narrative, elle voit le martyre prendre le relais du culte supprimé et interdit. Le culte était en effet confession de Dieu; célébrer la liturgie signifiait vénérer le Seigneur, l'adorer, lui rendre hommage. Or, c'est précisément la signification profonde du martyre! . . . Pour sa part, Sg 3,6 compare le martyre à l'offrande de l'holocauste parce que les deux sont agree par le Seigneur, et puisque les deux experiment le meme besoin d'honorer Dieu par les dons les plus grands.³³

This seems to indicate that the idea of sacrifice for the Jewish people signified one's devotion to God. It was an act of devotion by which the worshiper sought to please God. The authors of these writings seek to inspire Jews living in a hostile context to remain faithful to God and their Jewish heritage, even to the point of martyrdom. Lines of inclusion and exclusion are drawn by the use of sacrificial language.

Sirach / Ecclesiasticus

Sirach is also thought to be a response to the threat of Hellenism in the Jewish communities.³⁴ There are strong admonitions to remain faithful to Jewish laws and practices.

Importance of Levitical Sacrifices

In regard to sacrifices, several passages speak of the need to follow the sacrificial prescriptions of the Law. Sirach 7:31 reads, "Fear the Lord and honor the priest, and give him his portion, as you have been commanded: the first fruits, the guilt offering, the gift of the shoulders, the sacrifice of sanctification, and the first fruits of the holy things." In addition, Sirach

---

[31] Pr. Azar. 1:16-7.

[32] For dating, see page 105, footnote 25 in chapter 5.

[33] Adrian Schenker, "'Et comme le sacrifice de l'holocauste il les agréa' (Sg 3,6): les premières comparaisons du martyre avec un sacrifice dans l'Ancien Testament," in *Treasures of Wisdom: Studies in Ben Sira and the Book of Wisdom*, ed. Nuria Calduch-Benages and Jacques Vermeylen, BETL 143 (Leuven: Leuven University Press, 1999) 355.

[34] For dating, see page 66, footnote 15 in chapter 4.

35:6-7 states, "Do not appear before the Lord empty-handed, for all that you offer is in fulfillment of the commandment" (cf. 38:11). It is interesting to note that Ben Sira gives no other reason to offer sacrifices other than the fact that it was commanded. He is projecting a worldview in which the Law or Torah is the foundation of wisdom.

Ben Sira's attitude toward sacrifice can also be seen in his reverence for Aaron and his unique calling as priest. In reference to Aaron, he writes,

> His sacrifices shall be wholly burned twice every day continually. Moses ordained him, and anointed him with holy oil; it was an everlasting covenant for him and for his descendants as long as the heavens endure, to minister to the Lord and serve as priest and bless his people in his name. He chose him out of all the living to offer sacrifice to the Lord, incense and a pleasing odor as a memorial portion, to make atonement for the people. In his commandments he gave him authority and statutes and judgments, to teach Jacob the testimonies, and to enlighten Israel with his law (45:14-17).

It is this reverential attitude toward Aaron and his ministry of sacrifice that is to shape the readers' attitude. To Aaron belongs the honor of making atonement for the people, enabling them to draw near to God. The rhetorical function of these words is to legitimize Aaron and the sacrificial prescriptions of the Law.

Proper Attitude in Offering Sacrifices

The other major topic concerning sacrifice in Sirach has to do with the proper attitude in giving offerings. The worshiper is not to presume that God will automatically (*ex opere operato*) forgive him because of his many sacrifices. Ben Sira writes, "If one sacrifices ill-gotten goods, the offering is blemished; the gifts of the lawless are not acceptable. The Most High is not pleased with the offerings of the ungodly, nor for a multitude of sacrifices does he forgive sins" (34:21-23, cf. 7:9). J. G. Snaith comments on Ben Sira's words and writes, "The wrong attitude to ritual ceremonial is therefore to think that it is effective in itself without sincere intention to change on the part of the worshiper. His chief concern here appears to be with the inner devotion which should accompany the outward act."[35]

Ben Sira emphasizes as well that right conduct and charity are favorable sacrifices to the Lord. He writes,

---

[35] John G. Snaith, "Ben Sira's Supposed Love of Liturgy," *VT* 25 (1975) 169–70.

The one who keeps the law makes many offerings;[36] one who heeds the commandments makes an offering of well-being. The one who returns a kindness offers choice flour, and one who gives alms sacrifices a thank offering. To keep from wickedness is pleasing to the Lord, and to forsake unrighteousness is an atonement (35:1-5).

These do not replace sacrifices, but are necessary for the worshiper to be righteous and therefore acceptable before God (cf. 35:8-9).[37] Snaith writes, "Ben Sira is opposing false ideas on atonement, that if you have fallen down in obedience to God in practical social life you can make it up by offering extra sacrifices."[38]

The rhetoric used by Ben Sira here functions as polemic against those who adopt a more mechanical view of the sacrificial system. He seeks to persuade his readers to adopt his understanding of the kind of sacrifices that please God by painting the opposing view as ineffective in bringing about atonement and forgiveness (cf. 34:21-23).

Dead Sea Scrolls

The community at Qumran had a very high view of the Levitical sacrifices. It was their zeal for the proper administration of the cult sacrifices that led to the rejection of the corrupted priestly system in Jerusalem.[39] T.R.

---

[36] Snaith writes concerning verse 1, "(ὁ συντηρῶν νόμον πλεονάζει προσφοράς) could be interpreted as meaning that one who keeps the Law will offer many sacrifices. But a better interpretation is indicated by the infinitive construction in verse 5: εὐδοκία κυρί ου ἀποστῆναι ἀπὸ πονηρίας, 'the way to please the Lord is to renounce evil'. Verse 1 is therefore, more correctly translated: 'Keeping the Law is worth many offerings'"; ibid., 170.

[37] Robert Hayward tries to put a large wedge between Ben Sira's concern for piety and his adherence to the ritual law. He writes, "his [Ben Sira's] apparent interest in and affection for the cultus goes hand-in-hand with a kind of piety which many scholars regard as essentially non-cultic: he has a strongly personal, almost individualistic interior spirituality, characterized by moral and ethical values which at times seem to overshadow, or even to take the place of, such external things as sacrifice and priestly dues"; Robert Hayward, "Sacrifice and World Order: Some Observations on Ben Sira's Attitude to the Temple Service," in *Sacrifice and Redemption: Durham Essays in Theology*, ed. Stephen W. Sykes (Cambridge: Cambridge University, 1991) 23. Hayward seems to press this division too far. Ben Sira does not argue that the internal attitude and piety should replace the external ritual, but simply that the external ritual by itself is not enough.

[38] Snaith, "Ben Sira's Supposed Love of Liturgy," 170–71.

[39] Robert A. Kugler, "Rewriting Rubrics: Sacrifice and the Religion of Qumran," in *Religion in the Dead Sea Scrolls*, eds. John J. Collins and Robert A. Kugler (Grand Rapids: Eerdmans, 2000), 90. See also 4QpsMos^b 3 iii 6; 4QpsMos^e 1:1-2; 1QpHab 9:4; 1QpMic 11:1; 4QpNah 3-4 I 11; 3-4 ii 9.

Schreiner writes, "The Qumran community thought that the priesthood in Jerusalem was wicked and illegitimate, and looked forward to the day when a legitimate priesthood would be installed, and the sacrificial system would be practiced with integrity and propriety."[40] However, their critique of the Jerusalem cult never implied a complete replacement or annulment of the sacrificial system.

Because the community was removed from the Jerusalem cult, they had to make some provision for sacrifices. Therefore, as in the Prayer of Azariah and other apocryphal works, there is a tendency in the Dead Sea Scrolls to spiritualize sacrifices. Much of these writings indicate that the community's prayer and praise, Scripture reading and interpretation temporarily took the place of sacrifice.[41]

Guiding much of the sacrificial rhetoric in the Dead Sea Scrolls is the belief that the community constituted the faithful remnant of Israel. Therefore, their polemic against the Jerusalem cult sought to legitimize their community as those who alone had access to God through their sacrifices of praise, prayer, etc. It also functioned to subvert allegiance to the dominant Jewish sacrificial practice.

Temple Scroll (11Q19)

Perhaps the greatest evidence of the community's reverence for the sacrificial cult is found in the Temple Scroll. Columns 13-29 deal almost exclusively with the offerings made in the future ideal temple.[42] What is clear from a close analysis of these sacrifices is the fact that they correlate to the biblical prescriptions regarding sacrifices. In fact, Lawrence Schiffman argues that the author of the Temple Scroll sought to tie the sacrificial

---

[40] T. R. Schreiner, "Sacrifices and Offerings in the NT," *ISBE* 4:275. See also 1QM 2:5f.

[41] Kugler, "Rewriting Rubrics," 90. Others suggest that because the community saw itself as the temple community, there was no longer a need for sacrifices [see Kugler, "Rewriting Rubrics," 91; G. Klinzing, *Die Umdeutung des Kultus in der Qumrangemeinde und im Neuen Testament* (SUNT 7; Göttingen: Vandenhoeck & Ruprecht, 1971), 50-93]. Cf. Hermann Lichtenberger, "Atonement and Sacrifice in the Qumran Community," in *Approaches to Ancient Judaism: Volume 2* (ed. William Scott Green; BJS 9; Chico, Calif.: Scholars Press, 1980), 159-71.

[42] Lawrence Schiffman, "'ôlâ and ḥaṭṭā't in the *Temple Scroll*," in *Pomegranates and Golden Bells: Studies in Biblical, Jewish, and Near Eastern Ritual, Law, and Literature in Honor of Jacob Milgrom* (eds. D.P. Wright, D.N. Freedman, and A. Hurvitz; Winona Lake, Ind.: Eisenbrauns, 1995), 39. Hermann Lichtenberger raises the question as to whether the *Temple Scroll* was for the Qumran community or for another unknown Jewish sect. He suggests a relationship between the Qumran community and the *Temple Scroll* document, but does not say for certain that it is of Essene origin (Lichtenberger 1980, 165).

cult even more faithfully to the Law. Schiffman writes, "Our author, then, was both an innovator and a conservative. He tried to tie his every ruling to the biblical text, the words of which he felt free to adapt so as to assert that his law—the law of the Temple Scroll—was truly the word of God as revealed at Sinai."[43]

This would indicate that the community did not believe the sacrificial cult was annulled or abrogated, but would eventually be restored. Kugler writes, "In lieu of actually participating in the cult, the group's members satisfied themselves with redefining it according to their vision, surely in anticipation of their own return to the temple one day."[44]

RULE OF THE COMMUNITY (1QS)

The Rule of the Community makes very explicit the idea that prayer and piety functioned as sacrifices to the Lord in the Qumran community:

> They shall atone for guilty rebellion and for sins of unfaithfulness, that they may obtain loving-kindness for the Land without the flesh of holocausts and the fat of sacrifice. And prayer rightly offered shall be as an acceptable fragrance of righteousness, and perfection of way as a delectable free-will offering.[45]

1QS 10:6 connects praise with offerings, "I will bless Him with the offering of the lips according to the Precept engraved for ever." And again in 10:15-6 the author writes, "I will praise Him before I go out or enter, or sit or rise, and whilst I lie on the couch of my bed. I will bless Him with the offering of that which proceeds from my lips." What is clear from these connections is the idea that praise and prayer are acceptable forms of offering and sacrifice to the Lord.

Kugler argues that the community may have engaged in prayer and praise at the same time of day that specific liturgical rites occurred in the temple.[46] This would indicate that the community was seeking to essentially mirror the practice of the Jerusalem court with its own creative rendering of sacrifice and ritual.

---

[43] Lawrence Schiffman, "Priestly and Levitical Gifts in the *Temple Scroll*," in *Provo International Conference on the Dead Sea Scrolls: Technological Innovations, New Texts, and Reformulated Issues*, eds. Donald W. Parry and Eugene Ulrich (Leiden: Brill, 1999), 496. See also Schiffman, "'ôlâ and *ḥaṭṭa't* in the *Temple Scroll*," 48.

[44] Kugler, "Rewriting Rubrics," 92.

[45] 1QS 9:4-6. Cf. 4QFlor 1:6-7.

[46] Kugler, "Rewriting Rubrics," 91.

Hermann Lichtenberger identifies 1QS 2:25-3:13 as most important in describing the Qumran community's understanding of atonement.[47] The connection that is made in these passages is that atonement is not given to those who refuse to keep God's commands, even if they keep the ritual sacrifices. Lichtenberger writes, "Atoning rites do not function *ex opere operato*, for they demand total submission to God's will: 'Then he will be accepted through pleasing atonement before God, and it shall be to him a covenant of eternal community' (1QS 3,11f.)."[48]

Clearly what is implied is that only those who offer up sacrifices of praise and prayer coupled with piety will receive atonement and forgiveness. Only those in the community, who follow the community rule, will be accepted. The rhetoric here functions in forming boundaries for the community. It seeks to legitimize the community as the only true remnant, which alone has access to God.

Songs of the Sabbath Sacrifice (4Q400)

The *Songs of the Sabbath Sacrifice* describes the heavenly liturgy by angelic priests on thirteen successive Sabbaths. In the second song a sharp contrast is made between the heavenly cult and the earthly cult.

> for what shall we be counted among them? For what shall our priesthood be counted in their dwelling? [How shall our] ho[liness compare with their supreme] holiness? How does the offering of our tongue of dust compare with the knowledge of the divine [beings] . . . .[49]

According to Kugler, the community is able to peer into this heavenly liturgy but is not able to participate in it. The fact that the community was not able to sing with the angels in the heavenly cult indicates that both realms of worship must remain separate. This would imply then that the heavenly cult does not replace the earthly cult in Jerusalem.[50] The community still recognized the legitimacy of the earthly cultic institution itself. Kugler writes, "so in fact, the community's prayer, praise, study, and priestly-cultic self-definition did not replace the act of sacrifice; at best they mimicked or mirrored it."[51]

---

[47] Lichtenberger, "Atonement and Sacrifice in the Qumran Community," 162.
[48] Ibid., 163.
[49] 4Q400 2, 6-7.
[50] Kugler, "Rewriting Rubrics," 91–92.
[51] Ibid., 92.

What these songs also imply is the fact that the earthly cult is a replica of the heavenly cult. Therefore the language of purity and holiness in the heavenly realm is to inspire the same in the earthly realm. These songs function as a critique of the earthly cult. The author of the songs describes the heavenly priests and their sacrifices as having their legitimacy from God himself:

> [For he fo]unded them [for] himself as the most [holy, who minister in the h]oly of holies . . . do not endure [those who per]vert the way. There is [n]othing impure in their holy gifts. He engraved for them [precepts relating to ho]ly gifts; by them, all the everlasting holy shall sanctify themselves.[52]

The sacrificial language here is to inspire the community to remain zealous in their fidelity to the prescriptions of the cult established by God. By extolling the heavenly cult, there seems to be an implicit critique of the earthly cult. In the context of the Qumran community, the critique is directed toward the priests in Jerusalem. The criticism of the Jerusalem cult (those who pervert the way) functions to subvert the Jewish priestly leadership and legitimize the Qumran community.[53]

Miqsat Ma'aśê ha-Torah (4QMMT)

Miqsat Ma'aśê ha-Torah deals with matters relating to the cult and sacrifice. The rulings contained here are derived from an interpretation of Scripture. Kugler argues that meditation on Scripture describing the cult was how the community maintained their connection to the cult. This meditation was their "sacrifice" to the Lord. [54]

The author's exegesis of particular cultic texts reveals an even more stringent standard for priests and sacrifices than revealed in Scripture itself. For example, when wrestling with when to eat the last of a meal offering, the author navigates between two seemingly contradictory biblical passages, Lev 7:15 and 19:6. The former says that a peace offering should be eaten on the day of its offering, while the latter speaks of eating a peace offering "the same day you offer it, and the next day; but what remains until the third day shall be burned with fire" (19:6). In the author's ruling, he follows the more stringent principle. In regard to meal offerings,

---

[52] 4Q400 1, 10-15.
[53] See also 4Q405 23, i 10-11.
[54] Kugler, "Rewriting Rubrics," 95.

the community is not to follow the practice "of peace-off[erings] which they postpone from one day to the next. But [it is written (cf. Lev. 7:15)] that the meal-offe[ring] {is eaten} with the fat and the meat on the day of [their] being sacrifi[ced]."[55]

The community was clearly committed to upholding the strictest interpretation of the Law regarding sacrifices. These rulings function to distinguish who was on the inside and who was on the outside. They help forge the unique identity of the people as those who adhere to a very strict interpretation of the sacrificial law.

Philo

Philo's rhetorical goals are different from the writings previously surveyed. Rather than seeking to distinguish the Jewish community from the Gentile world, Philo seeks to make Judaism more appealing to the larger Gentile society. In his writings, he defends Judaism by demonstrating its compatibility with Greek philosophy. His treatment of sacrifice is placed within a system that values the spiritual over against the fleshly. Instead of seeing the Levitical sacrifices as an identity marker for those who belong to the community of faith, Philo sees them as a necessary condescension of God for those who need a tangible, physical experience. And yet, many of the same themes found in the other Second Temple writings are also found in Philo, namely the priority of internal devotion over external ritual, the spiritualizing of sacrifices, and the critique of an *ex opere operato* view of sacrifices.

Critique of the Levitical Sacrifices

What is driving Philo's critique of the Levitical sacrifices is his worldview that sets the spiritual over against the fleshly. In *Drunkenness*, Philo contrasts the ritual outside the holy of holies with that on the inside. The rituals outside are a condescension of God catering to the need of most of humanity for physical, tangible experiences of spirituality. But the inner altar deals with "what is bloodless, fleshless, bodiless, and is born of reason, which things are likened to the incense and the burnt spices."[56]

Philo understands sacrificial ritual as something more for man than for God. God does not need anything.[57] But for man, the sacrifices are

---

[55] MMT B 10-11 (4Q394 3-7 i conflated with 4Q395).

[56] *Drunkenness* 3.363, cf. Hos 6:6.

[57] See *Heir* 123; *Decalogue* 41; *Spec. Laws* 1.293; *QE* 2.50.

an exercise in devotion or piety;[58] or they function pedagogically to teach about equality or philanthropy.[59] Philo teaches that the sacrifice itself is of little importance, whether large or small.[60] These sacrifices are not ours, but God's own possession.[61] According to Philo, purity of heart is a prerequisite to approach the altar of God.[62]

Philo interprets Scripture to support his contention that the spiritual cult takes precedence over the fleshly. In *QE* 2.98, he comments that the etymology of θυσιαστήριον, (altar for whole-burnt offerings) comes from the word θυσία and the verb τηρεῖν. Thus he understands the offering of this sacrifice as that which destroys and conserves or keeps at the same time, "for the flesh is consumed by fire but the holiness of the sacrifice remains, for sacrifice is not flesh but the pure and unstained life of a holy (person)."[63] Hecht argues, "This means that the real sacrifice is an interior sacrifice, the engagement or intention of the sacrificer (προαίρεσιν τοῦ προσφέροντος), which is conserved in the sacrifice."[64]

Not only is there a contrast between internal and external sacrifices in Philo, but also a spiritualizing of sacrifices as praise. Jean Marc Laporte comments, "Philo interprets whole-burnt offerings as εὐχαριστία in the sense of praise and confession of God's gifts."[65] He does not see in Philo an atoning use of the daily sacrifice. Rather, the "high-priest, who is the Priest par excellence, is deeply connected with the sacrifice of praise and gratitude."[66] Though the idea of praise and gratitude as sacrifice is found in the previous Jewish writings examined, here in Philo, the concept serves a different rhetorical goal. Philo's critiques follow similar Hellenistic critiques of sacrifice. He seems to pick up on the themes that are found both in Judaism and the Hellenistic world, seeking to show the harmony be-

---

[58] See *Heir* 123.

[59] See Richard D. Hecht, "Patterns of Exegesis in Philo's Interpretation of Leviticus," in *Studia Philonica* 6 (1980) 80. Cf. *Spec. Laws* 1.294-295.

[60] See *Planting* 108; *Spec. Laws* 1.277.

[61] See *Sacrifices* 97.

[62] See Hecht, "Patterns of Exegesis," 80–81. Cf. *Spec. Laws* 1.203, 257, 269, 271.

[63] *QE* 2.98. Cf. *Moses* 2.106-108; *Spec. Laws* 1.274.

[64] Hecht, "Patterns of Exegesis," 81. Cf. *Dreams* 2.34, 217; *Worse* 21, *Drunkenness* 152; *Spec. Laws* 1.201, 277.

[65] Jean Marc Laporte, "Sacrifice in Origen in the Light of Philonic Models," in *Origen of Alexandria: His World and His Legacy,* ed. Charles Kannengiesser and William L. Petersen (Notre Dame, Ind.: University of Notre Dame Press, 1988) 256. Cf. *Spec. Laws* 1.169-176, 286; 2.161; *QE* 2.100-102.

[66] Laporte, "Sacrifice in Origen," 257.

tween the two cultures. Hecht argues that Philo's spiritualization of sacrifices is influenced "on the one hand, by the anti-ritualistic polemic already present in the Hebrew Bible and, on the other, by the Greek philosophical critique of ritual piety and popular cults, which was also very much a part of his social and intellectual milieu."[67]

Legitimacy of the Levitical Cult

Even though Philo criticizes the material, physical sacrificial cult and its temple, he still affirms the practical, pedagogical benefit of it. He does not go as far as the Hellenistic critique to say that material sacrifices and the temple should be rejected.[68] Laporte argues, "Like the prophets, Philo does not condemn purifications and sacrifices, but, precisely because he takes them very seriously as God-given remedies to sin, he opposes those who play the game but ignore the moral and religious implications of the ritual."[69] What Philo argues against is an *ex opere operato* view of sacrifices, which is criticized by both Jewish and Hellenistic writers.[70]

Philo writes of several pragmatic or practical benefits of ritual sacrifices: 1) the physical cult was a necessary condescension for those who desire to give thanks to God or ask for forgiveness of sins;[71] 2) the fact that people had to make a long journey to the one temple[72] was a way they were able to demonstrate true piety; 3) the temple cult drew people from all over the Mediterranean world, bringing about a national unity and identity;[73] and 4) the actual act of offering a sacrifice functioned in a certain sense to restore the one who has sinned back into the community. Laporte writes, "Philo notes that the flesh of his victim is not carried outside, in order to prevent the divulgation of his sin, but eaten by the priests,

---

[67] Hecht, "Patterns of Exegesis," 79. See also V. Nikiprowetzky, "La spiritualisation des sacrifices et le culte sacrificiel au temple de Jérusalem chez Philon d'Alexandrie," *Sem* 17 (1967) 79.

[68] Hecht, "Patterns of Exegesis," 84.

[69] Jean Marc Laporte, "Sacrifice and Forgiveness in Philo of Alexandria," in *Studia Philonica Annual: Studies in Hellenistic Judaism Volume I 1989*, ed. David T. Runia, BJS 185 (Atlanta: Scholars, 1989) 35.

[70] Hecht, "Patterns of Exegesis," 79.

[71] *Spec. Laws* 1.67.

[72] For Philo, the "one temple" reflects the oneness of God.

[73] *Spec. Laws* 1.70.

in order to indicate thereby that, since these holy men share with him in the banquet, he is now enjoying the mercy and peace of God."[74]

Some have argued that Philo was not intent on discarding the Law, but rather was writing to defend the Law. Laporte argues,

> The Philonic allegory does not propose to reduce the Law and its ritual to a pretext to extol Truth and Love and other Platonic Forms as Augustine does. It provides, on the contrary, a way to remain faithful to the Law, to become more faithful to the Law, to resist assimilation of Hellenism.[75]

Though Philo's motives may have been to preserve Judaism, there certainly is a sense that his writings present a non-traditional Judaism more acceptable (assimilated) to the Hellenistic world. Therefore, it may be better to speak of Philo seeking to resist a complete abandonment of Judaism to Hellenism.

Clearly the idea of sacrifice is important to Philo. His discussion of it reveals his desire to preserve it as a vital element of the Jewish faith and culture. However, his spiritualization of sacrifice opens the door for non-Jews to appreciate and perhaps participate in these sacrifices. Much of his discussion involves the general category of sacrifice, rather than the specific rituals of the Levitical sacrifice as prescribed by the Law. In this way, his writings concerning sacrifice do not seek to put a hedge around the community of faith as do other Second Temple writings.

Josephus

Like Philo, Josephus writes to a broader audience. His rhetorical goals are to defend and promote Judaism in the Gentile world.[76] As he recounts the history of the Jewish people, he demonstrates the importance of the sacrificial system to the identity of the Jews.

Jewish Antiquities

In his *Jewish Antiquities,* Josephus follows the scriptural account of the history of the Jewish people. His discussions regarding sacrifice also fol-

---

[74] Laporte, "Sacrifice and Forgiveness." Cf. *Spec. Laws* 1.226-256.

[75] Laporte, "Sacrifice in Origen," 252.

[76] *Ant.* 1:1-7. John Strugnell notes difficulties in translating Josephus' works because he is explaining to Greeks Semitic phenomena [John Strugnell, "Flavius Josephus and the Essenes: *Antiquities* 18:18-22," *JBL* 77 (1958): 108].

low this history, while keeping his Gentile readership in mind.[77] When describing the destruction of Nadab and Abihu as recorded in Leviticus 10:1,[78] Josephus paints the scene as an accident (rather than a direct act of God's judgment), though admitting that Aaron himself believed his sons died because they did not offer sacrifices according to the Law. Josephus writes,

> But the fire was also the cause of misfortune for Aaron, if regarded as a man and a father, albeit the blow was valiantly borne by him, because he had a soul steeled against accidents and believed that it was God's will that the tragedy befell. For he had four sons, as I have already mentioned, and of these the two eldest, Nadab and Abihu, having brought to the altar, not the incense which Moses had prescribed, but such as they had used aforetime, were burnt to death, the fire darting out upon them and beginning to consume their breasts and faces while none could extinguish it.[79]

What is communicated in this writing is the fact that for the Jews, sacrifices and keeping with the sacrificial law were very important.[80]

Josephus describes the on-going influence of Moses in the Jewish community, especially in regard to the Law and the sacrifices.

> But the admiration in which that hero was held for his virtues and his marvelous power of inspiring faith in all his utterances

---

[77] In *Ant.* 3:224-25; 233-37, Josephus describes the sacrificial practices of the Jews, emphasizing the prescriptions of the law (cf. *Ag. Ap.* 2:193-198). In *Ant.* 6:146-149, he reiterates God's preference for obedience over sacrifice in his retelling of Saul's disobedience in 1 Samuel 15:14-35.

[78] Cf. Numbers 3:2-4; 26:60-61.

[79] *Ant.* 3:208-9.

[80] Josephus describes the practice of the Essenes,

> They send votive offerings to the temple, but perform their sacrifices employing a different ritual of purification. For this reason they are barred from those precincts of the temple that are frequented by all the people and perform their rites by themselves. Otherwise they are of the highest character, devoting themselves solely to agricultural labor (*Ant.* 18:19).

The fact that they are excluded from the common court was a mark against the Essenes according to Josephus. In spite of this fact, he has a high regard for their character and piety. In this way, Josephus maintains the legitimacy of the temple and its sacrificial cult. For a fuller discussion of Josephus' reference to Essene sacrifices, see Strugnell, "Flavius Josephus and the Essenes," 106–15; David H. Wallace, "Essenes and Temple Sacrifice," *TZ* 13 (1957) 335–38; and Albert I. Baumgarten, "Josephus on Essene Sacrifice," *JJS* 45 (1994) 169–83.

were not confined to his lifetime: they are alive to-day. Certainly there is not a Hebrew who does not, just as if he were still there and ready to punish him for any breach of discipline, obey the laws laid down by Moses, even though in violating them he could escape detection.[81]

Josephus goes on to describe some Jewish travelers who traveled four months through many dangers and at great expense from beyond the Euphrates to come to the temple and worship. But when they came, they were forbidden to partake of their own sacrifices because the Law did not permit them for some reason.[82] Josephus describes their willingness to submit to the Law,

> ... some without sacrificing at all, others leaving their sacrifices half completed, many unable so much as to gain entrance to the temple, they went their way, preferring to conform to the injunctions of Moses rather than to act in accordance with their own will, and that from no fear of being reproved in this matter but solely through misgivings of conscience.[83]

But perhaps the greatest demonstration of the importance of keeping faithful to the Law and its sacrificial prescriptions are the descriptions of those Jews who died at the hands of their enemies while offering up sacrifices at the altar. Josephus recounts the fact that even when under siege, the Jews were faithful to their ritual requirements.

> And one may get an idea of the extreme piety which we show toward God and of our strict observance of the laws from the fact that during the siege the priests were not hindered from performing any of the sacred ceremonies through fear, but twice a day, in the morning and at the ninth hour, they performed the sacred ceremonies at the altar, and did not omit any of the sacrifices even when some difficulty arose because of the attacks. . . . . and the enemy rushed in and were slaughtering the Jews in the temple, those who were busied with the sacrifices none the less continued to perform the sacred ceremonies; nor were they compelled either by fear for their lives or by their great number of those already slain, to run away, but thought it better to endure whatever they

---

[81] *Ant.* 3:317.
[82] *Ant.* 3:318.
[83] *Ant.* 3:319-320.

might have to suffer there beside the altars than to neglect any of the ordinances.[84]

Jewish War

The emphasis by Josephus on the role and significance of the Jewish sacrificial system may have helped his Gentile audience understand the cultural factors influencing the Jewish revolt. Josephus describes the role of sacrifices in instigating the revolt. He describes Eleazar, the son of the high priest, persuading those officiating in the temple not to receive a gift or sacrifice from foreigners, including sacrifices for Caesar. Josephus then describes the efforts of several high priests and leaders to persuade Eleazar and the others to follow the tradition of their forefathers and accept the donations of foreigners. They pointed out that the decision to reject gifts and sacrifices from foreigners would bring about dire consequences.[85] Josephus writes of Eleazar and those who rejected sacrifices from foreigners:

> But now here were these men, who were provoking the arms of the Romans and courting a war with them, introducing a strange innovation into their religion, and, besides endangering the city, laying it open to the charge of impiety, if Jews henceforth were to be the only people to allow no alien the right of sacrifice or worship.[86]

The high priests' efforts at swaying the young men's practice were to no avail. Josephus identifies the decision to reject sacrifices from foreigners as that which instigated the Jewish revolt and war. "But not one of the revolutionary party would listen to them; even the Temple ministers failed to come to their support and were thus instrumental in bringing about the war."[87]

Josephus paints Eleazar as a maverick, who went against the Jewish custom of offering up sacrifices for the leaders of the land. By identifying Eleazar as going against what was traditionally Jewish, Josephus casts the larger Jewish society in a positive light. And yet Eleazar's actions seem consistent with the nationalistic desire of the Jews to retain and guard their identity, culture, and autonomy within the Gentile world.

---

[84] *Ant.* 14:65-67. Cf. *J.W.* 1:148-149.
[85] *J.W.* 2:409-413.
[86] *J.W.* 2:414.
[87] *J.W.* 2:417.

Against Apion

Like Philo, Josephus wants to emphasize those things that are Jewish that are also acceptable in the Gentile world. In his polemic against Apion, he aligns the Jews with the Greeks and Macedonians as those who offer sacrifices, while seeking to distance himself from Apion and Egyptians as those who do not.

> Well, the custom of slaughtering domestic animals we share with the rest of mankind; and Apion, by criticizing those who practise it, betrays his Egyptian birth. No Greek or Macedonian would have been moved to indignation. Their nations, indeed, vow sacrifices of hecatombs to the gods, and make a feast of the victims; yet this has not had the result, apprehended by Apion, of leaving the world without cattle.[88]

Josephus' rhetorical goals are to defend and promote Judaism to the Gentile world. He does not seek to build up walls around Judaism but present it in a more acceptable fashion. And yet what is communicated here is the importance of the sacrificial system to the identity of the Jewish people.

Conclusion

The importance of sacrifice in the life and community of Israel is demonstrated by the numerous discussions of it by Jewish writers. Many of the authors considered above argued for greater fidelity to the Law regarding the offering of sacrifices. Others criticized the sacrificial cult because those who gave the sacrifices were impure or unholy (both the priests and the worshiper). Still others criticized the cult because of a false understanding of how the cult worked. These polemical discussions only highlight how important the cultic institution was to the identity of the Jewish people.

What seems to be at the root of the discussion on sacrifice in these writings is the question, "What is the proper way to worship God," or "What is the acceptable way to approach God?" Each Jewish group had its own answer. Some emphasized keeping to the letter of the Law, others emphasized the priority of a righteous, God-fearing life. In each case, the rhetoric dealing with sacrifice promoted the view of the community represented. Boundaries were formed and the identity of the community was further defined by this sacrificial rhetoric. Not only did these discussions on sacrifice seek to subvert competing views, but they also functioned to

---

[88] *Ag.Ap.* 2:138.

socialize the members as to the practices that characterized the norms and customs of the community. Therefore, the sacrifices themselves functioned as identity markers for those who belonged to the community – even if the sacrifices were prayers, praises, and good works. The visible participation in these sacrifices would then strengthen the community's sense of identity, to the exclusion of others.

Analysis of Hebrews 10:1-10

As we turn our attention to Hebrews 10:1-10, what is important to note is the fact that the author of Hebrews comes to this same question, "What is the acceptable way to approach God?" but offers a radical alternative view. Like many of the Jewish authors mentioned above, the author of Hebrews also criticizes the Levitical cultus. But unlike them, he does not criticize the people or priests for improperly offering the sacrifices, but rather the Levitical institution itself. In this way, the author distances himself from the other Jewish writers. His polemic is the most radical in its implications.

At the same time, we realize that the author of Hebrews' sacrificial rhetoric follows the pattern set by many of the writers above. Like many of them, he defines what sacrifices are inadequate and what sacrifices are acceptable.[89] By showing the superiority of Christ's sacrifice over against the Levitical sacrifices, the author seeks to subvert the dominant Jewish view of sacrifice and further distinguish his community as the faithful remnant.[90] The author of Hebrews also seeks to socialize his members as to the proper way to approach God. In the end, he desires to rally his readers to a greater fidelity to their common community and faith, in a way similar to the Jewish authors mentioned above.

In the Second Temple Jewish writings, there has been an emphasis on discerning what God truly desires when his people approach him. This has led to a reinterpretation of sacrifice as praise, thanksgiving, good works, etc. The author of Hebrews also follows this trend and includes these things as acceptable sacrifices (13:15-16). Like the other Jewish writers, it seems that he was drawing these themes from the Hebrew Bible itself.[91] The radical statement in Hebrews, however, is not that praise and

---

[89] See above chapter 6, pages 148-167.

[90] This is similar to the polemic found in the Dead Sea Scrolls. See above chapter 6, pages 159-164.

[91] Perhaps what is motivating the author of Hebrews in reinterpreting sacrifices is the need to find some tangible replacements for the Levitical sacrifices. This seems to be the motivat-

good works are acceptable sacrifices, but rather that the Levitical sacrifices find their culmination in Christ's sacrifice.

Overview of the Argument

In chapter 10:1-18, the author of Hebrews concludes his discussion of the sacrifice of Christ first introduced in 5:1-10 and then picked up again in 8:1-5.[92] He understands this sacrifice as that which inaugurates the new covenant (9:15-22) and allows the worshiper to be made perfect and to draw near to God (10:1, 19-22). In 10:1-18, the author makes two contrasts: 1) between the Levitical sacrifices with the once-for-all sacrifice of Christ; and 2) between the priestly activity of the Levites and that of Christ.[93] Using a superior/inferior dialectic, the author seeks to persuade his readers to remain faithful to the better way of approaching God.

In verses 1-10, the author emphasizes the inadequacy of the Levitical offerings. While in verses 11-18, he emphasizes the superiority of the offering of Christ. The author uses a quotation from Psalm 39:7-9 (LXX) in verses 5-7 to argue that the Levitical sacrifices have been fulfilled. Therefore, since verses 1-10 speak more negatively toward the Jewish cultic institution, we will focus our analysis on these verses. The fruit of this analysis will determine the extent to which this passage can be considered anti-Semitic, anti-Judaic, or supersessionist.

We shall divide this passage into three major sections: 1) The imperfection of the Law and its sacrifices (10:1-4); 2) the use of Psalm 39:7-9 (10:5-7); and 3) the interpretation of Psalm 39:7-9 (10:8-10).

---

ing influence in the Qumran community as well.

[92] William Lane, *Hebrews 9–13*, WBC 47B (Dallas: Word, 1991) 257.

[93] Lane notes a concentric symmetry found in verses 1-18:

A The inadequacy of the provisions of the law for repeated sacrifices (10:1-4).
B The repeated sacrifices have been superseded by the one sacrifice of Christ in conformity to the will of God (10:5-10).
B' The Levitical priests have been superseded by the one priest enthroned at God's right hand (10:11-14).
A' The adequacy of the provisions of the new covenant, which render a sacrifice for sins no longer necessary (10:15-18). (Lane 1991b, 258).

Koester notes these division and describes the first and the last dealing with the law and the new covenant respectively and the two inner sections dealing with the superiority of Christ's sacrifice over against the Levitical sacrifices. See Craig R. Koester, *Hebrews*, AB 36 (New York: Doubleday, 2001) 436.

Imperfection of the Law and Its Sacrifices (10:1-4)

Levitical Sacrifices as Shadows

The conceptual framework in which the author of Hebrews is working is revealed in 10:1, "For the Law, since it has only a shadow [σκιάν] of the good things to come and not the very form [εἰκόνα] of things,[94] can never, by the same sacrifices which they offer continually year by year, make perfect those who draw near" (10:1).[95] The shadow/reality rhetoric reveals a redemptive-historical framework in which the climax of God's plan of salvation is foreshadowed throughout Israel's history.[96] Lane writes,

> ... the contrast implied is temporal and eschatological in character; the law is a past witness to a future reality...as a witness to the eschatological salvation that was clearly future from the vantage

---

[94] The shadows that are contained in the law are not the εἰκών. See Paul Ellingworth, *The Epistle to the Hebrews: A Commentary on the Greek Text*, NIGTC (Grand Rapids: Eerdmans, 1993) 490; Koester, *Hebrews*, 431. Cf. Plato, *Republic* 509E-510E, Philo, *Alleg. Interp.* 3.96; *Decalogue* 82; *Migration* 12; *Heir* 72; cf. Cicero, *De republica* 2.30 §52. P[46] has an alternate reading in verse 1. Instead of οὐκ αὐτὴν τὴν εἰκόνα, the text reads, καὶ τὴν εἰκόνα, which describes "image" as a synonym for "shadow." However, the construction of the sentence implies a contrast between the terms. In addition, other significant texts have the longer reading. Therefore we reject the reading in P[46] as an emendation of the original. See Lane, *Hebrews 9-13*, 254 n. b. Although εἰκών is often used synonymously with σκιά, here it speaks of the true form of the realities. See H. W. Montefiore, *The Epistle to the Hebrews*, Harper's New Testament Commentaries (New York: Harper & Row, 1964) 164; Philip E. Hughes, *A Commentary on the Epistle to the Hebrews* (Grand Rapids: Eerdmans, 1977) 390.

[95] Paul Ellingworth notes how radical the author's statement in verse 1 must have sounded to Jewish ears, "This statement would probably have been contested by the author's Jewish readers before they became Christian" (*Hebrews*, 490).

[96] It is unlikely that the author of Hebrews was following Philo or presupposing a Platonic framework as Spicq argues. See C. Spicq, *L'Epitre aux Hebreux*, 2 vols. (Paris: Gabalda, 1952–53) 1.39-91; cf. Marie E. Isaacs, *Sacred Space: An Approach to the Theology of the Epistle to the Hebrews*, JSNTSS 73 (Sheffield: JSOT Press, 1992) 49–56; Thompson, "Hebrews 9 and Hellenistic Concepts of Sacrifice," 567–78. R. Williamson has argued convincingly that though there may be verbal parallels, they do not share the same conceptual framework. See R. Williamson, *Philo and the Epistle to the Hebrews* (Leiden: Brill, 1970) 142–49. Hurst argues that what seems to be guiding the author of Hebrews' thought are Jewish apocalyptic and primitive Christian tradition. See L. D. Hurst, *The Epistle to the Hebrews: Its Background of Thought* (Cambridge: Cambridge University Press, 1990) 22–68; William Lane, *Hebrews 1–8*, WBC 47A (Dallas: Word, 1991) cviii.

point of the law, the law can be described as possessing a foreshadowing quality.[97]

It is within this framework that the author of Hebrews contrasts the sacrificial practices of the larger Jewish community and the practice of his own community. The final sacrifice of Christ is believed to be the true form of all the Levitical sacrifices prescribed in the Law. Thus the rhetoric automatically paints the Levitical sacrifices as inferior to the eschatological reality. Erich Grässer writes,

> Mit dem betont vorangestellten Partizipialsatz σκιὰν γὰρ ἔχων κτλ. wird das Unvermögen der alten Heilsordnung (νόμος) begründet: Die ihn legitimierende und tragende Kult-Tora hat es nur mit dem *Schatten* (σκιά) der eschatologischen Heilsgüter (μελλόντων ἀγαθῶν) zu tun, hat aber nicht αὐτὴν τὴν εἰκόνα τῶν πραγμάτων, die Gestalt der wahren (himmlischen) Wirklichkeit selbst.[98]

The author wants his Jewish readers to believe that they are part of the final culmination of God's redemptive plan. He wants them to think of Christ's sacrifice as the fulfillment of all the Levitical sacrifices that had gone before.

As we think about the author of Hebrews' polemic against the Levitical sacrifices we realize that instead of going from problem to solution, he likely started with the solution and then identified the problem. The development of the author's polemic goes in the reverse direction from the development at Qumran. The Qumran community started with a critique of the cult and its worship and then came to the solution that only in the eschatological temple will true, unadulterated worship be possible.[99] The author of Hebrews seems to begin with the eschatological revelation of Jesus as the perfect sacrifice and then work back from there to conclude that the Levitical sacrifices were inadequate. This would explain why the author was able to freely criticize the sacrifices themselves rather than an abuse or misunderstanding of how the sacrifices were offered. The eschatological act and revelation of Christ forced a reinterpretation of traditional Jewish categories and practices, which would have previously never been questioned.

---

[97] Lane, *Hebrews 9–13*, 259–60. See also F. F. Bruce, *The Epistle to the Hebrews*, rev. ed., NICNT (Grand Rapids: Eerdmans, 1990) 226. The phrase "good things to come," also indicates a temporal progression or contrast.

[98] Erich Grässer, *An die Hebräer*, 3 vols., EKK 17 (Zürich: Benziger, 1993) 2:205.

[99] See above chapter 6, pages 160-61.

Critique of the Sacrifices

Looking back then at the Levitical sacrifices in the light of Christ's sacrifice, the author states that they ultimately fail in bringing about God's intention for them, namely to make the worshiper complete or perfect as they approach God. This perfection entails the cleansing of one's consciousness of sins and the removal of sin as the barrier preventing the worshiper from drawing near to God.[100] Koester writes, "Hebrews argues that God brings his purposes to completion through Christ. Completion involves cleansing sin from the conscience (9:14; 10:2, 22) and the positive relationship that emerges as a result of the cleansing."[101] The two critiques of the Levitical sacrifices are 1) they do not cleanse the conscience but remind the worshipers of their sins; and 2) they cannot take away sin.

Reminder of Sins (10:2-3)

The author of Hebrews focuses on the repetitive nature of the Levitical sacrifices.[102] The inability of the Levitical sacrifices to perfect is proved by the fact that they continue year after year.[103] The author poses a contrafactual question to drive his point home to the readers, "Otherwise, would they not have ceased to be offered, because the worshipers, having once been cleansed, would no longer have had consciousness of sins?" (10:2)[104] Koester states, "Such questions help persuade listeners, because in answering the question, they themselves pass judgment on the matter."[105]

---

[100] David deSilva understands "perfect" in this context to refer to "removing the awareness of sin from the conscience of the worshiper (9:9,14) as well as ending the limitations on access to God so as to bring 'those who draw near' across the threshold into the true holy place"; *Perseverance in Gratitude: A Socio-Rhetorical Commentary on the Epistle 'to the Hebrews'* (Grand Rapids: Eerdmans, 2000) 316. See also Harold W. Attridge, *The Epistle to the Hebrews,* Hermeneia (Philadelphia: Fortress, 1989) 271–72; Grässer, *Hebräer,* 2:204.

[101] Koester, *Hebrews,* 437.

[102] The phrase, κατ' ἐνιαυτόν in 10:1 and 3 increases the sense of repetition. This creates weariness toward these sacrifices and implies that the ritual was formalistic and mechanical. These are the "same sacrifices which they offer continually year by year" (10:1).

[103] It seems clear that the Day of Atonement ritual (9:7; cf. Lev 16-17) is in the background of this discussion. See deSilva, *Perseverance in Gratitude,* 317; Lane, *Hebrews 9-13,* 260; and Bruce, *The Epistle to the Hebrews,* 227.

[104] Lane notes, "Reflecting a classical idiom, ἐπεί is used in an elliptical construction of a contrary-to-fact conditional clause cast in the form of a rhetorical question. The conj. ἐπεί presupposes an implied protasis: 'otherwise [if the law could have decisively purged its adherents], would these sacrifices not have ceased to be offered?'" (Lane 1991b, 255 n. h).

[105] Koester, *The Epistle to the Hebrews,* 437. Grässer also points out that putting the statement in the form of a question allows the readers to come to a personal realization of the

Some may argue that the repetition of the sacrifices were because the people continued to sin and not because of any inadequacy of the sacrifices themselves. The author of Hebrews seems to believe that if the sacrifices themselves were truly effective, they would have brought about a permanent change in the worshiper. He uses the perfect tense for the participle κεκαθαρισμένους (v. 2) to indicate that the sacrifices should have established a permanent cleansing.[106] In other words, the sacrifices were to bring about a heart change in addition to a cleansed conscience.[107]

The Levitical sacrifices seem to have just the opposite effect. Instead of causing the worshipers to forget about their sins, they remind them of their sins year by year (10:3), indicating that their consciences are still plagued by sin. But not only are the worshipers reminded year by year of their sins, but God himself is reminded of the worshipers' sins.[108] Therefore there is a sharp contrast between the old covenant and the new. In the old covenant, God is reminded of the people's sins year by year, but in the new covenant, God promises, "I will remember their sins no more" (8:12; 10:17).[109]

Otto Michel summarizes the hopeless condition of those living under the old covenant system:

> 1. Durch das Gesetz soll Reinheit und Vergebung gegeben werden, aber die Einmaligkeit und Ganzheit des Opfers, die für eine Umwandlung des Menschen notwendig wären, sind dem Gesetz unmöglich. 2. Jedes menschliche Handeln, das im Gehorsam gegen Gottes Gebot die Vergebung erbittet, erinnert tatsächlich an die Sünde der Vergangenheit und zeigt die menschliche Unfähigkeit, sich selbst zu helfen.[110]

---

inadequacies of the Levitical cult. "Da an die Erkenntnis der Adressaten appelliert wird, ist die Frageform wichtig"; Grässer, *Hebräer*, 2:208. See also deSilva, *Perseverance in Gratitude*, 317.

[106] Lane, *Hebrews 9–13*, 255 n. i.

[107] In 9:13-14, the author contrasts the Levitical sacrifices, which cleanse the flesh, with the sacrifice of Christ, which cleanses the conscience. In addition to the spatial and temporal contrasts mentioned earlier in the epistle, we have here evidence of a third category, where the author makes an internal-external contrast. This is perhaps an allusion or an explication of what was meant by having God's laws placed in one's mind and written on one's heart (8:10). See deSilva, *Perseverance in Gratitude*, 317.

[108] The actual referent of who is reminded of the sins is unclear in verse 3. It seems that it refers both to the worshiper, whose conscience is not clean and also to God, who in the new covenant remembers their sins no more (8:12; 10:17). See Hughes, *Hebrews*, 392.

[109] Bruce, *Hebrews*, 228–29.

[110] Otto Michel, *Der Brief an die Hebräer*, 13th ed., KEK (Göttingen: Vandenhoeck &

Clearly the author of Hebrews' critique is to persuade the readers to remain in the new covenant established by Jesus' sacrifice and not revert back to the old covenant. By repeatedly describing the Old Testament sacrifices as repetitive, the author paints sacrificial worship under the Levitical system as formalistic and ritualistic. He also gives the impression that these sacrifices were intended to drive the worshiper to look for something better.[111]

Impossible to Take Away Sins (10:4)

The radical statement in verse 4, "it is impossible for the blood of bulls and goats to take away sins," clearly separates the author of Hebrews' critique of the Levitical sacrifices from other Jewish writers. Unlike the critiques from the Second Temple Jewish writings, which were largely based on inadequacies of the worshipers or priests, the critique in this passage identifies a fundamental inadequacy of the sacrifices themselves.[112] Here in verse 4, we note a progression in the intensity of the author's polemic. The Levitical sacrifices do not merely fall short in bringing perfect cleansing; they are described here as completely unable to take away sin to any extent.[113] It is impossible, according to the author, for the blood of these sacrifices to accomplish what was presumed to be their intended goal.

And yet, we must keep in mind that what is driving this radical critique is the revelation of Jesus as the final sacrifice. Once the author was convinced that Jesus' blood alone is efficacious in cleansing sin, he must conclude that the shadowy Levitical sacrifices were deficient.[114] If indeed they were able to remove sin, then there would be no need for Jesus' sacri-

---

Ruprecht, 1975) 334.

[111] Lane notes, "the failure of the law in this respect is underscored by expressions that convey a notion of futility: the same sacrifices are offered continually (εἰς τὸ διηνεκές) year after year (κατ' ἐνιαυτόν)"; Lane, *Hebrews 9–13*, 260.

[112] deSilva, *Perseverance in Gratitude*, 319–20.

[113] Some may view the author as setting up a contrast between external cultic rites and internal obedience (cf. Attridge, *Hebrews*, 275), yet Koester is keen to comment,

> Hebrews' rejection of animal sacrifices (10:4) and its emphasis on obedience (10:5-10) might be taken to mean that the author thinks that material sacrifices cannot remove moral defilement or that animal sacrifices are merely external acts, whereas God desires internal obedience. The author, however, assumes that without blood there is no forgiveness (9:22). The blood of bulls and goats cannot take away sins, but *Christ's* blood does take away sins. Christ offered his body (10:10), not only his mind or will, which means that Hebrews' argument is primarily Christological rather than metaphysical or moral (Koester, *Hebrews*, 438).

[114] Grässer, *Hebräer*, 2:212.

fice. Even if the Levitical sacrifices only partially removed sins, the uniqueness and exclusive nature of Jesus' sacrifice would be jeopardized. Therefore the author is compelled to make the radical statement, "it is impossible for the blood of bulls and goats to take away sins" (10:4). He wants to leave his readers with no other choice, but to remain in his community, which approaches God through the sacrifice of Jesus.

Certainly there is some tension between the idea that the blood of bulls and goats cannot take away sins and the fact that God instituted the animal sacrifices for this very purpose. Lane approaches this tension by making a distinction between cleansing and decisive cleansing. He writes, "The issue is not whether the blood of bulls and goats sacrificed during the annual observances of the Day of Atonement (Lev 16:3, 6, 11, 14-16, 18-19) has any power to effect cleansing, but whether it has potency to effect a *decisive* cleansing."[115] This approach is a bit difficult to reconcile with the very clear statement by the author that it is impossible for the blood of bulls and goats to take away sin. The author of Hebrews seems to be making a stronger statement than Lane desires to admit. However, Lane does note, "the accent is placed on the insufficiency of the blood of sacrificial animals to remove the defilement of sins that constitutes a barrier to worship."[116]

Another approach is to view the Levitical system as ultimately established by God to point forward to the final sacrifice. Hughes writes that the whole Mosaic system was "in nature preparatory, or propaedeutic, showing in particular the seriousness of sin, the reality of the righteousness of God, and the necessity for atonement."[117] He also argues that these sacrifices have a forward-looking function,

> ... though itself the shadow and not the substance, and inherently incapable of achieving the reconciliation which it presaged, by its typical forms in association with the promises of the new covenant it pointed forward to the achievement of a full and final expiation through the Lamb which God would provide (7:11ff.; 8:1ff.; 9:11ff.; 10:11ff.).[118]

Roger Beckwith follows this line of thinking and writes, "The implication of this teaching evidently is that any grace which the OT sacrifices conveyed came not from themselves, but from the sacrifice of Christ

---

[115] Lane, *Hebrews 9-13*, 261–62.
[116] Ibid., 262.
[117] Hughes, *Hebrews*, 393.
[118] Ibid.

which they foreshadowed."[119] It seems that this approach is more consistent with the author of Hebrews. By stating that it is impossible for the blood of bulls and goats to take away sin, he implies that they were never established in and of themselves for this purpose.

Conclusion

What is important to note in this polemic is the fact that the author of Hebrews agrees with most of the Second Temple Jewish writers that sacrifices are for the ultimate purpose of enabling the worshiper to come near to God.[120] And like many of them, he is arguing that his particular view of sacrifice is the one that is most pleasing to God and provides the most intimate access to him. In this sense, his sacrifice rhetoric is very much a part of the Jewish milieu.

At the same time, his radical critique of the Levitical sacrifices separates him from mainstream Judaism and functions to set up boundaries between those in his community and those in the larger Jewish society. It also functions to socialize his constituent members as to their practice of sacrifice in the community. Those who belong to this community do not participate in sacrifices that are ineffective in enabling the worshiper to draw near to God.

Use of Psalm 39:7-9 (LXX 10:5-7)

Following the pattern established in his discussion on priesthood (7:11-28) and covenant (8:1-13), the author of Hebrews uses Scripture to support his argument and curtail any objections to his statements. His use of Scripture brings greater legitimacy to his statements on sacrifice as it appeals to an authority well recognized by the readers. Michel writes, "Wohl aber wird durch das Selbstzeugnis des Alten Bundes bestätigt, dass Gott das Tieropfer verwirft und einen neuen Gehorsam verlangt."[121]

---

[119] Roger T. Beckwith, "The Death of Christ as a Sacrifice in the Teaching of Paul and Hebrews," in *Sacrifice in the Bible,* ed. Roger T. Beckwith and Martin J. Selman (Grand Rapids: Baker, 1995) 134. Bruce also argues that God instituted these sacrifices to foreshadow things to come. He writes, "Such spiritual value as the sacrificial ritual might have lay in its being a material foreshadowing or object-lesson of a moral and spiritual reality" (Bruce, *Hebrews,* 230).

[120] Lane notes that the author of Hebrews believed that sacrifices were to bring about a cleansed conscience, which was a prerequisite to unhindered access to God (Lane 1991b, 261). See also Bruce, *The Epistle to the Hebrews,* 227.

[121] Michel, *Hebräer,* 335.

The use of Psalm 39:7-9 (LXX) functions to demonstrate that God himself acknowledges the inadequacies of Levitical sacrifices. David deSilva writes,

> Specific oracles such as Psalm 39:7-9 (LXX; MT 40:6-8) are read as authoritative proof that God has set aside the rites of the OT as inadequate and has prepared a body for the Son with which to accomplish at last God's will for the perfecting of his people, bringing them to that state in which they can enter their divinely appointed goal.[122]

William Spencer sees the use of Psalm 39:7-9 as an apologetic for the sacrifice of Christ against the Jewish background. He argues that the human sacrifice of Christ probably sounded very pagan to the Jews, and so the author of Hebrews uses Scripture to validate the place of Christ's sacrifice in removing sin. Spencer argues

> To readers and hearers of Hebrews a 'prepared body' must have set off warning signals. While the context is the superseding by Christ of the substitutionary sacrificial demands of Jewish ritual law, the introduction of a person's body being prepared for sacrifice may have summoned up as well Canaanite and even, perhaps, Greco-Roman religious demands for human sacrifice.[123]

Certainly the use of Psalm 39:7-9 would have helped defend the idea of Jesus as sacrifice to wary Jews.[124] Yet what seems to be the author's main motivation for his reference to Psalm 39 was to legitimize the claim that the old Levitical sacrifices would be replaced, given the context of the quotation in Hebrews.

---

[122] deSilva, *Perseverance in Gratitude*, 328. See also Montefiore, *Hebrews*, 168, Ellingworth, *Hebrews*, 498.

[123] Spencer, "Christ's Sacrifice as Apologetic," 190.

[124] Though the idea of pagan human sacrifices was abhorrent to Jews, the idea of martyrs functioning at least metaphorically as sacrifices was not uncommon. See above chapter 6, pages 156-57; Aharon R. E. Agus, *The Binding of Isaac and Messiah: Law, Martyrdom, and Deliverance in Early Rabbinic Religiosity* (Albany: SUNY Press, 1988). What also seems to have shaped the Jewish understanding of sacrifice was the Akedah or "Binding of Isaac" tradition. See Robert J. Daly, "Soteriological Significance of the Sacrifice of Isaac," *CBQ* 39 (1977) 74. Cf. James Swetnam, *Jesus and Isaac: A Study of the Epistle to the Hebrews in the Light of the Aqedah*, AnBib 94 (Rome: Biblical Institute Press, 1981).

Jesus as the Singer of the Psalm

The author introduces the quotation of Scripture by portraying Jesus as the singer of the Psalm.[125] He writes, "When He (Jesus) comes into the world, He says..."[126] DeSilva comments,

> Combining his conviction that certain Scriptures find their true meaning when placed on Jesus' lips and his understanding that a later word from God can correct, clarify, or nullify an earlier one, the author finds in this psalm strong scriptural support for the claim that the first kind of sacrifice is set aside in order to make room for the second (see his application of Jer. 31:31-34 to the two covenants).[127]

The author of Hebrews reads this Psalm Christocentrically in the sense that he sees the Psalm not only sung by Jesus, but that which speaks of Jesus. The Psalm's eschatological significance and meaning are found in Jesus.[128] Ellingworth notes, "It is probable that this Christ-centered understanding of Scripture was generally accepted in the community to which Hebrews was originally addressed. This in turn suggests a predominantly Jewish Christian community in which the OT was well known."[129]

What is subtly promoted in the author's use of Scripture is not simply the idea that the old Levitical sacrifices have been replaced, but also a Christ-centered hermeneutic. In this sense, the author is also socializing his audience as to how to read and think about Scriptural passages in light of the revelation of Jesus. The hermeneutic itself functions as an identity marker separating the community in Hebrews from the larger Jewish society.

---

[125] Cf. Heb 2:12-13. See Lane, *Hebrews 9–13*, 262; Hughes, *Hebrews*, 394; Attridge, *Hebrews*, 273.

[126] The idea of Jesus coming into the world seems to be a reference to the incarnation of Jesus Christ. See Koester, *Hebrews*, 438–39; Grässer, *Hebräer*, 2:214–15; Bruce, *Hebrews*, 234. The body prepared by God also strengthens the argument that the incarnation is in view (deSilva, *Perseverance in Gratitude*, 321). The reference to the incarnation further supports the argument that the author is working from a redemptive historical framework. It is the act of God in history in sending his Son that initiates the fulfillment of the older institutions. The coming of the Christ is to be seen as an eschatological act of God.

[127] deSilva, *Perseverance in Gratitude*, 320.

[128] This is a common hermeneutic for the early Christians (cf. Luke 24:27,44; Acts 8:35).

[129] Ellingworth, *Hebrews*, 499.

MT, LXX, and Hebrews

The quotation of Psalm 39:7-9 (LXX; 40:7-9 MT) in Hebrews generally follows the Septuagint reading. But the LXX version has a somewhat significant variation with the Masoretic text. The phrase אזנים כרית לי ("ears you dug for me") in 40:7b in the MT is replaced by σῶμα δὲ κατηρτίσω μοι "you fashioned a body for me," in the LXX.[130]

How are we to make sense of this change? Ellingworth suggests that it was because of a scribal error confusing ΗΘΕΛΗΣΑΣΩΤΙΑ with ΗΘΕΛΗΣΑΣ(Σ)ΩΜΑ.[131] Montefiore argues that this was an intentional corruption to support the interests of Jewish Messianism.[132] Bruce suggests another alternative, namely that this was an interpretive paraphrase of the Masoretic text. Bruce writes, "The Greek translator evidently regarded the Hebrew wording as an instance of *pars pro toto*; the 'digging' or hollowing out of the ears is part of the total work of fashioning a human body."[133]

Clearly the LXX rendering of the Psalm was much better than the MT in helping the author of Hebrews apply the passage to Jesus. The "body" that has been prepared is more easily identified with Jesus. The fact that it fits so nicely with the author's argument may indicate that the change from "ears" to "body" originated from the author of Hebrews himself. And yet, it is difficult to know for certain. It is more likely, however, that the version of the LXX used by the author already had σῶμα.[134]

A somewhat minor variation is found in verse 8 of the MT where במגלת־ספר "in the scroll of the book" is written, while in the LXX version ἐν κεφαλίδι βιβλίου "at the head of the book" is recorded.[135] What is the "head" of a book? The head likely refers to the knob on top of the rod, around which the scroll was wrapped. Therefore the phrase, "head of the book" is an example of synecdoche, where a part represents the whole. The "book" seems clearly to represent the Law.[136]

---

[130] The Göttingen LXX adopts ὠτία as the harder reading. But the author of Hebrews was likely using a version of the LXX that had σῶμα. See Ellingworth, *Hebrews*, 500.

[131] Ellingworth, *Hebrews*, 500.

[132] Montefiore, *Hebrews*, 167. Montefiore also notes another alteration that would further support the interests of Jewish Messianism. The LXX writers changed the MT text, which reads, "In the scroll of the book it is written for me," to "In the scroll of the book it is written about me"; see 167.

[133] Bruce, *Hebrews*, 232. See also Attridge, *Hebrews*, 274.

[134] See Ellingworth, *Hebrews*, 500.

[135] Koester, *Hebrews*, 432–33.

[136] Ibid., 433. The phrase that follows in the Masoretic text, "Your law is within my heart"

In addition to differences between the MT and the LXX version, there are also differences between the LXX version and the text of Hebrews. The author of Hebrews diverges from the LXX in two main instances.[137] First, instead of saying that God did not ᾔτησας "request" burnt offering and sin offerings as in 39:7 of the LXX, the author of Hebrews writes that you were not εὐδόκησας "pleased" with them. The idea of pleasing God is important to the author of Hebrews and so his use of εὐδόκησας helps develop this theme in his writing.[138] Second, the author of Hebrews shortens the quotation of verse 9 in the LXX, leaving off the verb, ἐβουλή-θην. What results is a change in translation from "I desire to do your will," to "to do your will."[139] Koester suggests that this was "perhaps to show that Christ did not merely 'wish' to do God's will, but came 'to do' it."[140] In this way, Christ's work is characterized as something secure and reliable, eliciting confidence in Jesus.

Sacrifices Versus a Body that Accomplishes God's Will (10:5b-7)

Verses 5b-7 can be divided into two parallel parts.

    A. Θυσίαν καὶ προσφορὰν οὐκ ἠθέλησας, (5b)
      B. σῶμα δὲ κατηρτίσω μοι. (5c)
    A'. ὁλοκαυτώματα καὶ περὶ ἁμαρτίας οὐκ εὐδόκησας. (6)
      B' τότε εἶπον, Ἰδοὺ ἥκω, ἐν κεφαλίδι βιβλίου γέγραπται

(Ps 40:8b), seems to indicate that the scroll is indeed the law: Bruce, *Hebrews*, 234–35. Cf. Ellingworth, *Hebrews*, 502.

[137] The LXX and the Hebrews text have a few other variants. The main differences in the LXX reading and Hebrews are in **bold**:

Psalm 39:7-9 LXX:
7. Θυσίαν καὶ προσφορὰν οὐκ ἠθέλησας **ὠτία** δὲ κατηρτίσω μοι **ὁλοκαύτωμα** καὶ περὶ ἁμαρτίας οὐκ **ᾔτησας**
8. τότε εἶπον ἰδοὺ ἥκω ἐν κεφαλίδι βιβλίου γέγραπται περὶ ἐμοῦ
9. τοῦ ποιῆσαι τὸ θέλημά σου ὁ θεός **μου ἐβουλήθην καὶ τὸν νόμον σου ἐν μέσω τῆς κοιλίας μου.**

Hebrews 10:5b-7:
5b. Θυσίαν καὶ προσφορὰν οὐκ ἠθέλησας, **σῶμα** δὲ κατηρτίσω μοι
6. **ὁλοκαυτώματα** καὶ περὶ ἁμαρτίας οὐκ **εὐδόκησας**
7. τότε εἶπον, Ἰδοὺ ἥκω ἐν κεφαλίδι βιβλίου γέγραπται περὶ ἐμοῦ, τοῦ ποιῆσαι ὁ θεὸς τὸ θέλημά σου

The LXX reading here adopts ὠτία as the harder reading, while other LXX manuscripts have σῶμα. As mentioned above, the author of Hebrews likely followed a LXX reading of this verse. Another minor variation is the pluralizing of ὁλοκαύτωμα in the Hebrews text (ὁλοκαυτώματα). This may be attributed to differing LXX versions.

[138] Cf. Heb 10:8, 38; 11:5-6; 13:16, 21.

[139] Attridge, *Hebrews*, 274.

[140] Koester, *Hebrews*, 433.

περὶ ἐμοῦ, τοῦ ποιῆσαι ὁ θεὸς τὸ θέλημά σου. (7)

There is a movement from A to A' in intensity and specificity. In A, the author states that God does not desire sacrifices and offerings. But in A' God is described as not taking pleasure in burnt offerings[141] and sin offerings.[142] The contrast to these offerings is found in B and B'. These are the things that God desires and bring him pleasure. There is also an increase in specificity from B to B'. The body, which has been prepared, is for the specific purpose of doing God's will. The author of Hebrews will interpret the doing of God's will as Jesus' once-for-all offering of his body (10:10). The contrast between the Levitical sacrifices and Jesus' once-for-all sacrifice serves to create two unequal options. Who would desire to come to God through sacrifices and offerings that God does not delight in or desire? The rhetoric contained within this quotation of Scripture serves the author's purpose. It paints those who bring the traditional offerings as those outside of God's pleasure and will.

Jesus as the singer of the Psalm reveals his intimacy with God by disclosing what does and does not please God.[143] By placing the Psalm on Jesus' lips, the author identifies Jesus as the authority to whom the readers are to pay close attention. In addition, Jesus is clearly identified as the one who accomplishes God's will.[144] What is emphasized is the fact that Jesus accomplishes by his sacrifice something that the Levitical sacrifices could never do. Therefore the Psalm itself seems to speak of the futility of the Old Testament sacrifices.

The language here evokes a sense of purposefulness, not only in Jesus' act of self-sacrifice, but also in the fulfillment of the Levitical sacrifices. If it was God's will that Jesus offer himself up once-for-all, then implicitly it was God's will that the former sacrifices be replaced. This legitimizes the polemic against the Levitical sacrifice by casting its replacement as part of God's divine plan, which in turn strengthens the legitimacy of the community that rests upon the once-for-all sacrifice of Christ.

---

[141] Whole burnt offerings were completely burned up to God. No portion was left for the worshiper. These sacrifices were used for: purification, expiation of sins, fulfillment of vows, freewill offerings, and festival offerings. Cf. Lev 14:19-20; Num 15:3. See ibid.

[142] Sacrifices for sins were not completely burned up, but a portion of the meat was given to the priests. Cf. Lev 4:1-5:13; 6:26. See ibid.

[143] This follows the introduction of the epistle, where Jesus, the Son of God, is identified as the one who speaks to us in the last days. He speaks to us the will and message of God (1:2).

[144] This idea is also found in other early Christian writings (Matt 5:17; 9:13; 10:34; 11:19; John 10:10).

Interpretation of Psalm 39:7-9 (LXX; 10:8-10)

The reason why the author quotes this passage is made clear as he interprets it in verses 8-10. In essence, he uses the passage to argue that the Levitical sacrifices have been displaced by the once-for-all sacrifice of Christ. The two different ways to approach God cannot co-exist, and so the arrival of the second necessarily requires the removal of the former. The author believes that Scripture itself speaks of the fulfillment of the Levitical sacrifices by the once-for-all sacrifice of Christ.

Summary of Psalm 39:7-9 (10:8-9a)

The author of the book begins his midrashic interpretation by summarizing the quotation.[145] And yet in his summary he rearranges things to rhetorically strengthen his argument. The author writes, "After saying above, 'Sacrifices and offerings and whole burnt offerings and sacrifices for sin you have not desired, nor have you taken pleasure in them' (which are offered according to the Law), then He said, 'Behold, I have come to do your will.'"[146] Instead of keeping the different categories for offerings separate, he lists them out together: sacrifices, offerings, whole burnt offerings, and sacrifices for sin (10:8). This creates rhetorically the wearying sense that these sacrifices just go on and on and on. Lane notes this rhetorical effect and writes that this rearrangement, "serves to intensify an impression of the divine disdain for the cultic provisions of the old covenant."[147] There is also the sense that the totality of sacrifices is in view. All sacrifices do not bring pleasure to God nor do they fulfill his desires.

The parenthetical statement, "which are offered according to the Law," seeks to tie together the Levitical sacrifices with the Law itself.[148] We have seen this "guilt by association" tactic in 10:1 as well, "For the Law, since it has only a shadow of the good things to come and not the very form of things, can never, by the same sacrifices which they offer continually year by year, make perfect those who draw near" (10:1). The author wants to transfer the explicit criticisms of the sacrifices in Psalm

---

[145] Donald Hagner, "Interpreting the Epistle to the Hebrews," in *The Literature and Meaning of Scripture*, ed. Morris A. Inch and C. Hassell Bullock (Grand Rapids: Baker, 1981) 229.

[146] Hebrews 10:8-9a.

[147] Lane, *Hebrews 9–13*, 264.

[148] It is this parenthetical statement that leads Montefiore to write, "Our author is not thinking here of particular ordinances: he is referring rather to the divine disapproval of the Law itself" (Montefiore, *Hebrews*, 168).

39:7-9 to the Law. Perhaps this is why he does not finish the quotation in 39:9, which reads, καὶ τὸν νόμον σου ἐν μέσῳ τῆς κοιλίας μου (Psalm 39:9 LXX).[149]

Removal (ἀναιρεῖ) of First to Establish (στήσῃ) the Second (10:9b)

The summary of the text gives way to perhaps the most radical statement in this section, "He takes away (ἀναιρεῖ) the first in order to establish the second."[150] The question that emerges, however, is what are the referents of "first" and "second?" Koester argues that the first refers to the first covenant and the second refers to the second covenant.

> The Law prescribed sacrifices that could not "take away" (*aphairein*) sins (10:4); therefore, when Christ accomplished God's purpose, the Law is "abolished" (*anairein*, 10:9). The problem is that God is the giver of the Law and to say that Christ "abolishes the first" covenant "in order to establish the second" (10:9) raises questions about God's own reliability.[151]

Koester sees a close parallel between the first covenant and the Law. If the first covenant is abolished, so also the Law associated with it. David deSilva sees the contrast as between the first cultus and the second cultus.[152] Lane identifies the first as the first arrangement and the second as the second arrangement. It seems that Lane also has covenant in mind when he speaks of "arrangement."[153]

Now certainly the idea of the old and new covenants is in the background, but the author of Hebrews seems much more focused on arguing

---

[149] While the phrase, "your law is within my heart," would not contradict the essential argument made by the author of Hebrews, it would detract from the intensity of the contrast that he seeks to make between all things belonging to the old covenant and all things belonging to the new. The law in its prescriptions regarding priesthood and sacrifice are viewed as belonging to what is replaced by Christ. Cf. Heb 7:11-12, 19, 28; 9:19-28.

[150] This pattern has been set with the author's discussion on priesthood and covenant. In each of these discussions, the arrival of the new renders the old: obsolete, set aside, and taken away (7:18-19, 8:13). Ellingworth notes that this term ἀναιρεῖ, "is the strongest negative statement the author has made or will make about the OT cultus: Christ by his sacrifice 'abolishes' or 'destroys' it"; *Hebrews,* 504. See also Koester, *Hebrews,* 434; Attridge, *Hebrews,* 275. Lane notes that the definition, "to suppress, to abolish, to annul," is not attested in the NT, but is well attested in classical and Hellenistic Greek; *Hebrews 9–13,* 256 n. r.

[151] Koester, *Hebrews,* 439–40.

[152] deSilva, *Perseverance in Gratitude,* 322.

[153] See Lane, *Hebrews 9–13,* 254, 264.

his particular point, namely that the sacrifice of Christ has rendered the Old Testament sacrifices obsolete. What is done away with is the Levitical offering for sin (10:18). Therefore, the "first" in this context likely refers to the Levitical sacrifices, while the "second" refers to Christ's once-for-all sacrifice (the accomplishment of God's will).[154] Montefiore writes, "Animal sacrifices have been superseded by the personal self-sacrifice of Jesus."[155] Surely the author of Hebrews' critique of the Levitical sacrifices has implications for the Law and covenant, but it seems that his immediate polemic in this passage is specifically with the Old Testament sacrifices.[156]

Sanctification Once-for-All

The connection between the will of God and the sacrifice of Christ is made explicit in verse 10; "By this will we have been sanctified through the offering of the body of Jesus Christ once for all."[157] Grässer writes, "Wegen seines Mißfallens an den iterativen Opfern ist es der Wille Gottes, Jesus zum Opfer zu begehren (V 10)."[158] Therefore the real contrast that is made is between what Jesus' sacrifice accomplishes and what the Levitical sacrifices could not accomplish.

The author of Hebrews argues that the Levitical sacrifices do not make the worshiper complete or perfect (10:1). The meaning of this is clarified as the author describes Jesus' offering making the worshiper sanctified once-for-all (10:10). Bruce writes, "And it is by His fulfilling the will of God to the uttermost that He has 'sanctified' His people and pro-

---

[154] Bruce, *Hebrews*, 235 n. 48. Hughes, *Hebrews*, 399; Ellingworth, *Hebrews*, 504–5.

[155] Montefiore, *Hebrews*, 168.

[156] Grässer identifies the first as the cultic offerings and the second as the obedience of the Son, but then goes on to broaden the scope of change. He writes,

> Und er ist von grundstürzender Tragweite: Die alte Heilsordnung wird annulliert, damit die neue in Kraft treten kann. Denn natürlich umgreift das πρῶτον und das δεύτερον auch den ‚ersten' und den ‚zweiten' Bund (8,7.13; 9,1.15.18), das ‚erste' und das ‚zweite' Zelt (9,2.6b.8b), ja selbst noch die letzte große μετάθεσις, bei der die alte Welt einer himmlischen, unvergänglichen weichen muß (12,27), in welcher die δικαιώματα σαρκός mitsamt Priester- und Opferkult keine Geltung mehr haben (Grässer, *Hebräer*, 2:222–23).

[157] See Lane, *Hebrews 9–13*, 265. Lane notes that shifting from the third person to the first person plural "we", "lends to the formulation of v 10 a confessional quality" (265). This would function then to unite the community around this truth and further define its identity.

[158] Grässer, *Hebräer*, 2:221.

vided the 'perfection', which was unattainable on the basis of the ancient sacrifices."[159]

The three deficiencies of the old cultic sacrifices outlined in 10:1-3 are resolved by the once-for-all sacrifice of Christ. Through Jesus' sacrifice: 1) worshipers are made perfect/complete;[160] 2) there is no longer a reminder of sin because the sacrifice was once-for-all;[161] and 3) the people are made holy (ἡγιασμένοι ἐσμέν),[162] indicating the removal of sins.[163]

Socio-Rhetorical Function

The author's polemic against the Old Testament sacrifices functions to dissuade his readers from participating in them. He does not want them to abandon his community and the sacrifice of Christ by which they approach God. The author sets up boundaries around his community and implies that those who are on the inside do not come to God through Levitical sacrifices. There is also a socializing function in that he teaches his readers how they should view the Levitical sacrifices, how they should read Scripture, and how they are to approach God in worship.

In this way, the author's community is clearly distinguished from the dominant Jewish culture. Those who remain in the community are built up and strengthened by their common beliefs regarding sacrifice. Richard Nelson points out that the author's portrayal of Christ's sacrificial act, not only has theological, but also psychological and social implications. He writes,

> Thus, sacrifice was believed to have a positive effect on one's relationship to God. At the same time, sacrifice provided its practitioners psychological and social gains...Hebrews uses the psychological aspect to assert that Christ's sacrifice cancels out feelings of guilt. The social aspects of sacrifice are used to build up a community of worship.[164]

---

[159] Bruce, *Hebrews*, 236. Michel argues similarly, "Was den Tieropfern unmöglich war— eine Umwandlung des Menschen in einen neuen Zustand vor Gott—ist durch christi Werk Wirklichkeit geworden" (Michel, *Hebräer*, 339).

[160] 10:14 connects the idea of the worshiper's sanctification and his or her perfection.

[161] 10:17 revisits the quotation of Jeremiah 31:34 describing God as no longer remembering the sins of those in the new covenant.

[162] The periphrastic perfect tense has the effect of stressing "a state of consecration resulting from some decisive event in the past" (Lane, *Hebrews 9–13*, 256 n. v, 264).

[163] 10:18 indicates that there is forgiveness of sins.

[164] Richard Nelson, "'He Offered Himself': Sacrifice in Hebrews," *Int* 57 (2003) 258–59.

Nelson gives examples of how sacrifice functions within a society and then states, "Hebrews takes up the social benefits inherent in sacrifice with its call to gather as a worshipping community, its reference to a communal sacrificial meal from the altar, and its renegotiation of the social categories of honor and shame."[165] Those who remain in communion with God through the sacrifice of Christ are defined as pleasing God, thus receiving his honor, which should take precedence over any shame they receive from the dominant Jewish society.[166]

By painting the Levitical sacrifices as abolished and ineffective for cleansing sin, the author leaves the readers with no alternative but to cling to the once-for-all sacrifice of Christ and abandon any thought of returning to the Levitical sacrifices.

And yet, we must note that the radical nature of the author's polemic is softened by his use of Scripture. By quoting Psalm 39:7-9 LXX, the author legitimizes his claims, which in turn legitimizes his community. The author aligns himself and his community with God. He is on God's side in criticizing the Old Testament cult. God approves and agrees with his statements that these sacrifices do not bring God pleasure nor fulfill his desires. In this way, the radical rhetoric of the abolishment of the Levitical sacrifices is seen as part of God's will.

Conclusion

Continuity/ Discontinuity

As we reflect upon the rhetoric used by the author of Hebrews, we affirm that it promotes a radical discontinuity with the Old Testament cultus. The author's rhetoric is effective in subverting allegiance to the Levicial system of approaching God in worship. At the same time, we must acknowledge that the new system, which replaces the old, has a conceptual framework that is built upon the old.[167]

The fact that what replaces the Levitical sacrifices is the sacrifice of Christ indicates that the Jewish conceptual category and function of

---

[165] Ibid., 263.

[166] Nelson indicates that the author is writing in a culture of honor and shame. Therefore, the author of the epistle needs to provide his audience, who may have experienced marginalization and reproach for joining the Christian community, a different definition of honor. The shame of the cross becomes the paradigm of honor for those in the community; ibid., 264.

[167] Cf. Roger L. Omanson, "A Superior Covenant: Hebrews 8:1—10:18," *RevExp* 82 (1985) 370.

sacrifice remain. The critique is not that the Old Testament worshipers were giving offerings with the wrong spirit, or that something was inherently wrong with the idea of sacrifice, rather the issue was efficacy. Olivier Herrenschmidt writes, "We see, then, that Christ's sacrifice is to be read and understood in direct comparison with the sacrifice in the Temple and, consequently, that what is being compared here is the respective efficacy of two rites."[168]

Nelson also notes how the author conceptualizes the deficiencies of the old sacrifices in light of the new. He writes, "Hebrews criticizes the previous sacrificial system to highlight, by contrast, the effectiveness of a 'better' sacrifice (9:23) that enacts a 'better covenant' (7:22) based on 'better promises' (8:26) made by Christ as the superior priest (7:11, 15, 26-27)."[169]

By using Scripture as the bedrock of his argument, the author establishes that he is speaking as a Jew to Jews. He appeals to the authority that binds both competing communities (Jewish and Christian) in order to show the fulfillment of one cultic system by another. In this way, he retains much of the Jewish heritage and history at the same time transforming it in the light of the revelation of Jesus Christ.[170]

ESCHATOLOGICAL CONTEXT

In essence, the author uses Psalm 39:7-9 to argue that the once-for-all sacrifice of Christ establishes (στήση)[171] the will or true intention of God. It accomplishes what the sacrifices under the Law could not do. Because it fulfills what the sacrifices looked forward to, it displaces and replaces the shadow. It is defined as the future reality that has come. Lane writes,

> The fulfillment of Ps 40:6-8 inaugurates the new arrangement. The quotation from the psalm and the event of Christ confirm that the old religious order has been abolished definitively. In the design of God, the two redemptive arrangements are irreconcilable; the

---

[168] Olivier Herrenschmidt, "Sacrifice: Symbolic or Effective," in *Between Belief and Transgression: Structuralist Essays in Religion, History, and Myth*, ed. Michel Izard and Pierre Smith, trans. John Leavitt (Chicago: University of Chicago, 1982) 36–37.

[169] Nelson, "He Offered Himself," 251.

[170] Although the author follows midrashic exegetical methods, his hermeneutic has been radically transformed by the revelation of Jesus Christ. See above chapter 4, pages 90-91.

[171] Lane notes that this word "is a preferred word in the LXX for expressing the creative activity of God in the establishing of a covenant or the giving of an unconditional promise" (Lane, *Hebrews 9–13*, 256 n. t).

one excludes the other. The suppression of the first occurs in order that (ἵνα) the validity of the new order of relationship may be confirmed (cf. 8:7, 13). Jesus Christ and the word of Scripture are agents of epochal change that introduce a radically new situation for the community of God's people.[172]

It is this redemptive historical framework that provides the context in which to speak of the abolishment of institutions and practices so closely tied to the Jewish identity and faith.

The difference between Qumran's eschatological views and the author of Hebrews' view may explain how the author of Hebrews' critique is more radical. The author places more emphasis on a realized eschatology compared with Qumran. Ellingworth writes that the author speaks of the "present effects of Christ's sacrifice in the lives of the believers, especially in their cleansing from sin."[173] The Qumran community was still anticipating the arrival of the future/heavenly temple. It seems that the author of Hebrews' higher realized eschatology demanded a greater degree of discontinuity with the older Jewish institutions.

Anti-Semitism, Anti-Judaism, Supersessionism in Hebrews 10:1-10

Can Hebrews 10:1-10 be considered anti-Semitic, anti-Judaic, or supersessionist? As we discussed previously, it would be anachronistic to describe the book of Hebrews as anti-Semitic. The nineteenth-century technical term referred to hatred, bias, abuse, and the destruction of Jews based on ethnic or racial differences. Our passage here deals specifically with theological differences among Jews.[174]

Anti-Judaism

Now certainly the Levitical sacrifices were very important to the identity and culture of the Jewish people. The Second Temple Jewish writings that we surveyed make this clear. Each Jewish community identified its members as those who offered sacrifices according to the Law or their particular interpretation of the Law.[175] Therefore, as we reflect upon the author of Hebrews' intention of distinguishing his community from the dominant

---

[172] Lane, *Hebrews 9–13*, 265.
[173] Ellingworth, *Hebrews*, 488.
[174] See above "Introduction," pages 2-3.
[175] See above chapter 6, pages 148-164.

Jewish society, it is possible to describe his critique of the Levitical sacrificial system in 10:1-10 as anti-Judaic. The author's rhetoric clearly seeks to subvert the dominant Jewish practice of approaching God through Levitical sacrifices. Unlike the critique of the cult in the Second Temple writings, the author's critique strikes at the very nature and effectiveness of the sacrifices themselves. He is promoting a sharp discontinuity with the dominant Jewish practice of sacrifice.

The question at hand, however, is whether this theological difference promotes hatred, or the destruction of the Jewish people? Now it is certainly true that the Levitical sacrifices were closely tied to the identity of the Jewish people. And we cannot deny that the author was speaking for the abrogation of these sacrifices. And yet, we must note that the core of the polemic in this section deals with the ineffectiveness of the Levitical sacrifices in enabling worshipers to draw near to God.[176] This is the same concern of many of the Second Temple Jewish writers.[177] The polemic against sacrifices in both Second Temple Jewish writings and Hebrews ultimately deals with the same questions, "What sacrifices please God?" or "What is the best way to approach God in worship?"

The author of Hebrews is not abandoning the essence of what makes the Jewish people uniquely Jewish, namely their relationship with God, but simply the means by which they draw near to him. Gunton writes,

> The relations of person to person in Israel are comprehended within the relations of them all to God, and the sacrifices are to do with the ordering of those relationships: with the establishing and re-establishing of the focus of Israel's life as a people. On such an understanding, the prophetic critique takes its place within that same network of relationships, anticipating the theology of the Letter to the Hebrews by highlighting the inadequacy of the sacrificial forms in themselves to secure true order in divine-human and consequently human-human relations.[178]

The reason why the Levitical sacrifices were held in such high esteem was because God himself ordained them in his law. Rabbi Johanan ben Zakkai[179] seems to echo a typical Jewish view of sacrifices. He responds to

---

[176] Heb 10:1, 4.

[177] See esp. Sir 34:21-23; 35:1-5.

[178] Colin Gunton, "Christ the Sacrifice: Aspects of the Language and Imagery of the Bible," in *The Glory of Christ in the New Testament: Studies in Christology in Memory of George Bradford Caird* (eds. L.D. Hurst and N.T. Wright; Oxford: Oxford University Press; New York: Clarendon Press, 1987), 235.

[179] Rabbi Johanan ben Zakkai lived in the first century AD.

his disciples, who asked him about the purifying effects of the ashes of the Red Heifer by saying,

> By your life! The corpse does not defile, nor do the waters (mixed with the ashes of the Heifer) purify. It is a decree of the king of the King of Kings. The Holy one, blessed be He, said I have ordained an ordinance and I have decreed a decree; no mortal is entitled to transgress it (though knowing no rational ground for it).[180]

Because God established the sacrifices, the people held them in high regard. Their importance and significance are intimately united with their function in ordering the people's relationship with God. In and of themselves, the sacrifices do not define Israel's identity. Therefore, we cannot say that the author of Hebrews' theological critique of the Levitical sacrifices promotes hatred toward the Jewish people or their destruction.

Supersessionism

We have stated previously that the author of Hebrews has indeed argued for the supersession or fulfillment[181] of the Levitical sacrifices by the once-for-all sacrifice of Christ. For the author, the appearance of the second necessitates the abrogation of the first.[182] Bruce argues that the once-for-all sacrifice of Christ has indeed superseded the Levitical sacrifices of the Old Testament. He writes, "The sacrifices in which God is said to take no pleasure are the sacrifices by the ancient cultic law of Israel; now that cultic law is to be superseded by a new order, inaugurated by Christ's perfect obedience to the will of God."[183] William Lane argues similarly, "In the following paragraph (vv 5-10) the writer argues that the ineffective sacrifices of the old covenant have been superseded by the sufficient sacrifice of Christ."[184]

What should be noted is the fact that the reason why both means of atonement cannot exist simultaneously is because the author believes there are only one people of God.[185] In other words, he understands his

---

[180] *Pesiqta de Rab Kahana* 40b. See Salomon Buber, *Pesikta de-Rav Kahana* (Yerushalaim: n.p., 1962 or 1963; repr. Lyck: Hevrat mekitse nirdamim, 1868). Though this is a late text, it may reflect earlier first century sentiments.

[181] See above pages 191-92.

[182] Heb 10:9b states, "He takes away the first in order to establish the second." The first must be removed before the second could be established. Cf. 8:8-10.

[183] Bruce, *Hebrews*, 235.

[184] Lane, *Hebrews 9–13*, 262. Cf. Nelson, "He Offered Himself," 258.

[185] Heb 3:1-6 indicates that both Jesus and Moses served the same house. In other words,

community as the rightful descendants or remnant of the Jewish people. He is not promoting a different faith from Judaism, but the eschatological climax of the Jewish faith. Therefore, there can only be one means to draw near for the one people of God.

The author of Hebrews is convinced that God himself has decreed the abolishment of the older means—the Levitical sacrifices—by the establishment of the eschatological means, Jesus' once-for-all self-sacrifice.[186] Therefore, in order to be faithful to the revelation of God, he is obliged to proclaim the fulfillment of the old at the arrival of the new. He understands his community, which in distinction from the dominant Jewish society, has the definitive means to approach God in worship.

What should be clear, however, is the fact that the author is not arguing for the complete abandonment of the Jewish people by God. He does not seek to destroy Judaism or the identity of the Jewish people, rather he seeks to promote his understanding of the fulfillment of the Levitical sacrifices and the God-defined means to approach God in the eschatological age.

Conclusion

Hebrews 10:1-10 can be considered anti-Judaic in the sense that it speaks of the abrogation of the Levitical sacrifices and seeks to distinguish the author's community from the larger Jewish community. Indeed the author uses a superior/inferior dialectic promoting the once-for-all sacrifice of Christ in order to subvert allegiance to the dominant Jewish practice of sacrifice. In his use of Psalm 39:7-9 (LXX), he seeks to legitimize his view of sacrifice in order to garner greater fidelity to his community. In the process, his rhetoric also socializes the readers as to how they are to view and practice sacrifice in their community as well as how to read and interpret Scripture. In this way, the author creates boundaries for his community. Those who come to God through the sacrifice of Christ are identified as those who are on the inside. Therefore, the language in Hebrews 10:1-10 is used to reinforce the unique identity of those in the community as the eschatological people of God.

However, the polemic in this section in no way promotes hatred toward the Jewish people or seeks to destroy the Jewish identity. Though the Levitical sacrifices were important, they did not in and of themselves define

---

the author of Hebrews believed that the community in Hebrews shared a common heritage with those in the Old Testament.

[186] Heb 10:8-10.

the identity of the Jews. What was of primary importance was the function and presumed goal of the sacrifices. The author argues simply that Christ's sacrifice fulfills the function and goal intended for the Levitical sacrifices. Therefore, in the author of Hebrews' polemic, the basic Jewish conception of sacrifice as the means to approach God remains and the identity of the Jewish people is not damaged. From the author's vantage point, Christ's sacrifice is for the ultimate benefit of the Jewish people in allowing them unprecedented access to God.

Conclusion

THE complexity in answering the question of whether the epistle to the Hebrews is anti-Semitic, anti-Judaic and/or supersessionistic has been demonstrated in our research. Throughout the epistle, the author describes his community as having both continuity and discontinuity with Judaism. This balance is appropriate in distinguishing the author's community from the larger Jewish society, while at the same time seeking to retain the community's Jewish roots and history. And yet it is this balance that makes the question of anti-Semitism, anti-Judaism, and supersessionism so difficult.

In the introduction of the dissertation we distinguished anti-Semitism from anti-Judaism. Anti-Semitism is a 19th century term used to describe ethnic or racial attacks against Jews from non-Jews. Anti-Judaism refers to theological disagreements either among Jews, between Jews and Jewish-Christians, or between Jews and Gentile Christians. But what was most important in our discussion was whether or not the anti-Judaism promotes hatred toward or the destruction of the Jewish people. We acknowledge that some forms of anti-Judaism are just as reprehensible as anti-Semitism. It does not matter whether a person receives hatred because of their ethnicity or because of their religion. Therefore, as we examined the polemical passages in Hebrews, we asked whether they were written for or against the Jewish people.

Also in the introduction, we qualified the term supersession. When applied to Judaism, what is traditionally meant is that Judaism is defunct and the church replaces Israel. This traditional understanding does not do justice to the fact that Christianity emerged from Judaism. The term in its traditional understanding implies the replacement of Judaism and the Jewish people by something completely new and foreign. Therefore, as we examined the polemical passages, we asked what specifically was being replaced? And what was the nature of the things that replaced them? Were they completely new institutions, or things that were informed by the old?

In our analysis, we identified the sociological context in which the author's polemic is used as that of a conflict between a counter-cultural sect with its parent group. The author was seeking to persuade those who were tempted to revert back to Judaism to remain faithful to his community, while strengthening and confirming the commitment of those who did remain. His polemic against the Levitical priesthood and law, Mosaic covenant, and Levitical sacrifices functions to legitimize his community and further distinguish it from the dominant Jewish society.

In our discussion of priesthood and polemic in Hebrews, we first established the importance of the Levitical priesthood for the Jewish people. Examining several Second Temple Jewish writings, we concluded that though there were critiques of individual priests, there was a high reverence for the priesthood as an institution. It was therefore, closely tied to the very identity of the Jewish people.

For this reason, we acknowledged the radical discontinuity implied in the author of Hebrews' polemic against the Levitical priesthood and law in 7:1-19. The author argues that the Levitical priesthood and law were not able to perfect and have been set aside (7:11-12, 18-19). He uses a superior/inferior dialectic, perfection rhetoric, and a Christocentric reading of Psalm 110:4 to legitimize Jesus' priesthood and dissuade his readers from utilizing the Levitical priesthood and submitting to the law. His midrashic reading of Psalm 110:4 also functions to socialize his readers, not only in how they are to relate to the Levitical priesthood, but also in how they are to read Scripture.

This radical discontinuity, however, is balanced by the fact that the author understood the priesthood of Christ as the fulfillment of the Levitical priesthood. There is a type/ anti-type relationship between them. The priesthood of Christ is informed and foreshadowed by the Levitical priesthood. Jesus' priesthood is able to bring about the perfection that was implicitly assumed to be the goal of the Levitical priesthood and law.

In our analysis of covenant and polemic in Hebrews, we first established the importance of the Mosaic covenant in forming the identity of the Jewish people. The covenant rhetoric found in much of the Second Temple Jewish writings was used to inspire Jews to remain faithful to their Jewish faith and heritage in the face of Gentile threats. The covenant language formed boundaries between those who were included in the community and those who were excluded. It served to solidify and legitimize the identity of the Jewish people.

This analysis highlights the radical nature of the author of Hebrews' statements in 8:1-13. To declare the old covenant as having fault (8:7) and as good as annulled (8:13) would have sounded quite alarming to Jewish ears. And yet what we find as we examine this passage is that the author uses new covenant rhetoric for the same general purpose as the other Jewish writers. He uses covenant language to rally his community to greater commitment and fidelity in the face of a threat from the larger Jewish society. The goal of his polemic against the Mosaic covenant was to persuade those in his community to remain and not align themselves with their former Jewish community.

By using an extended quotation of Jeremiah 31:31-34, the author legitimizes his claims that the old covenant was inadequate in fulfilling God's purposes. What is implied is that God himself declares the obsolescence of the old at the inauguration of the new. However, we must keep in mind that what replaces the old covenant is a covenant that is also informed and shaped by the old. There is a shadow/reality relationship between these covenants. Nevertheless, the benefit of the new is clearly outlined in the quotation and functions to persuade the readers to remain connected to the new covenant community promoted by the author.

In our analysis of sacrifice and polemic in Hebrews, we established that Levitical sacrifices did play a prominent role in the life and identity of the Jewish people. Our survey of Second Temple Jewish writings confirmed that adherence to the sacrificial prescriptions of the law functioned as an identity marker for the Jews. Those who sacrificed properly were on the inside of the community, while those who did not were on the outside. In addition, we also noted that the polemic against sacrifices was usually directed toward those who offered animals improperly or with an improper attitude or understanding.

Therefore, the radical nature of the author's polemic against the Levitical sacrifices in 10:1-10 was well noted. The impossibility of "the blood of bulls and goats to take away sins" (10:4) describes the Levitical sacrifices as useless for their presumed purpose. The implications would be that those who continued to use these sacrifices would not be cleansed of their sins or consciences (10:2) and would remain in an unfavorable relationship with God. On the other hand, what is implied is that those who come to God through the sacrifice of Christ will be made holy and able to draw near to God in worship (10:10).

However, it must be stated that the author depicts the final sacrifice of Christ as the reality to which the Levitical sacrifices foreshadowed (10:1). The author's conceptualization of Jesus' sacrifice is informed by the Levitical sacrifices. Christ's sacrifice fulfills what the Levitical sacrifices were not able to do. The author of Hebrews was addressing the questions that were posed by many Second Temple Jewish writers, namely, "What sacrifice(s) please(s) God?" or "What was the best way to approach God?"

The author again uses Scripture to prove his point. He quotes Psalm 39:7-9 (LXX) in order to persuade his readers that God himself initiated the change in sacrifices. God himself declares which sacrifice pleases him. The author's midrashic interpretation contrasts Jesus' body with the Levitical sacrifices (10:5), and emphasizes how God does not take pleasure in the Levitical offerings. This rhetoric is used to dissuade his readers from coming to God through ineffective sacrifices and to encourage them to make use of the once-for-all sacrifice of Christ. He also socializes them in how they are to relate to the Levitical offerings (do not participate in them) as well as how to read and interpret Scripture.

From our analysis of these polemical passages, we conclude that the author's use of a Christocentric hermeneutic, superior/inferior dialectic, type/anti-type rhetoric, and perfection language leaves his readers with the strongest reasons to remain connected to his community. The polemical rhetoric serves to further distinguish the author's community from the larger dominant Jewish society. In this way it shapes the identity of the counter-cultural Christian sect.

Some scholars have argued that the author was simply seeking to encourage apathetic Christians in his community to renew their commitment and faith. They do not see any direct polemic at work with the larger Jewish community, thus mitigating any sense of anti-Semitism or anti-Judaism in Hebrews. It has been shown, however, that this approach does not do justice to the sociological dynamic of the on-going separation of Christianity from Judaism. The need for the Christian community to form its identity in distinction from the larger Jewish society is made abundantly clear in the passages examined in this dissertation.

While the polemic in this context is clearly not anti-Semitic, it may be considered anti-Judaic in the sense that it speaks of the fulfillment of the Levitical priesthood and law, the Mosaic covenant, and the Levitical sacrifices. There was clearly a theological difference between the author of Hebrews and the larger Jewish community. The Levitical priesthood and law, the Mosaic covenant, and the Levitical sacrifices were closely tied to the very identity of the Jews. But the author of Hebrews argues that these things are of little use in gaining access to God.

It should be emphasized, however, that the polemic in the epistle cannot be charged with promoting hatred or the destruction of the Jewish people. Nor is it the case, as Gager maintains, that Hebrews contains the "most sustained and systematic case against Judaizing to be found anywhere in Christian literature of the first century."[1] The author's understanding of Jesus' priesthood, the new covenant, and Jesus' once-for-all sacrifice is shaped by the Levitical priesthood and law, Mosaic covenant, and Levitical sacrifices, respectively. The institutions of the new covenant are intimately connected to the old covenant. There is a shadow/reality, type-anti-type relationship. The function or intentions of the new institutions correspond to the presumed functions of the old ones.

The author of Hebrews is arguing that God himself has brought about the fulfillment of these institutions through his Son's priesthood, his once-for-all sacrifice, and the new covenant he inaugurated in the last days. These new institutions are never denied the Jews. In fact, the context of the epistle presumes that these are primarily for the Jews, considering that the author was speaking to a Jewish-Christian community. The author is not arguing for the abandonment by God of the Jewish people, but rather for the abandonment of the shadowy means by which God's people drew near to him. It is here we can speak of a qualified supersessionism. According to the author of Hebrews, the Levitical priesthood, the Mosaic covenant, and the Levitical sacrifices have been superseded by Jesus' priesthood, the new covenant, and Jesus' once-for-all sacrifice.

However, we conclude that the polemical passages in Hebrews do not promote hatred of the Jews, nor do they advocate the destruction of the Jewish people. Rather, the author of Hebrews stresses the fulfillment of specific Jewish institutions for the benefit of the Jews. It is this idea of fulfillment that rules out the charge that the epistle promotes the supersession of the Jewish people. Because of God's great love for his people, he has provided a superior way by which his people can draw near to him.

---

[1] John G. Gager, *The Origins of Anti-Semitism: Attitudes Toward Judaism in Pagan and Christian Antiquity* (New York: Oxford University, 1983) 183.

Bibliography

Commentaries

Attridge, Harold W. *The Epistle to the Hebrews: A Commentary on the Epistle to the Hebrews.* Hermeneia. Philadelphia: Fortress, 1989.
Bruce, A. B. *The Epistle to the Hebrews.* Edinburgh: T. & T. Clark, 1899.
Bruce, F. F. *The Epistle to the Hebrews.* Rev. ed. NICNT. Grand Rapids: Eerdmans, 1990.
Buchanan, George Wesley. *To the Hebrews: Translation, Comment and Conclusions.* AB 36. Garden City, N.Y.: Doubleday, 1972.
Delitzsch, Franz. *Commentary on the Epistle to the Hebrews.* 2 vols. Translated by T. L. Kingsbury. Edinburgh: T. & T. Clark, 1871. Reprint. Minneapolis: Klock & Klock, 1978.
deSilva, David A. *Perseverance in Gratitude: A Socio-Rhetorical Commentary on the Epistle "to the Hebrews."* Grand Rapids: Eerdmans, 2000.
Ellingworth, Paul. *The Epistle to the Hebrews: A Commentary on the Greek Text.* NIGTC. Grand Rapids: Eerdmans, 1993.
Gordon, Robert P. *Hebrews.* Readings: A New Biblical Commentary. Sheffield: Sheffield Academic, 2000.
Grässer, Erich. *An die Hebräer.* EKKNT 17. 3 vols. Zurich: Benziger, 1993.
Hagner, Donald A. *Hebrews.* NIBCNT 14. Peabody, Mass: Hendrickson, 1990.
———. *Encountering the Book of Hebrews.* Grand Rapids: Baker Academic, 2002.
Hugedé, Norbert. *Le sacerdoce du fils: commentaire de l'Epître aux Hébreux.* Paris: Fischbacher, 1983.
Hughes, Philip E. *A Commentary on the Epistle to the Hebrews.* Grand Rapids: Eerdmans, 1977.
Jewett, Robert. *Letter to Pilgrims: A Commentary on the Epistle to the Hebrews.* New York: Pilgrim, 1981.
Kistemaker, Simon J. *Exposition of the Epistle to the Hebrews.* NTC. Grand Rapids: Baker, 1984.
Koester, Craig R. *The Epistle to the Hebrews: A New Translation with Introduction and Commentary.* AB 36. New York: Doubleday, 2001.
Lane, William. *Hebrews 1–8.* WBC 47A. Dallas: Word, 1991.
———. *Hebrews 9–13.* WBC 47B. Dallas: Word, 1991.
Michel, Otto. *Der Brief an die Hebräer.* 13th ed. KEK. Göttingen: Vandenhoeck & Ruprecht, 1975.

Moffatt, James. *A Critical and Exegetical Commentary on the Epistle to the Hebrews.* ICC. Edinburgh: T. & T. Clark, 1924.
Montefiore, H. W. *The Epistle to the Hebrews.* HNTC. New York: Harper & Row, 1964.
Spicq, C. *L'Epitre aux Hebreux.* 2 vols. Paris: Gabalda, 1952–53.
———. *L'Epitre aux Hebreux.* SB. Paris: Gabalda, 1977.
Strack, Hermann L. and Paul Billerbeck. *Kommentar zum Neuen Testament aus Talmud und Midrasch.* 6 vols. Munich: Beck, 1922–1961.
Stuart, Moses. *A Commentary on the Epistle to the Hebrews.* Andover: Flagg, Gould, and Newman, 1833.
Weiss, H.-F. *Der Brief an die Hebräer.* KEK 13. Göttingen: Vandenhoeck & Ruprecht, 1991.
Westcott, Brooke Foss. *The Epistle to the Hebrews.* London: Macmillan, 1892.
Wilson, R. McL. *Hebrews.* NCBC. Grand Rapids: Eerdmans, 1987.

Monographs, Dissertations

A Theological Understanding of the Relationship Between Christians and Jews. New York: Office of the General Assembly of the Presbyterian Church (U.S.A.), 1987.
Abel, F. M. *Histoire de la Palestine depuis la conquête d'Alexandre jusqu'à l'invasion arabe.* 2 vols. Paris: Gabalda, 1952.
Agus, Aharon R. E. *The Binding of Isaac and Messiah: Law, Martyrdom, and Deliverance in Early Rabbinic Religiosity.* SUNY Series in Judaica. Albany: SUNY Press, 1988.
Anderson, R. Dean, Jr. *Ancient Rhetorical Theory and Paul.* CBET 17. Kampen: Kok Pharos, 1996.
Balla, Peter. *The Melchizedekian Priesthood.* Budapest: Ráday Nyomda, 1995.
Baum, Gregory. Introduction to *Faith and Fratricide,* by Rosemary Radford Ruether. 1974. Reprinted, Eugene, Ore.: Wipf & Stock, 1996.
Baumgarten, Joseph M. "Sacrifice and Worship among the Jewish Sectarians of the Dead Sea (Qumrân) Scrolls." *HTR* 46 (1953) 141–59.
———. *Studies in Qumran Law.* SJLA 24. Leiden: Brill, 1977.
Beck, N.A. *Mature Christianity: The Recognition and Repudiation of the Anti-Jewish Polemic of the New Testament.* 2d ed. New York: Crossroad, 1994.
Beckwith, Roger T., and Martin J. Selman. *Sacrifice in the Bible.* Grand Rapids: Baker, 1995.
Behm, J. *Der Begriff Διαθήκη im Neuen Testament.* Leipzig: Deichert, 1912.
Berger, Peter, and Thomas Luckmann. *The Social Construct of Reality: A Treatise in the Sociology of Knowledge.* Garden City, N.Y.: Doubleday, 1966.
Betz, Hans Dieter. *Galatians: A Commentary on Paul's Letter to the Churches in Galatia.* Hermeneia. Philadelphia: Fortress, 1979.
Bligh, John. *Chiastic Analysis of the Epistle to the Hebrews.* Oxford: Clarendon, 1966.
Blowers, Paul, editor. *In Dominico eloquio = In Lordly Eloquence: Essays on Patristic Exegesis in Honor of Robert Louis Wilken.* Grand Rapids: Eerdmans, 2002.
Boccaccini, Gabriele, editor. *The Origins of Enochic Judaism: Proceedings of the First Enoch Seminar, University of Michigan, Sesto Fiorentino, Italy, June 19–23, 2001.* Torino: Zamorani, 2002.
Boissevain, Jeremy. *Friends of Friends: Networks, Manipulators and Coalitions.* Oxford: Blackwell, 1974.

Borgen, Peder, and Søren Giversen. *The New Testament and Hellenistic Judaism*. Aarhus: Aarhus University Press, 1995.

Borgen, Peder, Vernon K. Robbins, and David B. Gowler, editors. *Recruitment, Conquest, and Conflict: Strategies in Judaism, Early Christianity, and the Greco-Roman World*. ESEC 6. Atlanta: Scholars, 1998.

Buber, Salomon. *Pesikta de-Rav Kahana*. Yerushalaim: n.p., 1962 or 1963. Reprinted, Lyck: Hevrat mekitse nirdamim, 1868.

Buck, Daniel E. "The Rhetorical Arrangement and Function of OT Citations in the Book of Hebrews." Ph.D. diss., Dallas Theological Seminary, 2002.

Burrows, Millar. *More Light on the Dead Sea Scrolls*. New York: Viking, 1958.

Charlesworth, James H. *Jesus and the Dead Sea Scrolls*. New York: Doubleday, 1992.

Charlesworth, James H., editor. *The Old Testament Pseudepigrapha*. 2 vols. Garden City, N.Y.: Doubleday, 1983.

Chilton, Bruce, and Jacob Neusner. *Judaism in the New Testament: Practices and Beliefs*. New York: Routledge, 1995.

Christiansen, Ellen Juhl. *The Covenant in Judaism and Paul: A Study of Ritual Boundaries as Identity Markers*. AGAJU 27. Leiden: Brill, 1995.

Classen, Carl Joachim. *Rhetorical Criticism of the New Testament*. WUNT 128. Tübingen: Mohr/Siebeck, 2000.

Cody, Aelred. *A History of Old Testament Priesthood*. AnBib 35. Rome: Pontifical Biblical Institute Press, 1969.

Cosby, Michael R. *The Rhetorical Composition and Function of Hebrews 11: In Light of Example Lists in Antiquity*. Macon, Ga.: Mercer, 1988.

Croy, N. Clayton. *Endurance in Suffering: Hebrews 12:1-13 in its Rhetorical, Religious, and Philosophical Context*. SNTSMS 98. Cambridge: Cambridge University, 1998.

Cryer, Frederick H., and Thomas L. Thompson. *Qumran between the Old and New Testaments*. JSOTSS 290. Sheffield: Sheffield Academic, 1998.

Danker, Frederick W., editor. *A Greek-English Lexicon of the New Testament and Other Early Christian Literature*. 3d ed. Based on Walter Bauer's *Griechisch-deutsches Worterbuch zu den Schriften des Neuen Testaments und der fruhchristlichen Literatur*, 6th edition, edited by Kurt Aland and Barbara Aland, with Viktor Reichmann and on previous English editions by W. F. Arndt, F. W. Gingrich, and F. W. Danker. Chicago: University of Chicago Press, 2000.

Davila, James R. *The Dead Sea Scrolls as Background to Postbiblical Judaism and Early Christianity: Papers from an International Conference at St. Andrews in 2001*. STDJ 46. Leiden: Brill, 2003.

Davis, Ronald Eugene. "The Function of Old Testament Texts in the Structure of Hebrews: A Rhetorical Analysis." Ph.D. diss., Southern Baptist Theological Seminary, 1994.

Demarest, Bruce A. "Priest After the Order of Melchizedek: A History of Interpretation of Hebrews 7 from the Era of the Reformation to the Present." Ph.D. diss., University of Manchester, 1973.

deSilva, David A. *Despising Shame: Honor Discourse and Community Maintenance in the Epistle to the Hebrews*. SBLDS 152. Atlanta: Scholars, 1995.

———. *Bearing Christ's Reproach*. North Richland Hills, Tex.: BIBAL, 1999.

———. *Introducing the Apocrypha: Message, Context, and Significance*. Grand Rapids: Baker, 2002.

Dey, Lala Kalyan Kumar. *The Intermediary World and Patterns of Perfection in Philo and Hebrews*. SBLDS 25. Missoula, Mont.: Scholars, 1975.

Douglas Mary. *Natural Symbols: Explorations in Cosmology.* 3d ed. New York: Pantheon, 1982.
Dubose, William Porcher. *High Priesthood and Sacrifice: an Exposition of the Epistle to the Hebrews.* London: Longmans, Green, 1908.
Dunn, James D. G. *The Partings of the Ways: Between Christianity and Judaism and their Significance for the Character of Christianity.* Philadelphia: Trinity, 1990.
Dunnill, John. *Covenant and Sacrifice in the Letter to the Hebrews.* SNTSMS 75. Cambridge: Cambridge University Press, 1992.
Eckardt, A. Roy. *Elder and Younger Brothers.* New York: Scribner, 1967.
Eckert, W. P., N. P. Levinson, and M. Stor, editors. *Antijudaismus im Neuen Testament? Exegetische und systematische Beitrage.* Munich: Kaiser, 1967.
Elliott, John H. *A Home for the Homeless: A Sociological Exegesis of 1 Peter, its Situation and Strategy.* 1981. Reprinted, Eugene, Ore.: Wipf & Stock, 2005.
———. *What is Social-Scientific Criticism?* GBS. Minneapolis: Fortress, 1993.
Evans, Christopher Francis. *The Theology of Rhetoric: The Epistle to the Hebrews.* London: Dr. Williams' Trust, 1988.
Evans, Craig, and Donald Hagner, editors. *Anti-Semitism and Early Christianity.* Minneapolis: Fortress, 1993.
Evans, Craig, and James A. Sanders. *Early Christian Interpretation of the Scriptures of Israel.* JSNTSS 148. Sheffield: Sheffield Academic, 1997.
Fannery, Austin P., editor. *Documents of Vatican II.* Grand Rapids: Eerdmans, 1975.
Freedman, David Noel, editor. *The Anchor Bible Dictionary.* 6 vols. New York: Doubleday, 1992.
Freeman, Gordon M. *The Rabbinic Understanding of Covenant as a Political Idea.* Ramat Gan, Israel: Bar-Ilan University, Dept. of Political Studies, 1977.
Freudmann, Lillian C. *Antisemitism in the New Testament.* Lanham, Md.: University Press of America, 1994.
Gager, John G. *Moses in Greco-Roman Paganism.* SBLMS 16. Nashville: Abingdon, 1972.
———. *The Origins of Anti-Semitism: Attitudes Toward Judaism in Pagan and Christian Antiquity.* Oxford: Oxford University, 1983.
Gärtner, Bertil E. *The Temple and the Community in Qumran and the New Testament: A Comparative Study in the Temple Symbolism of the Qumran Texts and the New Testament.* SNTSMS 1. Cambridge: Cambridge University Press, 1965.
Gordon, V. R. "Studies in the Covenantal Theology of the Epistle to the Hebrews in Light of its Setting." Ph.D. diss., Fuller Theological Seminary, 1979.
Green, William S., editor. *Approaches to Ancient Judaism,* Vol. 2. BJS 9. Missoula, Mont.: Scholars, 1980.
Guthrie, George H. *The Structure of Hebrews: A Text-Linguistic Analysis.* NovTSup 73. Leiden: Brill, 1994.
Halpern-Amaru, Betsy. *Rewriting the Bible: Land and Covenant in Post-Biblical Jewish Literature.* Valley Forge, Pa.: Trinity, 1994.
Haran, Menahem. *Temples and Temple Service in Ancient Israel.* Oxford: Clarendon, 1978.
Harrisville, Roy A. *The Concept of Newness in the New Testament.* Minneapolis: Augsburg, 1960.
Hartman, David. *A Living Covenant: The Innovative Spirit in Traditional Judaism.* Woodstock, Vt.: Jewish Lights, 1997.
Helyer, Larry R. *Exploring Jewish Literature of the Second Temple Period: A Guide for New Testament Students.* Downers, Grove, Ill.: InterVarsity, 2002.
Henrichsen, Walter A. *After the Sacrifice.* Grand Rapids: Zondervan, 1979.

Hens-Piazza, Gina. *Of Methods, Monarchs, and Meanings: A Sociorhetorical Approach to Exegesis*. SOTI 3. Macon: Mercer University, 1996.
Hoffman, Lawrence A. *Covenant of Blood: Circumcision and Gender in Rabbinic Judaism*. CSHJ. Chicago: University of Chicago Press, 1996.
Hughes, Graham. *Hebrews and Hermeneutics: The Epistle to the Hebrews as a New Testament Example of Biblical Interpretation*. SNTSMS 36. Cambridge: Cambridge University Press, 1979.
Hurst, Douglas C. "The Resurrected Word: An Investigation of the Audience and the Author of Hebrews." Ph.D. diss., Garrett Evangelical Theological Seminary, 1990.
Hurst, Lincoln D. *The Epistle to the Hebrews: Its Background of Thought*. SNTSMS 65. Cambridge: Cambridge University, 1990.
Isaac, Jules. *The Teaching of Contempt: Christian Roots of Anti-Semitism*. New York: McGraw-Hill, 1964.
———. *Jesus and Israel*. Translated by Helen Weaver. New York: Holt, Rinehart and Winston, 1971.
Isaacs, Marie E. *Sacred Space: An Approach to the Theology of the Epistle to the Hebrews*. JSNTSS 73. Sheffield: JSOT Press, 1992.
Isaak, Jon M. *Situating the Letter to the Hebrews in Early Christian History*. SBEC 53. Lewiston, N.Y.: Mellen, 2002.
Jennrich, Walter A. "Rhetorical Style in the New Testament: Romans and Hebrews." Ph.D. diss., Washington University, 1947.
Johnson, Richard Warren. *Going outside the Camp: The Sociological Function of the Levitical Critique in the Epistle to the Hebrews*. JSNTSS 209. Sheffield: Sheffield Academic, 2001.
———. "The Sociological Function of the Critique of the Levitical System in the Epistle to the Hebrews." Ph.D. diss., New Orleans Baptist Theological Seminary, 1998.
Johnsson, William G. "Defilement and Purgation in the Book of Hebrews." Ph.D. diss., Vanderbilt University, 1973.
Josephus. Translated by H. St. J. Thackeray et al. 10 vols. LCL. Cambridge: Harvard University Press, 1926–1965.
Kennedy, George A. *New Testament Interpretation through Rhetorical Criticism*. Chapel Hill: University of North Carolina Press, 1984.
Kim, Ui-won. "An Eschatological Examination of the New Covenant Based on the Dead Sea Scrolls." Ph.D. diss., New York University, 1983, 1981.
Kistemaker, Simon J. *The Psalm Citations in the Epistle to the Hebrews*. Amsterdam: Van Soest, 1961.
Klinzing, G. *Die Umdeutung des Kultus in der Qumrangemeinde und im Neuen Testament*. SUNT 7. Göttingen: Vandenhoeck & Ruprecht, 1971.
Kohlenberger, John R. editor. *The Parallel Apocrypha: Greek Text, King James Version, Douay Old Testament, the Holy Bible by Ronald Knox, Today's English Version, New Revised Standard Version, New American Bible, New Jerusalem Bible*. New York: Oxford University Press, 1997.
Kosmala, H. *Hebräer, Essener, Christen: Studien zur Vorgeschichte der frühchristlichen verkündigung*. SPB 1. Leiden: Brill, 1959.
Kurianal, James. *Jesus our High Priest: Ps. 110,4 as the Substructure of Heb 5,1-7,28*. European University Studies 693. Frankfurt: Lang, 2000.
Langmuir, Gavin I. *History, Religion, and Anti-Semitism*. Berkeley: University of California Press, 1990.

———. *Toward a Definition of Anti-Semitism*. Berkeley: University of California Press, 1990.
Larcher, C. *L'actualite chrétienne de l'Ancien Testament d'apres le Nouveau Testament*. Paris: Cerf, 1962.
Lascelle, Ruth Specter. *We Have a Great High Priest: A Brief Study on the Book of Hebrews*. Arlington, Wash.: Bedrock, 1997.
Lehne, Susanne. *The New Covenant in Hebrews*. JSNTSS 44. Sheffield: JSOT Press, 1990.
Lim, Timothy H. et al., editors *The Dead Sea Scrolls in Their Historical Context*. Edinburgh: T. & T. Clark, 2000.
Linafelt, Tod. *A Shadow of Glory: Reading the New Testament after the Holocaust*. New York: Routledge, 2002.
Lindars, Barnabas. *The Theology of the Letter to the Hebrews*. NTT. Cambridge: Cambridge University Press, 1991.
Littell, Franklin H. *The Crucifixion of the Jews*. New York: Harper & Row, 1975.
Livingstone, Elizabeth A. *Studia Biblica 1978, 1: Papers on Old Testament and Related Themes*. JSOTSS 11. Sheffield: JSOT Press, 1979.
Loader, William. *Sohn und Hoherpriester*. WMANT 53. Neukirchen-Vluyn: Neukirchener, 1981.
Lohfink, Norbert. *The Covenant Never Revoked: Biblical Reflections on Christian-Jewish Dialogue*. New York: Paulist, 1991.
Lohse, Eduard. *The Formation of the New Testament*. Translated by M. Eugene Boring. Nashville: Abingdon, 1981.
Longenecker, Bruce W. *Eschatology and the Covenant: A Comparison of 4 Ezra and Romans 1–11*. JSNTSS 57. Sheffield: JSOT Press, 1991.
Lovsky, F. *Antisémitisme et mystère d'Israel*. Paris: Michel, 1955.
Lussier, Ernest. *Christ's Priesthood According to the Epistle to the Hebrews*. Collegeville, Minn.: Liturgical, 1975.
Mack, Burton L. *Rhetoric and the New Testament*. GBS. Minneapolis: Fortress, 1990.
Malina, Bruce J. *The New Testament World: Insights from Cultural Anthropology*. 3d ed. Louisville: Westminster John Knox, 2001.
Malone, Fred Anderson. "A Critical Evaluation of the Use of Jeremiah 31:31-34 in the Letter to the Hebrews." Ph.D. diss., Southwestern Baptist Theological Seminary, 1989.
Margolin, Ron, editor. *Proceedings of the Twelfth World Congress of Jewish Studies, Jerusalem, July 29—August 5, 1997, Division A: the Bible and its World*. WCJS 12. Jerusalem: World Union of Jewish Studies, 1999.
Maxey, Lee Zachary. "The Rhetoric of Response: A Classical Reading of Heb 10:32—12:13." Ph.D. diss., Claremont Graduate University, 2002.
McKenzie, Steven. *Covenant*. St. Louis: Chalice, 2000.
Medebielle, A. *L'Expiation dans l'Ancien Testament et Nouveau Testament*. 2 vols. Rome: Institut Biblique Pontifical, 1923.
Metzger, Bruce M., and Roland E. Murphy, editors. *The New Oxford Annotated Apocrypha: The Apocryphal/Deuterocanonical Books of the Old Testament*. New York: Oxford University Press, 1991.
Meynet, Roland. *Rhetorical Analysis: An Introduction to Biblical Rhetoric*. Translation and Revised edition of *L'Analyse Rhétorique: une nouvelle méthode pour comprendre la Bible: textes fondateurs et exposé systématique*. Paris: Cerf, 1989. JSNTSS 256. Sheffield: Sheffield Academic, 1998.

Moore, George Foot. *Judaism: In the First Centuries of the Christian Era, the Age of the Tannaim.* Cambridge: Harvard University Press, 1927–30.
Nairne, Alexander. *The Epistle of Priesthood: Studies in the Epistle to the Hebrews.* Edinburgh: T. & T. Clark, 1913.
Najman, Hindy, and Judith H. Newman, editors. *The Idea of Biblical Interpretation: Essays in Honor of James L. Kugel.* Leiden: Brill, 2004.
Neusner, Jacob. *Judaism When Christianity Began.* Louisville: Westminster John Knox, 2002.
Nicene and Post-Nicene Fathers. Series 2. Edited by Philip Schaff and Henry Wace. 1890–1900. 14 vols. Reprinted, Peabody, Mass.: Hendrickson, 1994, 1995.
Parkes, James. *The Conflict of the Church and the Synagogue: A Study in the Origins of Antisemitism.* Philadelphia: Jewish Publication Society of America, 1961.
Pawlikowski, John and Hayim Goren Perelmuter. *Reinterpreting Revelation and Tradition: Jews and Christians in Conversation.* Franklin, Wisc.: Sheed & Ward, 2000.
Perelman, Chaim, and Lucie Olbrechts-Tyteca. *The New Rhetoric: A Treatise on Argumentation.* Notre Dame: University of Notre Dame, 1969.
Peterson, David Gilbert. *Hebrews and Perfection: An Examination of the Concept of Perfection in the "Epistle to the Hebrews."* SNTSMS 47. Cambridge: Cambridge University Press, 1982.
Philo. Translated by F. H. Colson, G. H. Whitaker, and R. Marcus. 12 vols. LCL. Cambridge: Harvard University Press, 1929-1953.
Porter, Stanley E. *Handbook of Classical Rhetoric in the Hellenistic Period 330 B.C.—A.D. 400.* Leiden: Brill, 1997.
———, editor. *Handbook to Exegesis of the New Testament.* NTTS 25. Leiden: Brill, 1997.
———, and Jeffrey T. Reed, editors. *Discourse Analysis and the New Testament.* JSNTSS 170. Sheffield: Sheffield Academic, 1999.
———, and Jacqueline C. R. De Roo, editors. *The Concept of the Covenant in the Second Temple Period.* Leiden: Brill, 2003.
Rapoport-Albert, Ada, and Steven J. Zipperstein, editors. *Jewish History: Essays in Honour of Chimen Abramsky.* London: Halban, 1988.
Rayburn, Robert S. *The Contrast Between the Old and New Covenants in the New Testament.* Seattle: Pfefferle, 1998.
Renaud, Bernard. *Nouvelle ou éternelle alliance? Le message des prophètes.* Paris: Cerf, 2002.
Reventlow, Henning, and Yair Hoffman, editors. *Politics and Theopolitics in the Bible and Postbiblical Literature.* JSOTSS 171. Sheffield: JSOT Press, 1994.
Riggenbach, Eduard. "Der Begriff der ΔΙΑΘΗΚΗ im Hebraerbriefes." In *Theologische Studien,* edited by T. Zahn, 300–311. Leipzig: Deichert, 1908.
Robbins, Vernon K. *Exploring the Texture of Texts: A Guide to Socio-Rhetorical Interpretation.* Valley Forge, Pa.: Trinity, 1996.
———. *The Tapestry of Early Christian Discourse: Rhetoric, Society, and Ideology.* London: Routledge, 1996.
Röth, E. M. *Epistolam vulgo "ad Hebraeos" inscriptam non ad Hebreos, id est christianos genere judaeos.* Frankfurt: Schmerberi, 1836.
Ruether, Rosmary Radford. *Faith and Fratricide: The Theological Roots of Anti-semitism.* 1974. Reprinted, Eugene, Ore.: Wipf & Stock, 1996.
Salevao, Iutisone. *Legitimation in the Letter to the Hebrews.* JSNTSS 219. Sheffield: Sheffield Academic, 2002.

Sanders, E. P. *Paul and Palestinian Judaism: A Comparison of Patterns of Religion.* Philadelphia: Fortress, 1977.

Sandmel, Samuel. *The First Christian Century in Judaism and Christianity: Certainties and Uncertainties.* New York: Oxford University Press, 1969.

———. *Anti-Semitism in the New Testament?* Philadelphia: Fortress, 1978.

———. *Philo of Alexandria: An Introduction.* New York: Oxford University Press, 1979.

Scholer, John M. *Proleptic Priests: Priesthood in the Epistle to the Hebrews.* JSNTSS 49. Sheffield : JSOT Press, 1991.

Schwartz, Seth. *Josephus and Judean Politics.* Columbia Studies in the Classical Tradition 18. Leiden: Brill, 1990.

Seid, Tim Wayne. "The Rhetorical Form of the Melchizedek/Christ Comparison in Hebrews 7." Ph.D. diss., Brown University, 1996.

Simon, Marcel. *Verus Israel: étude sur les relations entre chrétiens et juifs dans l'empire romain (135-425).* Paris: Boccard, 1948. Reprinted 1964. English Translation: *Verus Israel: A Study of the Relations between Christians and Jews in the Roman Empire (135–425).* Translated by H. McKeating. Oxford: Oxford University Press, 1986.

Sowers, Sidney G. *The Hermeneutics of Philo and Hebrews: A Comparison of the Interpretation of the Old Testament in Philo Judaeus and the Epistle to the Hebrews.* BST 1. Zurich: EVZ, 1965.

Swetnam, James. *Jesus and Isaac: A Study of the Epistle to the Hebrews in the Light of the Aqedah.* AnBib 94. Rome: Biblical Institute Press, 1981.

Talmon, Shemaryahu. *The "Dead Sea Scrolls" or "The Community of the Renewed Covenant."* Tucson: University of Arizona Press, 1993.

Taubenschlag Raphael. *The Law of Greco-Roman Egypt in the Light of the Papyri 332 B.C—A.D. 640.* New York: Herald Square, 1944.

Taylor, Miriam S. *Anti-Judaism and the Early Christian Identity: A Critique of the Scholarly Consensus.* SPB 46. Leiden: Brill, 1995.

Thompson, John Lee. *Writing the Wrongs: Women of the Old Testament among Biblical Commentators from Philo through the Reformation.* Oxford: Oxford University Press, 2001.

Turner, Victor. *The Forest of Symbols: Aspects of Ndembu Ritual.* Ithaca, N.Y.: Cornell University Press, 1967.

Übelacker, Walter G. *Der Hebräerbrief als Appell.* ConBNT 21. Stockholm: Almqvist & Wiksell, 1989.

Ulrich, Eugene C., and James C. VanderKam, editors. *The Community of the Renewed Covenant: The Notre Dame Symposium on the Dead Sea Scrolls.* Notre Dame, Ind.: University of Notre Dame Press, 1994.

Vanhoye, Albert. *Our Priest Is Christ: The Doctrine of the Epistle to the Hebrews.* Rome: Pontifical Biblical Institute Press, 1977.

———. *Prêtres anciens, prêtre nouveau selon le Nouveau Testament.* PD 20. Paris: Éditions du Seuil, 1980.

———. *Structure and Message of the Epistle to the Hebrews.* Translated by James Swetnam. Subsidia Biblica 12. Rome: Pontifical Biblical Institute, 1989.

Vermès, Géza. *Jesus in his Jewish Context.* Minneapolis: Fortress, 2003.

———. *The Complete Dead Sea Scrolls in English.* London: Penguin, 1997.

Vos, Geerhardus. *Redemptive History and Biblical Interpretation: The Shorter Writings of Geerhardus Vos,* edited by Richard B. Gaffin. Phillipsburg, N.J.: Presbyterian and Reformed, 1980.

———. *The Teaching of the Epistle to the Hebrews*. Edited and revised by Rev. J. Vos. 1956. Reprinted Eugene, Ore.: Wipf and Stock, 1998.
Wallace, Daniel. *Greek Grammar Beyond the Basics*. Grand Rapids: Zondervan, 1996.
Watson, Duane F. and Alan J. Hauser. *Rhetorical Criticism of the Bible: A Comprehensive Bibliography with Notes on History and Method*. BibIntSer 4. Leiden: Brill, 1994.
Whiston, W. *The Works of Josephus: Complete and Unabridged*. New updated ed. Peabody, Mass.: Hendrickson, 1993.
Wilder, Amos N. *Early Christian Rhetoric: The Language of the Gospel*. Cambridge: Harvard University, 1964.
Wildgube, E. "Sociological Study of the Addressees of the Epistle to the Hebrews." Ph.D. diss., Lutheran Theological Seminary, 1984.
Williams, Arthur Lykyn. *Adversus Judaeos: A Bird's Eye View of Christian Apologiae until the Renaissance*. Cambridge: Cambridge University, 1935.
Williamson, Clark M. *A Guest in the House of Israel: Post-Holocaust Church Theology*. Louisville: Westminster John Knox, 1993.
Williamson, Ronald. *Philo and the Epistle to the Hebrews*. ALGHJ 4. Leiden: Brill, 1970.
Wilson, Bryan R. *Sects and Society: A Sociological Study of the Elim Tabernacle, Christian Science, and Christadelphians*. Berkeley: University of California Press: 1961.
Wilson, Stephen G. *Related Strangers: Jews and Christians 70–170 C.E.* Minneapolis: Fortress, 1995.
Wimbush, Vincent, editor. *Rhetorics of Resistance: A Colloquy on Early Christianity as Rhetorical Formation*. Semeia 79. Atlanta: Scholars, 1997.
Wright, David P., David Noel Freedman, and Avi Hurvitz, editors. *Pomegranates and Golden Bells: Studies in Biblical, Jewish, and Near Eastern Ritual, Law, and Literature in Honor of Jacob Milgrom*. Winona Lake, Ind: Eisenbrauns, 1995.
Xeravitis, Géza G. *King, Priest, Prophet: Positive Eschatological Protagonists of the Qumran Library*. STDJ 47. Leiden: Brill, 2003.
Yadin, Yigael. *The Temple Scroll*. 3 vols. Jerusalem: Israel Exploration Society, 1983.
Yonge, C.D., trans. *The Works of Philo: Complete and Unabridged*. Peabody, Mass.: Hendrickson, 1993.
Young, Richard. *Intermediate New Testament Greek*. Nashville: Broadman and Holman, 1994.
Yu, Young Ki. "The New Covenant: The Promise and its Fulfillment: An Inquiry into the Influence of the New Covenant Concept of Jeremiah 31:31-34 on Later Religious Thought with Particular Reference to the Dead Sea Scrolls and the New Testament." Ph.D. diss., University of Durham, 1989.
Zenger, Erich, editor. *Der Neue Bund im Alten: Zur Bundestheologie der beiden Testamente*. QD 146. Freiburg: Herder, 1993.

Articles and Essays

Abusch, Raanan. "Sevenfold Hymns in the Songs of the Sabbath Sacrifice and the Hekhalot Literature: Formalism, Hierarchy and the Limits of Human Participation." In *Dead Sea Scrolls as Background to Postbiblical Judaism and Early Christianity: Papers from an International Conference at St. Andrews in 2001*, edited by James R. Davila, 220–47. Leiden: Brill, 2003.

Allison, Dale C., Jr. "The Silence of Angels: Reflections on the Songs of the Sabbath Sacrifice." *RevQ* 13 (1988) 189–97.

Anderson, Charles P. "Who are the Heirs of the New Age in the Epistle to the Hebrews?" In *Apocalyptic and the New Testament: Essays in Honor of J. Louis Martyn,* edited by Joel Marcus and Marion L. Soards, 255–77. JSNTSS 24. Sheffield: Sheffield Academic Press, 1989.

Anderson, Richard H. "The Cross and Atonement from Luke to Hebrews." *EvQ* 71 (1999) 127–49.

Ashley, Benedict M. "The Priesthood of Christ, the Baptized, and the Ordained." In *Theology of Priesthood,* edited by Donald J. Goergen and Ann Garrido, 139–64. Collegeville, Minn.: Liturgical, 2000.

Attridge, Harold W. "New Covenant Christology in an Early Christian Homily." *QR* 8 (1988) 89–108.

———. "Paraenesis in a Homily (λόγος παρακλήσεως) The Possible Location of, and Socialization in, the 'Epistle to the Hebrews.'" *Semeia* 50 (1990) 211–26.

———. "The Uses of Antithesis in Hebrews 8–10." *HTR* 79 (1986) 1–9.

Baker, Cynthia. "Pseudo-Philo and the Transformation of Jephthah's Daughter." In *Anti-Covenant: Counter-Reading Women's Lives in the Hebrew Bible,* edited by Mieke Bal, 195–209. JSOTSS 81. Sheffield: Almond Press, 1989.

Barton, Stephen C. "Historical Criticism and Social-Scientific Perspectives in New Testament Study." In *Hearing the New Testament: Strategies for Interpretation,* edited by Joel B. Green, 61–89. Grand Rapids: Eerdmans, 1995.

Baumgarten, Albert I. "Josephus on Essene Sacrifice." *JJS* 45 (1994) 169–83.

Beckwith, Roger T. "The Death of Christ as a Sacrifice in the Teaching of Paul and Hebrews." In *Sacrifice in the Bible,* edited by Roger T. Beckwith and Martin J. Selman, 130–35. Grand Rapids: Baker; Carlisle, Eng: Paternoster, 1995.

Beentjes, Pancratius C. "The 'Praise of the Famous' and Its Prologue: Some Observations on Ben Sira 44:1-15 and the Question on Enoch in 44:16." *Bijdr* 45 (1984) 374–83.

Begg, Christopher T. "Rereading of the 'Animal Rite' of Genesis 15 in Early Jewish Narratives." *CBQ* 50 (1988) 36–46.

Benetreau, Samuel. "La mort de Jésus et le sacrifice dans l'épître aux Hébreux." *FoiVie* 95 (1996) 33–45.

Betz, Hans Dieter. "The Literary Composition and Function of Paul's Letter to the Galatians." *NTS* 21 (1975) 353–79.

Black, C. Clifton. "Keeping up with Recent Studies XVI. Rhetorical Criticism and Biblical Interpretation." *ExpTim* 100 (1989) 253–54.

———. "Rhetorical Criticism." In *Hearing the New Testament: Strategies for Interpretation,* edited by Joel Green, 256–77. Grand Rapids: Eerdmans; Carlisle: Paternoster, 1995.

———. "The Rhetorical Form of the Hellenistic Jewish and Early Christian Sermon: A Response to Lawrence Wills." *HTR* 81 (1988) 1–18.

Black, David Alan. "Heb 1:1-4: A Study in Discourse Analysis." *WTJ* 49 (1987) 175–94.

Bloesch, Donald G. "'All Israel Will Be Saved': Supersessionism and the Biblical Witness." *Int* 43 (1989) 130–42.

Bourke, Myles M. "The Priesthood of Christ." In *To Be a Priest,* edited by Robert E. Terwilliger and Urban T. Holmes III, 55–62. New York: Seabury, 1975.

Breidenthal, Thomas. "Neighbor-Christology: Reconstructing Christianity Before Supersessionism." *CrossCurr* 49 (1999) 319–48.

Brooks, Walter Edward. "Perpetuity of Christ's Sacrifice in the Epistle to the Hebrews." *JBL* 89 (1970) 205–14.

Bruce, F. F. "To the Hebrews or to the Essenes?" *NTS* 9 (1963) 217–32.
Bulley, Alan D. "Death and Rhetoric in the Hebrews 'Hymn of Faith.'" *SR* 25 (1996) 409–23.
Burgmann, Hans. "11QT: The Sadducean Torah." In *Temple Scroll Studies*, edited by George J. Brooke, 257–63. Journal for the Study of the Pseudepigrapha Supplement Series 7. Sheffield: Sheffield Academic, 1989.
Caird, George B. "The Epistle of Priesthood: Studies in the Epistle to the Hebrews." *ExpTim* 72 (1961) 204–6.
———. "The Exegetical Method of the Epistle to the Hebrews." *CJT* 5 (1959) 44–51.
Campbell, K. M. "Covenant or Testament: Heb 9:16, 17 Reconsidered." *EvQ* 44 (1972) 107–11.
Carpenter, E. E. "Sacrifices and Offerings in the OT." In *ISBE* 4:260–73.
Chester, A. N. "Hebrews: The Final Sacrifice." In *Sacrifice and Redemption: Durham Essays in Theology*, edited by Stephen W. Sykes, 57–72. Cambridge: Cambridge University, 1991.
Clements, Ronald E. "The Use of the Old Testament in Hebrews." *SwJT* 28 (1985) 36–45.
Cockerill, G. L. "The Better Resurrection: Heb 11:35" *TynBul* 51 (2000) 215–34.
Cohn, R. "The Second Coming of Moses: Deuteronomy and the Construction of Israelite Identity." In *Proceedings of the Twelfth World Congress of Jewish Studies, Jerusalem, July 29–August 5, 1999*, edited by Ron Margolin, 59–71. Jerusalem: World Union of Jewish Studies, 1999.
Cosby, Michael R. "Hebrews 11 and the Art of Effective Preaching." *Covenant Quarterly* 48 (1990) 29–33.
———. "The Rhetorical Composition of Hebrews 11." *JBL* 107 (1988) 257–73.
Craven, Toni. "Tradition and Convention in the Book of Judith." *Semeia* 28 (1983) 49–61.
Culpepper, R. Alan. "Mapping the Textures of the New Testament Criticism: A Response to Socio-Rhetorical Criticism." *JSNT* 70 (1998) 71–77.
Culpepper, Robert H. "The High Priesthood and Sacrifice of Christ in the Epistle to the Hebrews." *TTE* 32 (1985) 46–62.
Daly, Robert J. "Soteriological Significance of the Sacrifice of Isaac." *CBQ* 39 (1977) 45–75.
Daniels, Richard. "How Does the Church Relate to the New Covenant? Or, Whose New Covenant Is It, Anyway?" *FM* 16 (1999) 64–98.
Davies, Philip R. and Bruce D. Chilton. "The Aqedah: A Revised Tradition History." *CBQ* 40 (1978) 514–46.
Delorme, Jean. "Sacrifice, sacerdoce, consécration: typologie et analyse sémantique du discours." *RechScRel* 63 (1975) 343–66.
deSilva, David A. "Epistle to the Hebrews in Social Scientific Perspective." *ResQ* 36 (1994) 1–21.
———. "Exchanging Favor for Wrath: Apostasy." *JBL* 115 (1996) 91–116.
———. "Hebrews 6:4-8: A Socio-Rhetorical Investigation (Part 1)." *TynBul* 50 (1999) 33–57.
———. "Hebrews 6:4-8: A Socio-Rhetorical Investigation (Part 2)," *TynBul* 50 (1999) 225–36.
Dieterlé, Christiane. "Par-delà le voile: l'Épitre aux Hébreux et le sacrifice (Hébreux 6,13 à 10,21)." *FoiVie* 95 (1996) 47–51.

Di Lella, A. A. "Authenticity of the Geniza Fragments of Sirach." *Bib* 44 (1963) 171–200.

Dimant, Devorah. "The Hebrew Bible in the Dead Sea Scrolls: Torah Quotations in the Damascus Covenant." In *Sha'arei Talmon: Studies in the Bible, Qumran, and the Ancient Near East Presented to Shemaryahu Talmon,* edited by Michael Fishbane and Emanuel Tov, 113–22. Winona Lake, Ind.: Eisenbrauns, 1991.

Doran, Robert. "Pseudo-Hecataeus." In *OTP* 2:905–19.

Dunn, James D. G. "The Question of Anti-Semitism in the New Testament Writings of the Period." In *Jews and Christians: The Parting of the Ways A.D. 70 to 135,* edited by James D. G. Dunn, 177–211. Rev. ed. Grand Rapids, 1999.

Ellingworth, Paul. "Just Like Melchizedek." *BT* 28 (1977) 236–39.

———. "The Unshakable Priesthood: Hebrews 7:24." *JSNT* 23 (1985) 125–26.

Elliott, John H. "Phases in the Social Formation of Early Christianity: From Faction to Sect—A Social Scientific Perspective." In *Recruitment, Conquest, and Conflict,* edited by Peder Borgen, Vernon K. Robbins, and David Gowler, 273–313. ESEC 6. Atlanta: Scholars, 1998.

Fearghail, Fearghas O. "Sir 50:5-21: Yom Kippur or the Daily Whole-Offering?" *Bib* 59 (1978) 301–16.

Fischer, John. "Covenant, Fulfillment and Judaism in Hebrews." *EvRT* 13 (1989) 175–87.

Fisher, Eugene J. "The Church's Teaching on Supersessionism." *BAR* 17 (1991) 58.

Fitzmyer, Joseph A. "Further Light on Melchizedek from Qumran Cave 11." *JBL* 86 (1969) 25–41.

———. "'Now this Melchizedek' (Heb 7:1)." *CBQ* 25 (1963) 305–21.

Floor, L. "The General Priesthood of Believers in the Epistle to the Hebrews." In *Ad Hebraeos: Essays on the Epistle to the Hebrews,* 72–82. Pretoria: Die Nuwe-Testamentiese Werkgemeenskap van Suid-Afrika, 1971.

Fonseca, L. G. da. "Διαθήκη—Foedus an testamentum?" *Bib* 8 (1927) 31–50; 161–81; 290–319; 418–41; 9 (1928) 26–40; 143–60.

Frey, Jörg. "Die alte und die neue diatheke nach dem Hebräerbrief." In *Bund und Tora,* edited by Friedrich Avemarie and Hermann Lichtenberger, 263–310. WUNT 92. Tübingen: Mohr/Siebeck, 1996.

Freyne, Sean. "Reading Hebrews and Revelation Intertextually." In *Intertexuality in Biblical Writings: Essays in Honour of Bas van Iersel,* edited by S. Draisma, 83–93. Kampen: Kok, 1989.

Gallazzi, Sandro "'Worthless is the Fat of Whole Burnt Offerings': A Critique of the Sacrifice of the Second Temple." In *Subversive Scriptures: Revolutionary Readings of the Christian Bible in Latin America,* edited by Leif E. Vaage, 124–41. Valley Forge, Pa: Trinity, 1997.

Gitay, Yehoshua. "Rhetorical Criticism." In *To Each Its Own Meaning: An Introduction to Biblical Criticisms and Their Application,* edited by Steven L. McKenzie and Stephen R. Haynes, 135–49. Louisville: Westminster John Knox, 1993.

Gordon, Robert P. "Better Promises: Two Passages in Hebrews Against the Background of the Old Testament Cultus." In *Templum Amicitiae: Essays on the Second Temple Presented to Ernst Bammel,* edited by William Horbury, 434–49. Sheffield: JSOT Press, 1991.

Grimm, Werner. "Die Preisgabe eines Menschen zur Rettung des Volkes: priesterliche Tradition bei Johannes und Josephus." In *Josephus-Studien: Untersuchungen zu Josephus, d. antiken Judentum u. d. Neuen Testament: Otto Michel z. 70. Geburtstag gewidmet,* edited by Otto Betz, Klaus Haacker, and Martin Hengel, 133–46. Göttingen: Vandenhoeck & Ruprecht, 1974.

Gunton, Colin. "Christ the Sacrifice: Aspects of the Language and Imagery of the Bible." In *The Glory of Christ in the New Testament: Studies in Christology in Memory of George Bradford Caird*, edited by L. D. Hurst and N. T. Wright, 229–38. Oxford: Clarendon, 1987.

Hagner, Donald A. "Interpreting the Epistle to the Hebrews." In *The Literature and Meaning of Scripture*, edited by Morris A. Inch and C. Hassell Bullock, 217–42. Grand Rapids: Eerdmans, 1981.

———. "A Positive Theology of Judaism from the New Testament." *SEÅ* 69 (2004) 7–28.

Hann, Robert R. "Supersessionism, Engraftment, and Jewish-Christian Dialogue: Reflections on the Presbyterian Statement on Jewish-Christian Relations." *JES* 27 (1990) 327–42.

Harding, Vincent. "In the Company of the Faithful: Journeying Toward the Promised Land." In *Rise of Christian Conscience: The Emergence of a Dramatic Renewal Movement in the Church Today*, edited by Jim Wallis, 273–84. San Francisco: Harper & Row, 1987.

Hare, Douglas R. A. "The Rejection of the Jews in the Synoptics and Acts." In *Anti-Semitism and the Foundations of Christianity*, edited by A. T. Davies, 27–47. New York: Paulist, 1979.

Harrelson, Walter J. "Ezra Among the Wicked in 2 Esdras 3–10." In *Divine Helmsman: Studies on God's Control of Human Events, Presented to Lou H. Silberman*, edited by James L. Crenshaw and Samuel Sandmel, 21–40. New York: Ktav, 1980.

Harrington, D.J. "Pseudo-Philo." In *OTP* 2:297–303.

Harrisville, Roy A. "The Concept of Newness in the New Testament." *JBL* 74 (1955) 69–79.

Harvey, Anthony. "Forty Strokes Save One." In *Alternative Approaches to New Testament Study*, edited by A. E. Harvey, 79–96. London: SPCK, 1985.

Hayward, Robert. "Sacrifice and World Order: Some Observations on Ben Sira's Attitude to the Temple Service." In *Sacrifice and Redemption: Durham Essays in Theology*, edited by Stephen W. Sykes, 22–34. Cambridge: Cambridge University Press, 1991.

———. "The Present State of Research into the Targumic Account of the Sacrifice of Isaac." *JJS* 32 (1981) 127–50.

Hecht, Richard D. "Patterns of Exegesis in Philo's Interpretation of Leviticus." *SPhilo* 6 (1980) 77–155.

Herrenschmidt, Olivier. "Sacrifice: Symbolic or Effective." In *Between Belief and Transgression: Structuralist Essays in Religion, History, and Myth*, edited by Michel Izard and Pierre Smith, 24–42. Translated by John Leavitt. Chicago: University of Chicago, 1982.

Hoehner, H. W. "Hasmoneans." In *ISBE* 2:621–27.

Horbury, William. "The Aaronic Priesthood in the Epistle to the Hebrews." *JSNT* 19 (1983) 43–71.

Hughes, John J. "Hebrews 9:15ff and Galatians 3:15ff: A Study in Covenant Practice and Procedure." *NovT* 21 (1979) 27–96.

Hughes, Philip Edgcumbe "The Blood of Jesus and his Heavenly Priesthood in Hebrews Part II: The High Priestly Sacrifice of Christ." *BSac* 130 (1973) 195–212.

Humphreys, Fisher. "Articles on Hebrews." *TTE* 32 (1985) 20–81.

Hunt, B. P. W. S. "The Epistle to the Hebrews or against the Hebrews? Anti-Judaic treatise?" *SE* 2 (1964) 408–10.
Isaacs, Marie E. "Hebrews." In *Early Christian Thought in Its Jewish Context,* edited by John Barclay and John Sweet, 145–59. Cambridge: Cambridge University Press, 1996.
Jennrich, Walter A. "Rhetoric in the New Testament: The Diction in Romans and Hebrews." *CTM* 20 (1949) 518–31.
Jobes, Karen H. "Rhetorical Achievement in the Hebrews 10 'Misquote' of Psalm 40." *Bib* 72 (1991) 387–96.
———. "The Function of Paronomasia in Hebrews 10:5-7." *TJ* 13 (1992) 181–91.
Johnson, Luke Timothy. "The New Testament's Anti-Jewish Slander and the Conventions of Ancient Polemic." *JBL* 108 (1989) 419–44.
Johnson, William G. "The Pilgrimage Motif in the Book of Hebrews." *JBL* 97 (1978) 239–51.
Jones, Peter R. "The Figure of Moses as a Heuristic Device for Understanding the Pastoral Intent of Hebrews." *RevExp* 76 (1979) 95–107.
Jonge, Marinus, and Adam S. Woude. "11Q Melchizedek and the New Testament." *NTS* 12 (1966) 301–26.
Kaiser, Walter C., Jr. "The Abolition of the Old Order and the Establishment of the New: A Study of Psalm 40:6-8 and Hebrews 10:5-10." In *Tradition and Testament: Essays in Honor of Charles Lee Feinberg,* edited by John S. Feinberg and Paul D. Feinberg, 19–37. Chicago: Moody, 1981.
Karlberg, Mark W. "Justification in Redemptive History." *WTJ* 43 (1981) 213–46.
Kee, Howard Clark. "*Testament of the Twelve Patriarchs.*" In *OTP* 1:775–81.
Kent, Homer A. "The New Covenant and the Church." *GTJ* 6 (1985) 289–98.
Kidner, Derek. "Sacrifice: Metaphors and Meaning." *TynBul* 33 (1982) 119–36.
Klassen, W. "To the Hebrews or against the Hebrews? Anti-Judaism and the Epistle to the Hebrews." In *Anti-Judaism in Early Christianity.* Vol. 2 of *Separation and Polemic,* edited by Stephen G. Wilson, 1–16. Waterloo, Ont.: Wilfred Laurier University Press, 1986.
Kleinig, John W. "The Blood for Sprinkling: Atoning Blood in Leviticus and Hebrews." *LTJ* 33 (1999) 124–35.
Kline, Meredith G. "Canon and Covenant." *WTJ* 32 (1970) 49–67; 179–200.
Koester, Helmut. "'Outside the Camp': Hebrews 13:9-14." *HTR* 55 (1962) 299–315.
Konkel, August. "The Sacrifice of Obedience." *Did* 2 (1991) 2–11.
Koosed, Jennifer L. "Double Bind: Sacrifice in the Epistle to the Hebrews," In *A Shadow of Glory: Reading the New Testament after the Holocaust,* edited by Tod Linafelt, 89–101. New York: Routledge, 2002.
Kugler, Robert A. "Rewriting Rubrics: Sacrifice and the Religion of Qumran." In *Religion in the Dead Sea Scrolls,* edited by John J. Collins and Robert A. Kugler, 90–112. Grand Rapids: Eerdmans, 2000.
Ladd, George Eldon. "Apocalyptic Literature." In *ISBE* 1:151–61.
Lane, William L. "Hebrews: A Sermon in Search of a Setting." *SwJT* 28 (1985) 13–18.
———. "Social Perspectives on Roman Christianity during the Formative Years from Nero to Nerva." In *Judaism and Christianity in First-Century Rome,* edited by Karl P. Donfried and Peter Richardson, 196–244. Grand Rapids: Eerdmans, 1998.
Laporte, Jean Marc. "Sacrifice and Forgiveness in Philo of Alexandria." In *Studia Philonica Annual: Studies in Helenistic Judaism Volume I, 1989,* edited by David T. Runia, 34–42. BJS 185. Atlanta: Scholars, 1989.

———. "Sacrifice in Origen in the Light of Philonic Models." In *Origen of Alexandria: His World and His Legacy*, edited by Charles Kannengiesser and William L. Petersen, 250–76. Notre Dame, Ind: University of Notre Dame Press, 1988.

Leithart, Peter J. "The Priests of Culture." *FT* 27 (1992) 10–12.

———. "Womb of the World: Baptism and the Priesthood of the New Covenant in Hebrews 10.19-22." *JSNT* 78 (2000) 49–65.

Levine, Amy-Jill. "Sacrifice and Salvation: Otherness and Domestication in the Book of Judith." In *No One Spoke Ill of Her: Essays on Judith*, edited by James C. VanderKam, 17–30. SBLEJL 2. Atlanta: Scholars, 1992.

Levinson, John R. "Torah and Covenant in Pseudo Philo's *Liber Antiquitatum Biblicarum*." In *Bund und Tora*, edited by Friedrich Avemarie and Hermann Lichtenberger, 111–27. WUNT 92. Tübingen: Mohr/Siebeck, 1996.

Liao, Paul S. H. "The God of the Covenant: Toward an Understanding of God Language in the Epistle to the Hebrews." *TaiJT* 20 (1998) 13–47.

Lichtenberger, Hermann. "Atonement and Sacrifice in the Qumran Community." In *Approaches to Ancient Judaism*, edited by William Scott Green, 2:159–71. BJS 9. Chico, Calif.: Scholars, 1980.

Lincoln, Lucy. "Translating Hebrews 9:15-22 in its Hebraic Context." *JOTT* 12 (1999) 1–29.

Lindars, Barnabas. "Hebrews and the Second Temple." In *Templum Amicitiae: Essays on the Second Temple Presented to Ernst Bammel*, edited by William Horbury, 410–33. JSNTSS 48. Sheffield: JSOT Press, 1991.

———. "The Rhetorical Structure of Hebrews." *NTS* 35 (1989) 382–406.

Lundquist, J. M. "Temple, Covenant, and Law in the Ancient Near East and in the Old Testament." In *Israel's Apostasy and Restoration*, edited by A. Gileadi, 293–305. Grand Rapids: Baker, 1988.

MacLeod, David J. "The Cleansing of the True Tabernacle." *BSac* 152 (1995) 60–71.

———. "The Present Work of Christ in Hebrews." *BSac* 148 (1991) 184–200.

Malina, Bruce J. "A Conflict Approach to Mark 7." *Forum* 4.3 (1988) 3–30.

———. "Rhetorical Criticism and Social-Scientific Criticism: Why Won't Romanticism Leave Us Alone?" In *Rhetoric Scripture and Theology: Essays from the 1994 Pretoria Conference*, edited by Stanley E. Porter and Thomas H. Olbricht, 72–101. JSNTSS 131. Sheffield: Sheffield Academic, 1996.

Martin, Dale. "Social-Scientific Criticism." In *To Each its Own Meaning*, edited by Steven L. McKenzie and Stephen R. Haynes, 103–20. Louisville: Westminster John Knox, 1993.

Mayhue, Richard L. "Heb 13:20: Covenant of Grace or New Covenant? An Exegetical Note." *MSJ* 7 (1996) 251–57.

McCarthy, Dennis J. "Covenant in Narratives from Late OT Times." In *Quest for the Kingdom of God: Studies in Honor of George E. Mendenhall*, edited by Herbert B. Huffmon, Frank A. Spina, and A. R. W. Green, 77–94. Winona Lake, Ind: Eisenbrauns, 1983.

Meeks, Wayne. "The Man from Heaven in Johannine Sectarianism," *JBL* 91 (1972) 44–72.

Metzger, Bruce M. "The Fourth Book of Ezra." In *OTP* 1:517–24.

Michaud, Jean P. "Le passage de l'ancien au nouveau, selon l'épître aux Hébreux." *ScEs* 35 (1983) 33-52.

Mitchell, Alan C. "The Use of πρέπειν and Rhetorical Propriety in Hebrews 2:10." *CBQ* 54 (1992) 681–701.

Moe, Olaf. "Der Gedanke des allgemeinen Priestertums im Hebräerbrief." *TZ* 5 (1949) 161–69.
Moore, George Foot. "Christian Writers on Judaism." *HTR* 14 (1921) 197–254.
Morrice, William G. "New Wine in Old Wine-Skins, XI: Covenant." *ExpTim* 86 (1975) 132–36.
Murphy, Frederick J. "The Eternal Covenant in Pseudo-Philo." *JSP* 3 (1988) 43–57.
Nauck, Wolfgang. "Zum Aufbau des Hebräerbriefes." In *Judentum, Urchristentum, Kirche: Festschrift für Joachim Jeremias*, edited by Walther Eltester, 199–206. BZNW 26. Berlin: Töpelmann, 1960.
Nelson, Richard. "'He Offered Himself': Sacrifice in Hebrews." *Int* 57 (2003) 251–65.
Neusner, Jacob. "Varieties of Judaism in the Formative Age." In *Formative Judaism, Second Series*, 59–89. BJS 41. Chico, Calif.: Scholars, 1983.
Nikiprowetzky, V. "La spiritualisation des sacrifices et le culte sacrificiel au temple de Jérusalem chez Philon d'Alexandrie." *Sem* 17 (1967) 96–110.
Nomoto, Shinya. "Herkunft und Struktur der Hohenpriestervorstellung im Hebräerbrief." *NovT* 10 (1968) 10–25.
O'Hagan, Angelo. "The Martyr in the Fourth Book of Maccabees." *LibA* 24 (1974) 94–120.
Olbricht, Thomas H. "Hebrews as Amplification." In *Rhetoric and the New Testament: Essays From the 1992 Heidelberg Conference*, edited by Stanley E. Porter and Thomas H. Olbricht, 375–87. JSNTSS 90. Sheffield: Sheffield Academic, 1993.
Omanson, Roger L. "A Superior Covenant: Hebrews 8:1–10:18." *RevExp* 82 (1985) 361–73.
Paul, André. "Flavius Josephus' *Antiquities of the Jews*: An Anti-Christian Manifesto." *NTS* 31 (1985) 473–80.
Paul, M. J. "The Order of Melchizedek (Ps 110:4 and Heb 7:3)." *WTJ* 49 (1987) 195–211.
Payne, Philip Barton. "A Critical Note on Ecclesiasticus 44:21's Commentary on the Abrahamic Covenant." *JETS* 15 (1972) 186–87.
Perdue, Leo G. "The Social Character of Paraenesis and Paraenetic Literature." *Semeia* 50 (1990) 5–39.
Perrot, Charles. "L'Épitre aux *Hébreux*." In *Ministère et les ministères selon le Nouveau Testament*, edited by Paul Bony and Jean Delorme, 118–37. Paris: Seuil, 1974.
Perry, Tim. "The Historical Jesus, Anti-Judaism, and The Christology of Hebrews: A Theological Reflection." *Did* 10 (1999) 69–78.
Peterson, David Gilbert. "The Prophecy of the New Covenant in the Argument of Hebrews." *RTR* 38 (1979) 74–81.
Phillips, Anthony C J. "Respect for Life in the Old Testament." *KTR* 6 (1983) 32–35.
Pretorius, E.A.C. "*Diatheke* in the Epistle to the Hebrews." *Neot* 5 (1971) 37–50.
Priest, J. "Testament of Moses." In *OTP* 1:919–26.
Robbins, Vernon K. "Response." *JSNT* 70 (1998) 101–7.
Robinson, W. Gordon. "Historical Summaries of Biblical History." *EvQ* 47 (1975) 195–207.
Rooke, Deborah W. "Jesus as Royal Priest: Reflections on the Interpretation of the Melchizedek Tradition in Heb 7." *Bib* 81 (2000) 81–94.
Roth, Cecil. "The Debate on the Loyal Sacrifice, AD 66." *HTR* 53 (1960) 93–97.
Ruether, Rosmary Radford. "Theological Anti-Semitism in the New Testament." *ChrCent* 85 (1968) 191–96.

Rylaarsdam, J. C. "Jewish-Christian Relationships: The Two Covenants and the Dilemmas of Christology." In *Grace upon Grace: Essays in Honor of Lester J. Kuyper*, edited by James I. Cook, 70–84. Grand Rapids: Eerdmans, 1975.

Sanders, E. P. "Covenant as a Soteriological Category and the Nature of Salvation in Palestinian and Hellenistic Judaism." In *Jews, Greeks and Christians: Religious Cultures in Late Antiquity Essays in Honor of William David Davies*, edited by Robert Hamerton-Kelly and Robin Scroggs, 11–44. SJLA 21. Leiden: Brill, 1976.

———. "Patterns of Religion in Paul and Rabbinic Judaism: A Holistic Method of Comparison." *HTR* 66 (1973) 455–78.

Sänger, D. "Neues Testament und Antijudaismus: Versuch einer exegetischen und hermeneutischen Vergewisserung im innerchristlichen Gespräch." *KD* 34 (1988) 210–31.

Schenker, Adrian. "'Et comme le sacrifice de l'holocauste il les agréa' (Sg 3,6) les premières comparaisons du martyre avec un sacrifice dans l'Ancien Testament." In *Treasures of Wisdom: Studies in Ben Sira and the Book of Wisdom*, edited by Nuria Calduch-Benages and Jacques Vermeylen, 351–56. BETL 143. Leuven: Leuven University Press, 1999.

———. "Welche Verfehlungen und welche Opfer in Lev 5,1-6?" In *Levitikus als Buch*, edited by Heinz-Josef Fabry and Hans-Winfried Jüngling, 259–61. Bonner biblische Beiträge 119. Berlin: Philo, 1999.

Schiffman, Lawrence H. " '*ôlâ* and *ḥaṭṭā't* in the *Temple Scroll*." In *Pomegranates and Golden Bells: Studies in Biblical, Jewish, and Near Eastern Ritual, Law, and Literature in Honor of Jacob Milgrom*, edited by David P. Wright, David Noel Freedman, and Avi Hurvitz, 39–48. Winona Lake, Ind.: Eisenbrauns, 1995.

———. "Priestly and Levitical Gifts in the *Temple Scroll*." In *Provo International Conference on the Dead Sea Scrolls: Technological Innovations, New Texts, and Reformulated Issues*, edited by Donald W. Parry and Eugene Ulrich, 480–96. Leiden: Brill, 1999.

———. "The Rabbinic Understanding of Covenant." *RevExp* 84 (1987) 289–98.

Schmidt, T.E. "Moral Lethargy and the Epistle to the Hebrews." *WTJ* 54 (1992) 167–73.

Schreckenberg, H. "Josephus, Flavius." In *ISBE* 2:1132–33.

Schreiner, T. R. "Sacrifices and Offerings in the NT." In *ISBE* 4:273–77.

Schunack, Gerd. 'Jesu Opfertod' im Hebräerbrief." In *Bezwingende Vorsprung des Guten: exegetische und theologische Werkstattberichte FS Wolfgang Harnisch*, edited by Ulrich Schoenborn and Stephan Pfürtner, 209–31. Münster, Germany: Lit, 1994.

Schüssler Fiorenza, Elisabeth. "Cultic Language in Qumran and in the NT." *CBQ* 38 (1976) 159–77.

Scott, William M. F. "Priesthood in the New Testament." *SJT* 10 (1957) 399–415.

Segal, Alan F. "Covenant in Rabbinic Writings." *SR* 14 (1985) 53–62.

Seid, Tim Wayne. "Synkrisis in Hebrews 7: Rhetorical Structure and Strategy." In *Rhetorical Interpretation of Scripture: Essays from the 1996 Malibu Conference*, edited by Stanley E. Porter and Dennis L. Stamps, 322–47. JSNTSS 180. Sheffield: Sheffield Academic, 1999.

Seland, Torrey. "Jesus as a Faction Leader: On the Exit of the Category 'Sect.'" In *Context*, edited by P. W. Böckman and R. E. Kristiansen, 197–211. Trondheim: TAPIR, 1987.

Siegman, E. F. "The Blood of the Covenant." *AER* 136 (1957) 167–74.

Sigal, Phillip. "A Prolegomenon to Paul's Judaic Thought: The Death of Jesus and the Akedah." In *Proceedings, Eastern Great Lakes and Midwest Biblical Societies, Vol. 4*, 222–36. Grand Rapids: Eastern Great Lakes Biblical Society, 1984.

Snaith, John G. "Ben Sira's Supposed Love of Liturgy." *VT* 25 (1975) 167–74.
Snell, Antony. "We Have an Altar." *RTR* 23 (1964) 16–23.
Soden, H. von. "Der Hebräerbrief." *JPT* 10 (1884) 435–93; 627–56.
Songer, Harold S. "A Superior Priesthood: Hebrews 4:14—7:27." *RevExp* 82 (1985) 345–59.
Spencer, William David. "Christ's Sacrifice as Apologetic: An Application of Hebrews 10:1-18." *JETS* 40 (1997) 189–97.
Spicq, C. "La theologie des deux alliances dans l'Epitre aux Hebreux." *RSPT* 33 (1949) 15–30.
Stanley, Steve. "The Structure of Hebrews from Three Perspectives." *TynBul* 45 (1994) 245–71.
Stott, Wilfrid. "Conception of 'offering' in the Epistle to the Hebrews." *NTS* 9 (1962) 62–67.
Strugnell, John. "Flavius Josephus and the Essenes: Antiquities 18:18-22." *JBL* 77 (1958) 106–15.
Swetnam, James. "Form and Content of Hebrew 1–6." *Bib* 53 (1972) 268–85.
———. "Form and Content of Hebrew 7–13." *Bib* 55 (1974) 333–48.
———. "On the Imagery and Significance of Hebrews 9:9-10." *CBQ* 28 (1966) 155–73.
———. "Sacrifice and Revelation in the Epistle to the Hebrews: Observations and Surmises on Hebrews 9:26." *CBQ* 30 (1968) 227–34.
———. "Why Was Jeremiah's New Covenant New?" In *Studies on Prophecy: A Collection of Twelve Papers,* 111–15. VTSup 26. Leiden: Brill, 1974.
Teicher, J. Louis. "Priests and Sacrifices in the Dead Sea Scrolls: A Question of Method in Historical Research." *JJS* 5 (1954) 93–99.
Thoma, Clemns. "The High Priesthood in the Judgment of Josephus." In *Josephus, the Bible, and History,* edited by Louis H. Feldman and Gohei Hata, 196–215. Detroit: Wayne State University Press, 1989.
Thompson, James W. "Hebrews 9 and Hellenistic Concepts of Sacrifice." *JBL* 98 (1979) 567–78.
Tigchelaar, Eibert J.C. "Reconstructing 11Q17 Shirot 'Olat Ha-Shabbat." In *Provo International Conference on the Dead Sea Scrolls: Technological Innovations, New Texts, and Reformulated Issues,* edited by Donald W. Parry and Eugene Ulrich, 171–85. Leiden: Brill, 1999.
Unnik, Willem Cornelis van. "Eine merkwürdige liturgische Aussage bei Josephus (Jos Ant 8, 111-113)." In *Josephus-Studien: Untersuchungen zu Josephus, d. antiken Judentum u. d. Neuen Testament: Otto Michel z. 70. Geburtstag gewidmet,* edited by Otto Betz, Klaus Haacker, and Martin Hengel, 362–69. Göttingen: Vandenhoeck & Ruprecht, 1974.
Vaganay, Leon. "Le Plan de L'Épître aux Hébreux." In *Memorial Lagrange,* edited by L.-H. Vincent, 269–77. Paris: J. Gabalda, 1940.
Vanhoye, Albert. "Esprit éternel et feu du sacrifice en He 9:14." *Bib* 64 (1983) 263–74.
———. "Le Dieu de la nouvelle alliance dans l'Epitre aux Hébreux." In *Le notion biblique de Dieu: Le Dieu de la Bible et le Dieu des Philosophes,* edited by J. Coppens, 315–30. BETL 41. Louvain: Louvain University Press, 1976.
Wall, Robert, and William Lane. "Polemic in Hebrews and the Catholic Epistles." In *Anti-Semitism and Early Christianity: Issues of Polemic and Faith,* edited by Craig Evans and Donald Hagner, 166–98. Minneapolis: Fortress, 1993.
Wallace, David H. "Essenes and Temple Sacrifice." *TZ* 13 (1957) 335–38.
Walters, J.R. "The Rhetorical Arrangement of Hebrews." *AsTJ* 51 (1996) 59–70.

Watson, Duane F. "Rhetorical Criticism of Hebrews and the Catholic Epistles Since 1978." *CurBS* 5 (1997) 175–207.
Werline, Rodney A. "The Curses of the Covenant Renewal Ceremony in 1QS 1.16—2.19 and the Prayers of the Condemned." In *For a Later Generation: The Transformation of Tradition in Israel, Early Judaism, and Early Christianity,* edited by Randal A. Argall, Beverly A. Bow and Rodney A. Werline, 280–88. Harrisburg, Pa.: Trinity, 2000.
Wenschkewitz, H. "Die Spiritualisierung der Kultusbegriffe Tempel, Priester und Opfer im Neuen Testament." *AfNZK* 4 (1932) 70–230.
Whitcomb, John C. "Christ's Atonement and Animal Sacrifices in Israel." *GTJ* 6 (1985) 201–17.
Williamson, Clark M. "Anti-Judaism in Hebrews?" *Int* 57 (2003) 266–79.
Williamson, Ronald. "Background of the Epistle to the Hebrews." *ExpTim* 87 (1976) 232–37.
Wills, Lawrence. "The Form of the Sermon in Hellenistic Judaism and Early Christianity." *HTR* 77 (1984) 277–99.
Wilson, R. M. "Philo Judaeus." In *ISBE* 3:847–50.
Wintermute, O. S. "Jubilees." In *OTP* 2:35–51.
Wolmarans, Johannes L P. "The Text and Translation of Hebrews 8:8." *ZNW* 75 (1984) 139–44.
Worley, David R. "Fleeing to Two Immutable Things: God's Oath Taking and Oath Witnessing." *ResQ* 36 (1994) 223–36.
Wright, R. B. "Psalms of Solomon." In *OTP* 2:639–50.
Yadin, Yigael. "The Dead Sea Scrolls and the Epistle to the Hebrews." *ScrHier* 4 (1958) 36–55.
Young, Norman H. "The Gospel according to Hebrews 9." *NTS* 27 (1981) 198–210.

www.ingramcontent.com/pod-product-compliance
Lightning Source LLC
Chambersburg PA
CBHW070250230426
43664CB00014B/2469